# AXIS OF AUTHORITARIANS
*Implications of China-Russia Cooperation*

# AXIS OF AUTHORITARIANS
*Implications of China-Russia Cooperation*

*Edited by*

Richard J. Ellings and Robert Sutter

*With contributions from*

Richard J. Ellings, Peter Mattis, James B. Steinberg, Angela Stent,
Robert Sutter, Richard Weitz, and Charles E. Ziegler

**THE NATIONAL BUREAU *of* ASIAN RESEARCH**

Published in the United States of America by
The National Bureau of Asian Research, Seattle, WA, and Washington, D.C.
www.nbr.org

Copyright © 2018 by The National Bureau of Asian Research

All rights reserved. No part of this publication may be reproduced, stored in a retrieval system, or transmitted in any form or by any means, electronic, mechanical, photocopying, recording, or otherwise, without prior permission of the publisher.

Front cover image: Chinese president Xi Jinping (r) welcomes Russian president Vladimir Putin (l) at the G20 summit in Hangzhou © plavevski / Shutterstock.com

Back cover images (left to right): Russian fighter bomber Sukhoi Su-34 during a rehearsal of the victory parade © Grigorii Pisotsckii / Shutterstock.com; A Chinese military memorial in Hebei, China © Terry J. King / Shutterstock.com; and Oil pump at the Luanhe River in the north of China © Qui Ju Song / Shutterstock.com

ISBN (print): 978-1-939131-55-3

ISBN (electronic): 978-1-939131-56-0

Design and publishing services by The National Bureau of Asian Research

# Contents

Foreword ............................................................... vii
*Angela Stent*

Preface ................................................................ xiii
*Richard J. Ellings and Robert Sutter*

Chapter 1 – The Strategic Context of China-Russia Relations .......... 3
*Richard J. Ellings*

    Sino-Soviet Relations after World War II ............................. 9

    The Contemporary Strategic Context ................................. 19

    Strategic Questions ................................................ 44

Chapter 2 – China-Russia Relations in Energy, Trade, and Finance: Strategic Implications and Opportunities for U.S. Policy ............. 51
*Charles E. Ziegler*

    Trade, Finance, and Infrastructure ................................. 55

    Energy ............................................................. 66

    Implications ....................................................... 71

    Conclusion ......................................................... 77

Chapter 3 – Growing China-Russia Military Relations: Implications and Opportunities for U.S. Policy ...................... 81
*Richard Weitz*

    Regional Security .................................................. 83

    Functional Security Cooperation .................................... 88

    Scenarios .......................................................... 97

Policy Implications . . . . . . . . . . . . . . . . . . . . . . . . . . . . . . . . . . . . . . . . . . . . . . . . 101

Conclusion . . . . . . . . . . . . . . . . . . . . . . . . . . . . . . . . . . . . . . . . . . . . . . . . . . . . . . 105

## Chapter 4 – Russian and Chinese Political Interference Activities and Influence Operations . . . . . . . . . . . . . . . . . . . 109
*Peter Mattis*

Chaos and Construction: Active Measures vs. United Front Work . . . . . . . . 112

Organizing for Influence . . . . . . . . . . . . . . . . . . . . . . . . . . . . . . . . . . . . . . . . . 118

Comparing and Contrasting Tactics. . . . . . . . . . . . . . . . . . . . . . . . . . . . . . . . 127

Challenges and Opportunities. . . . . . . . . . . . . . . . . . . . . . . . . . . . . . . . . . . . 138

Conclusion . . . . . . . . . . . . . . . . . . . . . . . . . . . . . . . . . . . . . . . . . . . . . . . . . . . . 142

## Chapter 5 – China-Russia Cooperation: How Should the United States Respond? . . . . . . . . . . . . . . . . . . . . . . . . . . . 145
*James B. Steinberg*

The Shadow of the Past. . . . . . . . . . . . . . . . . . . . . . . . . . . . . . . . . . . . . . . . . . 147

The Reality of the Present. . . . . . . . . . . . . . . . . . . . . . . . . . . . . . . . . . . . . . . . 150

Net Assessment . . . . . . . . . . . . . . . . . . . . . . . . . . . . . . . . . . . . . . . . . . . . . . . . 158

Policy Options . . . . . . . . . . . . . . . . . . . . . . . . . . . . . . . . . . . . . . . . . . . . . . . . . 163

## Chapter 6 – U.S. Policy Opportunities and Options. . . . . . . . . . . . . . . . . 171
*Robert Sutter*

Context for Current U.S. Policy: Consensus on Five Policy Judgments . . . . . . 174

U.S. Policy Opportunities and Options . . . . . . . . . . . . . . . . . . . . . . . . . . . . 178

An Uncertain Future. . . . . . . . . . . . . . . . . . . . . . . . . . . . . . . . . . . . . . . . . . . . 187

# Foreword

*Angela Stent*

In June 2018, Chinese president Xi Jinping described Russian president Vladimir Putin as his "best, most intimate friend," terming relations between their two countries as the most significant between major powers in the world, as Richard Ellings notes in the opening chapter to this volume.[1] Putin returned the compliment, lauding Xi as a "reliable friend and good partner."[2] Troops from China's People's Liberation Army took part in Russia's massive Vostok (East) military exercises in September 2018, the first time that China has joined Russia in these war games. But while Putin and Xi were praising each other and conducting joint maneuvers, the Trump administration's National Security Strategy had issued a warning: "China and Russia challenge American power, influence and interests, attempting to erode American security and prosperity."[3]

Today, Washington faces a triple challenge: dealing individually with both China and Russia and confronting the threats that each poses to U.S. security; and the even more complex issue of how to approach the increasingly robust Sino-Russian partnership and minimize its potential to disrupt and adversely affect the United States' global interests. This volume addresses the triple Sino-Russian challenge in its political, economic, and security dimensions and suggests an array of possible U.S. responses to the budding China-Russia axis.

---

**ANGELA STENT** is Director of the Center for Eurasian, Russian and East European Studies and Professor of Government and Foreign Service at Georgetown University. She is the author of *The Limits of Partnership: U.S.-Russian Relations in the Twenty-First Century* (2014) and of the forthcoming *Putin's World*. She can be reached at <stenta@georgetown.edu>.

---

[1] Ben Blanchard and Denis Pinchuk, "China's Xi Awards 'Best Friend' Putin Friendship Medal, Promises Support," Reuters, June 8, 2018.

[2] Xu Wei, "Putin Hails Xi as His Reliable Partner," Xinhua, June 7, 2018.

[3] White House, *National Security Strategy of the United States of America* (Washington, D.C., 2017), 2, https://www.whitehouse.gov/wp-content/uploads/2017/12/NSS-Final-12-18-2017-0905.pdf.

With increasingly public affirmations of the closeness of Sino-Russian ties, it is instructive to remember that 50 years ago the Soviet Union and China were engaged in cross-border military clashes on the Ussuri River border between the two countries. Chinese soldiers, brandishing both their guns and their copies of Mao Zedong's Little Red Book, shouted accusatory slogans at their Soviet "brothers," who replied with commensurate vituperation. This was the culmination of a decade of growing Sino-Soviet tensions and mutual ideological invective. Some Western observers spoke of a coming war between the two countries. For the Soviet leadership, China arguably represented a greater ideological threat than did the United States because Beijing challenged the very legitimacy of the Soviet Union as a socialist state and its mantle as the leader of the Communist world and revolutionary movements. Mao's death and Deng Xiaoping's rise led to a diminution of bilateral tensions, but only after the Soviet collapse did ties between Beijing and Moscow begin to improve significantly. It is remarkable how the relationship has evolved in the nearly two decades of Putin's time in office. Indeed, the improvement of ties with China has been one of the signatory achievements of his foreign policy, one that he is not about to jettison.

The authors of this volume discuss the ties that bind China and Russia and their two leaders. Both Putin and Xi are authoritarian rulers who support a strong state, are determined to suppress any opposition, and are allergic to a "unipolar" world and to U.S. attempts to promote democracy and the rule of law that might undermine their power. Regime survival is their foremost goal, and Western actions present a potential challenge to that overriding aim. Both feel that the current world order dominated by the United States disadvantages them and fails to accommodate their legitimate interests. As Richard Ellings points out in his chapter, Xi and Putin are the world's two leading dissatisfied powers and "share interests in subverting many of the values and rules that are embedded in the post–World War II order." They are also both nationalists and have to ensure that their respective nationalisms do not clash. A similar worldview and values have apparently cemented what have become productive personal ties.

In a number of concrete areas, the Sino-Russian relationship has improved exponentially over the past few years. Richard Weitz discusses the dramatic increase in military ties, culminating in the joint participation in Vostok 2018. This military cooperation, he points out, is increasingly and explicitly directed against the United States, so much so that the Chinese defense minister has publicly promised that China would come to Russia's defense in the event of a war with the United States.[4] Weitz also stresses that neither country believes that North Korea would attack it; instead, they tend to view Pyongyang's nuclear program as a defense against the United States. Although China continues to reverse-engineer Russian weapons, Russia will continue selling advanced weaponry to China because it needs the revenue and this strengthens their relationship, given that sanctions prevent Beijing from purchasing weapons from the West. But while Russia's security priorities remain focused on Europe, China's are focused on Asia, although both are also concerned about security and terrorism in Central Asia, their common neighborhood.

Economic ties remain modest—especially when compared with the vastly more important U.S.-China economic relationship. But they have become more important since the imposition of Western sanctions on Russia following its annexation of Crimea and its launch of a war in southeastern Ukraine. Russia has turned to China for new energy deals and is seeking more Chinese investment in the Russian Far East. Thus, as Charles Ziegler observes, Western sanctions against Russia and the Trump administration's trade war with China are pushing the two countries closer together. It is unclear what kind of role Russia and its Eurasian Economic Union will have in China's massive, ambitious infrastructure project—the Belt and Road Initiative—but so far Chinese leaders continue to promise that this will be a "win-win" situation for both sides.

The United States has become increasingly concerned about both Russian and Chinese political interference operations. As Peter Mattis points out, both Putin and Xi see political influence operations as a routine part of statecraft, and both countries engage in aggressive activities to diminish the possibility of threats to their respective systems. This includes everything from cyber intrusions and spreading disinformation to kidnapping and poisoning opponents in the West. There is no evidence that China and Russia coordinate their political influence operations, so the United States has to deal separately with these challenges. Taken together, they have the potential to if not undermine the U.S. political system, then at least help fuel greater political discord.

James Steinberg summarizes the totality of the Sino-Russian challenge to the United States: their cooperation is driven by a mutual interest in promoting an international order that will ensure the survival of their authoritarian, mercantilist regimes. How, then, should the United States respond?

---

[4] "New Chinese Defense Minister Says China Will 'Support' Russia against U.S.: Tass," *Asia Times*, April 5, 2018, http://www.atimes.com/article/new-chinese-defense-minister-says-china-will-support-russia-us-tass.

As several of the authors point out, during the period between Richard Nixon's opening to China and Putin's ascent to the Kremlin, the United States enjoyed better relations with both China and Russia than either country did with the other. Washington was able to play the China card to its advantage as long as relations between Moscow and Beijing remained adversarial. But in the nearly two decades that Putin has been in power, the situation has dramatically changed. Today the relationship between Moscow and Washington is the worst it has been since Mikhail Gorbachev entered the Kremlin in 1985, while the relationship between Beijing and Washington, although less adversarial, is beset by tensions over trade and China's actions in the South China Sea. Nevertheless, China retains a significant economic stake in relations with the United States, whereas Russia does not. Today, China enjoys better relations with the United States and Russia than they do with each other. The United States and China are highly integrated in terms of finance and supply chains, whereas the main issue that necessitates U.S.-Russia engagement is the fact that they are the world's two nuclear superpowers.

Donald Trump has consistently argued that the United States should improve ties with Russia and embark on a new relationship with it in order to persuade the Kremlin to distance itself from Beijing and join Washington in putting pressure on China. The authors in this volume disagree about both the advisability and feasibility of this strategy. Some view China as a much greater longer-term threat to the United States than is Russia, and they urge a reconciliation with Russia to contain China. Others believe that Russia and China, both separately and jointly, present an equal threat to the United States, and argue for a dual policy that seeks to contain both countries but also to work with them on issues of mutual interest, where such cooperation is feasible.

Is the nature of the triple challenge changing? Steinberg argues that the principal challenge to the United States stems from the individual policies of China and Russia rather than from their combined efforts. But he also discerns a greater willingness from both countries to coordinate their efforts against the United States. Sino-Russian cooperation in the UN Security Council has certainly thwarted a variety of Western attempts to resolve crises in Syria and Ukraine, and China has enabled Russia to avoid the international isolation the West sought to impose after the annexation of Crimea. Their partnership often reinforces the ability of both countries to work separately against U.S. interests, even if Beijing and Moscow do not always agree on everything. Their grievances against the United States override their differences of interest on a number of issues.

Given that China has been instrumental in facilitating Russia's increasingly assertive presence on the world stage, it is highly unlikely, in contrast to President Trump's entreaties, that Putin would jeopardize this key relationship by joining the United States to pressure China. From the Kremlin's perspective, the United States is a far less predictable partner than is China, and Putin's anti-Western views appear to be deeply held. Whatever concerns Russia may have about China's longer-term ambitions and how they might affect Russia's security—including the future of the sparsely populated Russian Far East—they have so far been dwarfed by a belief that the United States represents a greater threat to the Putin regime. This suggests that the pursuit of an anti-Chinese U.S.-Russian partnership would be doomed to failure.

The authors in this volume consider a variety of ways in which the United States could respond to the China-Russia relationship. All agree that Washington should eschew policies that drive the two countries closer together to cooperate against U.S. interests. In this context, the Trump administration would be well advised to review its economic policies toward both countries. Waves of sanctions on Russia—in response to its actions in Ukraine, its election interference, and the poisoning of former military intelligence agent Sergei Skripal and his daughter in the United Kingdom—have had an economic impact in Russia and have also adversely affected the interests of several Russian business magnates. But they have done little to induce Moscow to cease its malign activities and instead have driven it into a closer embrace with China. Similarly, the trade war with China has complicated the Trump administration's efforts to secure Beijing's cooperation on dealing with North Korea. Moreover, both Russia and China have responded to sanctions and tariff hikes by exploring the feasibility of creating an alternative international payment system to the current SWIFT system in which the United States plays such a predominant role.

The other major theme of this book is that, in order to deal successfully with the separate and joint Chinese and Russian challenges it faces, the United States should seek to mend its relations with many of its allies. Several authors emphasize that Washington needs to reassert its commitment to the postwar liberal international order that has served the United States and its European and Asian allies so well for the past seven decades. The United States needs a strong and united NATO to counter Russian challenges to European security, just as it needs robust alliances with Japan, South Korea, and other Asia-Pacific nations to meet challenges from China. As Steinberg argues, the best way to deal with China and Russia is to strengthen U.S. international engagement and support allies who share the United States' values and interests, given that there is little that Washington can do to discourage Sino-Russian cooperation. Robert Sutter adds that the United States also needs to strengthen itself domestically. A less partisan and contentious polity could more effectively and convincingly face China and Russia, both of which seek to exploit existing differences within U.S. society to their own benefit.

China and Russia repeatedly point out that the U.S.-led unipolar world that immediately followed the collapse of the Soviet Union has been eclipsed by a new, multipolar world in which they are destined to play a far greater role than before and in which U.S. influence will be diminished. They call for a post-West order in which they have greater agency in setting the rules, an order that takes their interests into account much more than the previous one. China has already taken the initiative by creating the Asian Infrastructure Investment Bank, and it will continue to pursue its global economic interests whether or not the United States participates in the organizations that it leads. Russia has limited economic clout internationally, but it emphasizes the need to renegotiate Euro-Atlantic security arrangements as part of the new post-West order. That said, there is no united Sino-Russian view of what the post-West order should look like, other than diminishing the United States' ability to adversely affect the two countries' interests, and it is highly questionable whether Beijing and Moscow could agree on both the contours and details of this new order. But they will continue to challenge the United States around the world.

If the United States wants to avoid the creation of a post-West order designed by China and Russia, it should rededicate itself to its allies in the pursuit of consistent policies that deal with Beijing and Moscow as both Washington's competitors and sometimes partners on issues of mutual interest. The Sino-Russian partnership is here to stay, and the United States can best deal with it from a position of strength, not disunity and unpredictability.

# Preface

*Richard J. Ellings and Robert Sutter*

This volume is the culmination of the National Bureau of Asian Research (NBR) project "Strategic Implications of China-Russia Relations," which spanned 2016–18 and was supported by a generous grant from the Carnegie Corporation of New York. The project's findings are based on 50 commissioned papers as well as formal presentations at workshops and panel discussions in Washington, D.C., in December 2016, January 2017, March 2017, July 2017, and May 2018. Participants in these deliberations included 80 leading U.S. specialists and 30 leading specialists from China, Russia, Japan, South Korea, and Europe. The project was likewise informed by in-depth briefings with relevant officials at the U.S. National Security Council, the Department of Defense, and the Department of State; multiple briefings for U.S. congressional staff; and conferences in Seoul, Singapore, and several locations in the United States. Interim findings and policy options were published in two NBR Special Reports: "Russia-China Relations: Assessing Common Ground and Strategic Fault Lines" and "Japan and the Sino-Russian Entente: The Future of Major-Power Relations in Northeast Asia."[1] These findings were also discussed in a roundtable in the journal *Asia Policy* and an article in the *Diplomat*.[2]

---

**RICHARD J. ELLINGS** is President and Co-founder of the National Bureau of Asian Research (NBR) and Affiliate Professor of International Studies in the Henry M. Jackson School of International Studies at the University of Washington. He is a senior adviser to the NBR project "Strategic Implications of China-Russia Relations." Dr. Ellings can be reached at <ellings@nbr.org>.

**ROBERT SUTTER** is Professor of Practice of International Affairs at George Washington University and the principal investigator of the project "Strategic Implications of China-Russia Relations" at NBR. He can be reached at <sutterr@gwu.edu>.

[1] Michael S. Chase et al., "Russia-China Relations: Assessing Common Ground and Strategic Fault Lines," NBR, NBR Special Report, no. 66, July 2017; and Shoichi Itoh et al., "Japan and the Sino-Russian Entente: The Future of Major-Power Relations in Northeast Asia," NBR, NBR Special Report, no. 64, April 2017.

[2] "The Strategic Implications of Russia-China Relations: Regional Perspectives," *Asia Policy* 13, no. 1 (2018); and Robert Sutter, "When Will Closer China-Russia Cooperation Impact U.S. Policy Debate?" *Diplomat*, September 14, 2018.

The first goals of the project were to assemble the pertinent facts, look for trends, and place these into strategic perspective, assessing their significance to the interests of the United States and its allies and partners. The second purpose was to identify and assess policy options. The project's experts provided a rich and wide range of perspectives. Chinese and Russian specialists offered insights on their countries' common interests and challenges from the West, whereas U.S. specialists and those from allied countries varied more widely in their net assessments of the challenges presented by Chinese-Russian alignment and of the efficacy and wisdom of a range of policy responses.[3]

Most participants were in agreement on two aspects. The first is that relations between China and Russia have grown closer in ways that are troubling for the United States and its allies and partners. As Chinese and Russian authoritarianism has strengthened, the two countries have transcended the "axis of convenience" concept that Bobo Lo used to characterize the relationship ten years ago.[4] In its place, they have cultivated an axis that has strategic and other ambitious goals. While not leading yet, nor perhaps ever, to a formal alliance, China and Russia are taking steps to undermine the United States and other liberal nations and to expand their own influence abroad. The other point of majority agreement is that the United States and its allies and partners need to strengthen their capacities to defend their interests.

The volume explores the strategically significant cooperation between China and Russia and the implications of this cooperation for the United States, including a thorough assessment of policy options. It begins with Richard Ellings examining the strategic context of contemporary China-Russia cooperation as it is influenced by the fast-changing balance of power. He addresses the question of how the two countries' positions in the world, ideologies, and political systems shape their national interests and strategies. He shows the ways China and Russia perceive new opportunities, individually and together, for weakening liberal democracies and eroding key tenets of the post–World War II international system. At the same time, he argues, because Russian interests to align with China are mixed, and Russia exhibits major vulnerabilities, there may be more opportunities to change Moscow's strategic calculations than Beijing's.

The volume then addresses functional areas of strategic cooperation. Charles Ziegler's chapter tackles China-Russia relations in the domains

---

[3] An NBR Special Report presenting Chinese, Russian, and other regional perspectives on the growing ties between China and Russia is forthcoming.

[4] Bobo Lo, *Axis of Convenience: Moscow, Beijing, and the New Geopolitics* (Washington, D.C.: Brookings Institution Press, 2008).

of energy, trade, and finance. Like Ellings, Ziegler contends that China and Russia seek to reshape international institutions and that China's vastly superior power has created some distance in the relationship. Beijing has the economic upper hand over Moscow, and its close ties to the Russian economy give it leverage with Washington—but only to a point. The Chinese economy remains deeply intertwined with that of the United States. Toughened U.S. trade policies toward China, U.S. allies, and multilateral institutions could drive Beijing and Moscow closer together.

In his chapter, Richard Weitz charts the remarkable deepening of China-Russia military ties in recent years. He predicts that the two countries will continue their cooperation on regional security, joint exercises, and arms sales—though, similar to China's economic success, China's rising military is discomfiting to many in the Kremlin. The strength of U.S. alliances and partnerships will be central to limiting the authoritarians' defense ties and maintaining U.S. strategic advantages where possible, and Weitz stresses the need for the United States and its allies and partners to strengthen their security cooperation.

Peter Mattis examines Chinese and Russian political interference activities and influence operations, a topic that has catapulted to international prominence in the last few years, particularly in light of Russia's malign activities in the 2016 U.S. presidential election. The two authoritarians' operations largely differ and, to date, show little evidence of direct coordination, but there is evidence of intelligence sharing between the two countries and the replication of more aggressive Russian tactics by China on some fronts. Each country has developed formidable tactics to weaken democratic governments and institutions. Like the other authors, Mattis prescribes collective measures for the United States and other liberal democracies to counter Chinese and Russian influence and interference.

James Steinberg looks at the big diplomatic picture, providing historical context and surveying the security, economic, and political dimensions of Sino-Russian relations. For Steinberg, the critical question is not the extent of bilateral cooperation itself, but whether that cooperation harms fundamental U.S. interests. In his assessment, the challenges that Russia and China pose to the United States stem less from their collaboration than from their individual policies. Nonetheless, where their growing coordination can negatively affect U.S. interests, he argues that a policy of international engagement and support for U.S. allies and partners provides the best remedy.

In the volume's concluding chapter, Robert Sutter synthesizes what these chapters and the full findings of this multiyear NBR project mean for U.S. policy. U.S. and allied-country experts agree that the United States must strengthen its position economically, diplomatically, and militarily to deal with the significant challenges posed by China and Russia. They differ, however, on the degree of strengthening needed in each area and whether the United States should accommodate Chinese and Russian interests. Nonetheless, a position of general accommodation toward both authoritarian powers is not favored by the project's participants (other than by the experts from China and Russia).

## *Acknowledgments*

This volume is the capstone to two years of considerable effort. An immense debt is owed to Stephen Del Rosso of the Carnegie Corporation, whose early insights helped frame the major issues our team subsequently tackled. We also owe enormous gratitude to the authors of each chapter in this volume and to the scores of individuals from across the United States and around the globe who participated in the numerous workshops and events. They helped shape and refine the project's scope and output at each stage. A formidable team of senior advisers—Aaron Friedberg, Admiral Jonathan Greenert, Ambassador J. Stapleton Roy, James Steinberg, and Angela Stent—offered critical feedback during workshops and on papers. NBR was fortunate to have such a high level of scholarly and practitioner expertise on hand throughout the project.

An additional debt is owed to the team of editors and researchers at NBR. NBR's publications team, led by Joshua Ziemkowski with the assistance of Jessica Keough and Alexandria Baker, checked every footnote, comma, and turn of argument. Their editing improved both the logic and form of the chapters. Researchers in NBR's Washington, D.C., and Seattle offices—Meagan Araki, Melanie Berry, Karolos Karnikis, Seo Jung Kim, Ian McManus, and Stella Robertson—located and verified sources, tracked down and compiled data, and constructed charts. Brian O'Keefe's contributions in terms of research support and editorial assistance were instrumental to the timely production of this volume. The team was overseen by Roy Kamphausen, NBR's senior vice president for research and a key contributor to every phase of the project.

Finally, the volume and entire effort were ably organized and managed on a day-to-day basis by NBR senior project manager Brian Franchell. Brian has devoted much of his time and energy to seeing the project through, from its earliest conceptualization to this volume. His diligence and commitment deserve our highest commendation.

# EXECUTIVE SUMMARY

This chapter places into historical and strategic perspective the known and potential significance to the United States of China-Russia strategic cooperation.

## MAIN ARGUMENT

As authoritarian, nationalist powers, China and Russia share interests and cooperate to weaken the U.S. and the other democracies. The two regimes perceive strategic opportunities in the changing global and regional balances of power to enhance their influence abroad. They share interests in subverting many of the values and rules that are embedded in the post–World War II order, such as freedom of navigation and skies, the free flow of information across borders, international rule of law, and international institutions. As nations that covet different regions—Asia and Europe, respectively—China and Russia have complementary interests that form their major strategic challenges to the U.S. Yet the two countries also have interests that conflict, stemming from their histories, competition for influence in Eurasia, disputed borders, and the widening asymmetry in their relative power. Their autocratic histories and ideological propensities suggest that China's and Russia's alignment calculations are apt to change when international and domestic circumstances make realignment advantageous.

## POLICY IMPLICATIONS

- The perceived weakness of U.S. international leadership has encouraged Chinese and Russian aggression, which is often coordinated. Consequently, the fundamentals of U.S. and allied power, economic as well as military, require immediate and sustained attention.

- China-Russia strategic cooperation poses the worst-case threat to the U.S. due to the potential for the two to wage simultaneous wars in Asia and Europe, respectively. U.S. defense planners should make this scenario their top concern, both to mitigate this threat and to win the wars should mitigating policies, including deterrence, fail.

- Because Russian interests to align with China are mixed, and Russia exhibits major weaknesses that likely make it more susceptible to Western policies than China, there may be more opportunities to alter Russia's alignment calculations than China's.

Chapter 1

# The Strategic Context of China-Russia Relations

*Richard J. Ellings*

President Putin is the leader of a great country who is influential around the world....He is my best, most intimate friend....Myself and President Putin agreed, in the face of a complex international situation, that China and Russia will increase mutual support and coordination in international affairs, and deepen strategic cooperation.

—Xi Jinping

I see this as an acknowledgement and an evaluation of Russia's efforts to develop a comprehensive strategic partnership with China....This is an indication of the special attention and respect on which our mutual national interests are based, the interests of our peoples, and, of course, our personal friendship.

—Vladimir Putin

Most importantly...we [Putin and I] have things to talk about...everything from trade to military to missiles to nuclear to China...[and] our mutual friend President Xi.

—Donald Trump

These statements by Xi Jinping, Vladimir Putin, and Donald Trump, made in the summer of 2018, are poignant reminders of the centrality of great-power relations in international affairs and the special nature and collaboration of the two leading authoritarian powers of our time.[1]

---

**RICHARD J. ELLINGS** is President and Co-founder of the National Bureau of Asian Research (NBR) and Affiliate Professor of International Studies in the Henry M. Jackson School of International Studies at the University of Washington. He is a senior adviser to the NBR project "Strategic Implications of China-Russia Relations." Dr. Ellings can be reached at <ellings@nbr.org>.

[1] The statements from Xi and Putin are quoted by Ben Blanchard and Denis Pinchuk, "China's Xi Awards 'Best Friend' Putin Friendship Medal, Promises Support," Reuters, June 8, 2018, https://www.reuters.com/article/us-china-russia/chinas-xi-awards-best-friend-putin-friendship-medal-promises-support-idUSKCN1J41RO. The statement by Trump was made during opening remarks at the Trump-Putin meeting in Helsinki on July 16, 2018. "Watch Trump and Putin Speak ahead of Summit," CNN, July 16, 2018, https://www.cnn.com/videos/politics/2018/07/16/trump-putin-helsinki-summit-one-on-one-full-comments-vpx.cnn.

China and Russia loom large today indeed. The U.S. National Security Strategy released in December 2017 and National Defense Strategy released in January 2018 name them as the two greatest security challenges facing the United States. Neither strategy document, however, explores the issue of strategic alignment between these two U.S. rivals.[2] How best to understand the strategic alignment of China and Russia, its implications for the United States, and the options available to U.S. policymakers to respond are the topics of this volume.

We start with an examination of the background and context. Highlighting this context is the remarkable dynamism in the international system today, most notably China's meteoric rise and expanding influence and Russia's provocations and revanchism. There are historical antecedents. "The fundamental problem in international relations in the contemporary world," the late, eminent scholar Robert Gilpin wrote, "is the problem of peaceful adjustment to the consequences of uneven growth of power among states, just as it was in the past."[3] Twenty-four centuries earlier Thucydides made the rise of Athens the focus of the first historical study—his recounting and analysis of the Peloponnesian War. The rise and fall of the great powers, their coalitions, and the seeming inevitability of war between them have consumed the attention of some of the best minds over the past two millennia. The fortunes of the great powers set the rhythm of history.

While leading nations seek to maximize their power by acting alone and by positioning themselves internationally, they invariably contest ideologies—ideas and ideals. Their ideologies and even perceptions of the international environment are shaped by historical and cultural legacies and the nature of their domestic political systems.[4] Underlying the analyses in this volume is an appreciation for the impact of power on international relations, history, ideologies, and political systems. Combined, these forces make the struggle between nations especially dangerous, so very often resulting in war.

---

[2] White House, *National Security Strategy of the United States of America* (Washington, D.C., 2017), https://www.whitehouse.gov/wp-content/uploads/2017/12/NSS-Final-12-18-2017-0905.pdf; and U.S. Department of Defense, "Summary of the 2018 National Defense Strategy of the United States of America: Sharpening the American Military's Competitive Edge," January 2018, https://dod.defense.gov/Portals/1/Documents/pubs/2018-National-Defense-Strategy-Summary.pdf.

[3] Robert Gilpin, *War and Change in World Politics* (Cambridge: Cambridge University Press, 1981), 230.

[4] For further discussion, see Ashley J. Tellis, "Overview," in *Strategic Asia: 2017–18: Power, Ideas, and Military Strategy in the Asia-Pacific*, ed. Ashley J. Tellis, Alison Szalwinski, and Michael Wills (Seattle: National Bureau of Asian Research [NBR], 2017), 3–16, 5–7. See also Ashley J. Tellis, Alison Szalwinski, and Michael Wills, eds., *Strategic Asia: 2015–16: Foundations of National Power in the Asia-Pacific* (Seattle: NBR, 2015); Ashley J. Tellis, Alison Szalwinski, and Michael Wills, eds., *Strategic Asia: 2016–17: Understanding Strategic Cultures in the Asia-Pacific* (Seattle: NBR, 2016); and Samuel P. Huntington, *The Clash of Civilizations and the Remaking of World Order* (New York: Simon and Schuster, 1996).

More than at any time since the Cold War, ideologies are at stake in great-power relations. The world's major industrial power today, China, is governed by Xi Jinping, the formidable leader of a Leninist party that is conducting an extraordinary totalitarian experiment by exploiting cutting-edge surveillance technology and data analytics.[5] His purpose is to exert unprecedented control of the country's 1.4 billion people. Russia too is led by a powerful authoritarian, Vladimir Putin, who controls the Russian media, propaganda, and cyber operations to deceive, spread rumors, twist news, infiltrate databases, steal information, and disrupt and manipulate political institutions at home and abroad. As in China, the trend in Russia is toward further repression.

Inherently insecure and fearful, these authoritarians are threatened by foreign as well as domestic forces. Concepts and examples of freedom and democracy, especially examples located near their borders, pose dangers. After a careful analysis of their behavior, Aaron Friedberg concludes the following:

> Today's Russian and Chinese leaders want, above all, to survive, to preserve their grip on political power, and to maintain their present form of government in the face of Western efforts to promote liberalization and democratization. This is the master key, the single factor that goes furthest in explaining virtually every aspect of...[their] behavior both at home and abroad....As nationalistic authoritarian capitalists in a world still dominated by liberal democracies, both have an additional motive, rooted in ideology, to want to push the West and its contaminating influence back from their frontiers and to control events around their peripheries.[6]

As Mark Katz observes about Russian leadership, "because [regime change] is what the Russian elite genuinely fears, its focus on the combined threat of the United States externally and a color revolution internally has understandably led to a more aggressive strategy."[7] Eugene Rumer agrees. His assessment is that Russian foreign policy is the purview of Putin and a small cadre of elites that surrounds him, and serves first and foremost to ensure regime survival.[8] Putin equates himself with Russian superiority, contriving and pouncing on evidence of the unscrupulous policies and aspects of

---

[5] Louise Lucas and Emily Feng, "Inside China's Surveillance State," *Financial Times*, July 20, 2018, https://www.ft.com/content/2182eebe-8a17-11e8-bf9e-8771d5404543; and Carl Minzner, *End of an Era: How China's Authoritarian Revival Is Undermining Its Rise* (Oxford: Oxford University Press, 2018).

[6] Aaron L. Friedberg, "The Authoritarian Challenge: China, Russia, and the Threat to the Liberal International Order," Sasakawa Peace Foundation, August 2017, 50. Friedberg has been a senior adviser to the NBR project that produced this volume since the project's inception in 2016.

[7] Mark N. Katz, "Putin and Russia's Strategic Priorities," in Tellis et al., *Strategic Asia: 2017–18*, 55.

[8] Eugene B. Rumer, "Russia's China Policy: This Bear Hug Is Real," in "Russia-China Relations: Assessing Common Ground and Strategic Fault Lines," NBR, NBR Special Report, no. 66, July 2017, 13–25.

the decadent West that threaten Russia and his own rule. He manifests an ideological zeal, the "additional motive" that Friedberg references.

China's case is similar. According to Christopher Ford, the legitimacy of Chinese Communist Party (CCP) leaders is underpinned by perceptions that they occupy the moral high ground and at the same time are powerful realists—hence, their continuous effort to portray themselves as successfully fighting evil forces at home and abroad:

> [B]eing exposed as corrupt, selfish, and immoral—and as being incompetent or incapable enough so as to allow disorder and injustice to flourish in society—would drive directly at the core of the virtuocratic legitimacy narrative of every Chinese regime, including the contemporary CCP. Such criticism strikes, in effect, at its "mandate of heaven."[9]

As if it were not complex and unruly enough, given the diverse actors involved, the international contest over power and ideologies is especially difficult to predict and prone to war because actors' capabilities can change rapidly. With this dynamism, uncertainty spreads among states. A practitioner no less enamored with history than the ancients and modern international relations theorists, Senator Henry (Scoop) Jackson, framed the effects of uneven growth thusly: "Like popularity in politics, strategic advantage may be difficult to define, but when it shifts, those who gain it and those who lose it are bound to be sensitive to the change." The inevitable ambiguities that result from evolving power relations tend to stimulate fear, investments in defense, and coalition behavior. In Senator Jackson's assessment, the Soviet Union's increasingly advantageous arsenal in the late 1970s and early 1980s enabled it "directly or by proxies, to expand its influence and power." Consequently, he argued at the time, the United States lost much freedom of action, concluding that "the element of uncertainty in crisis situations is now more serious." There was an opportunity, he pointed out, to better balance the Soviet Union and reduce strategic uncertainty through continued, careful development of the United States' relations with another great nation that shared the Soviet threat, China.[10]

Four decades later, China-Russia-U.S. relations are again assuming enormous importance in human affairs. At stake are not just bilateral or trilateral diplomatic relations. Also in play are the fundamental organizing

---

[9] Christopher A. Ford, "Realpolitik with Chinese Characteristics: Chinese Strategic Culture and the Modern Communist Party-State," in Tellis et al., *Strategic Asia: 2016–17*, 60; and Christopher A. Ford, "Puncturing Beijing's Propaganda Bubble: Seven Themes," New Paradigms Forum, November 20, 2015, http://www.newparadigmsforum.com/NPFtestsite/?p=1993.

[10] Henry M. Jackson, "Foreword," in *The Sino-Soviet Conflict: A Global Perspective*, ed. Herbert J. Ellison (Seattle: University of Washington Press, 1982), viii.

principles and regimes in the international system; the prospects for a world again divided into two or three hostile, competing zones of influence and political organization; and the prospects for war—in the worst-case scenario, an unimaginably horrific nuclear World War III. Once more it appears that the constant struggle over power and ideologies has reached a critical stage. Today, out of fear of weakening international leadership and the growth of Chinese and Russian influence, a loose collection of countries—Western nations, Japan, South Korea, India, and some lesser powers—are grappling internally and with each other over ways to respond. We again live in a period of polarization and heightened uncertainty, this time arguably more acute than at any point since the 1930s.

The period before World War I and the interwar period leading up to World War II are frequently seen as analogous to the international environment today.[11] The similarities start with balances of power that were in great flux—what might be characterized as "skewed multipolar balances."[12] Twice in the twentieth century, rising, dissatisfied, authoritarian powers—primarily Germany and Japan—emerged and prepared to expand their influence dramatically, taking advantage of the two major potential impediments: the slower growing, and thus weakening, dominant political power, Great Britain, and the dominant economic power still deeply resistant to assuming international leadership, the United States. From a global perspective, a process of polarization ensued, as the ambitious and status quo powers alike expanded their military capacities—in the former cases to acquire influence and domination through intimidation and outright aggression, and in the latter cases simply to avoid or deter aggression and, as needed, defend themselves. Many formed alliances as best they could to maximize their positions. The development of extraordinary economic interdependence in the early twentieth century was hailed by some as the ultimate self-interest-based deterrent.[13] But this trend failed to hold back other forces—notably, faltering global leadership and rising nationalism

---

[11] World War II and the preceding interwar period were in many ways a continuation of World War I and its prewar era.

[12] In 1992, Edward Olsen and I invoked the term "skewed multipolarity" to describe the balance of power unfolding and destined to persist in Asia for maybe two decades. That condition changes fundamentally with the polarization that takes place when the likelihood of war looms, as the principal rising and status quo powers accelerate military preparations and strengthen coalitions. The rise of China was probable then: "[B]etween 2000 and 2010 we may see a confident China turn its attention to regional affairs, feeling no special need to work closely with the United States. At that time Japan and the United States may once again have a clear strategic basis for cooperation." Richard J. Ellings and Edward A. Olsen, "A New Pacific Profile," *Foreign Policy*, Winter 1992–93, 116, 124–25; and Richard J. Ellings, "Preface," in Tellis et al., *Strategic Asia: 2017–18*, viii.

[13] The most famous case is Norman Angell, *The Great Illusion: A Study of the Relation of Military Power to National Advantage* (London: William Heinemann, 1909).

driven by industrialization and authoritarianism—from propelling the outbreak of World War I. Of special note were the enduring regional interests between the Axis powers that drove their strategic collaboration during World War II. Japan set its sights on Asia, and Germany on Europe. These enduring interests were complementary, not shared. Their shared interest was expedient: dividing the attention and forces of the Allied powers, and primarily of the United States, the great power that presented the biggest potential hurdle.

Today there are many features of international affairs that echo the first half of the last century. International economic integration is high, giving some caution to China but seemingly less to Russia. Some of the principal players are new; most are not. The two leading dissatisfied powers are once again authoritarian, with starkly different ideologies than the democracies, and covet, as they have for centuries, different parts of the globe. Russia covets Europe, while China covets Asia (and beyond). They fear democracy yet sense its declining position in international leadership, and they share an expedient interest in dividing and weakening their major external worry, the United States. They work together in the Shanghai Cooperation Organisation, coordinate in the United Nations, conduct joint military exercises, circumvent UN sanctions to support the North Korean economy,[14] threaten Japanese airspace daily with armed aircraft, mount cyberattacks around the clock against Western institutions and companies, and leap on opportunities to divide the United States and its allies. This is just a sample. The details of their extraordinary cooperation are examined in subsequent chapters.

Unlike Germany and Japan, however, Russia and China are each other's primary neighbor, and they have a history of conflict and border disputes extending back to the mid-seventeenth century. Besides Europe, Russia's enduring interests include its near abroad to the south—Central Asia and the border regions with China and Mongolia. China too sees these regions to its north and west as enduring interests. Predating the Russian intrusions, the Great Wall was built and extended over the centuries to protect China from invaders from the north and west. Moreover, working to divide the two

---

[14] See, for example, Ian Talley and Anatoly Kurmanaev, "Thousands of North Korean Workers Enter Russia despite UN Ban," *Wall Street Journal*, August 2, 2018, https://www.wsj.com/articles/russia-is-issuing-north-korean-work-permits-despite-u-n-ban-1533216752; Ian Talley, "UN Report Faults China, Russia for Subverting North Korea Sanctions," *Wall Street Journal*, February 2, 2018, https://www.wsj.com/articles/u-n-report-faults-china-russia-for-subverting-north-korea-sanctions-1517610153; and Gardiner Harris, "New U.S. Sanctions Target Russia for Defying Rules on North Korea," *New York Times*, August 21, 2018, https://www.nytimes.com/2018/08/21/us/politics/new-us-sanctions-target-russia-for-defying-rules-on-north-korea.html.

nations' interests today is the gross disparity in their economic, political, and military power—the sheer dominance of China.

The starting point for this volume is placing into historical and strategic perspective the known and potential significance of China-Russia relations. The chapter seeks to answer several questions. What are the relevant lessons from the post–World War II experience? How does the fast-changing Eurasian balance of power, which has turned upside down since the Cold War, with China now enjoying tremendous advantages, raise uncertainties and affect the strategic calculus from each power's perspective? What role do ideologies play in each nation's strategic behavior? What are these countries' interests, and how might their leaders' assessments of these interests change? Finally, what core strategic issues do China-Russia relations pose for the policies of the United States and its allies?

## Sino-Soviet Relations after World War II

The record of Sino-Soviet relations during the Cold War is one of distinctive authoritarians operating according to their interests, which were shaped by national and international circumstances and these leaders' insecurities, ideologies, and assessments. One side attacked the political legitimacy of the other, which led to a strategic miscalculation of historic proportions that both sides wish to avoid repeating today.

### *The Sino-Soviet Alliance*

As World War II drew to a close, the Chinese civil war expanded, with Communist forces eventually victorious and Mao Zedong formally establishing the People's Republic of China (PRC) on October 1, 1949. As he is said to have proclaimed, "The Chinese have stood up." Mao knew, in fact, that the CCP was standing on shaky ground. China's economy was devastated. Tibet and the vast border regions were floating free of control. And in the midst of it all, Chiang Kai-shek was plotting to retake the mainland and receiving U.S. support, as he had during the civil war. Under such trying conditions, Mao had good reason to "lean to one side"—the Soviet Union—and form tight relations with China's socialist "big brother."[15]

---

[15] The official announcement came in the *Renmin Ribao* [People's Daily] on July 1, 1949, three months before the founding of the PRC and well before the mutual security treaty of February 1950. Recently declassified archives suggest that Mao reached the decision sometime in the prior year. See Zhihua Shen and Yafeng Xia, *Mao and the Sino-Soviet Partnership, 1945–1959: A New History* (Lanham: Lexington Books, 2015).

For Joseph Stalin, the initial Soviet priority in China immediately after World War II was restoring tsarist rights lost in 1905 in Russia's war with Japan. Stalin at one point even counseled the Communists to accept the Nationalist government, offering to mediate a solution to the conflict, which Mao refused. Leading figures in the People's Liberation Army (PLA) noted that Stalin's ideological commitment to socialism was taking a backseat to other Soviet interests.[16] However, as the Communists made significant gains in 1947, Stalin shifted to supporting Mao directly over Chiang. By the summer of 1948, he was supplying the CCP with arms.[17]

If a shared Communist ideology did not in and of itself prompt Stalin's military support for Mao, it also could not resolve all the sore points between the two leaders. In addition to conflicting interests over the Changchun Railway, the port at Dalian, Port Arthur, and the status of Outer Mongolia, questions lingered over whether the Soviets would insist on preserving the treaty signed with the Nationalists in 1945 or aid the PRC in capturing Taiwan. Stalin feared that Mao might be a nationalist at heart, like Tito in Yugoslavia, and did not want Mao insisting on independence from the Soviet-led movement.[18] He knew as well that the United States was actively working to split the new "brothers" apart, and to prove this he relayed intelligence to the CCP. In the treaty negotiations, Mao gained points for conceding Outer Mongolian "independence," which Stalin pursued as a territorial buffer between the Soviet Union and China. Stalin followed with major concessions on the Changchun Railway, Port Arthur, and Dalian and a large loan for China, not simply in return for Mao's concession of Outer Mongolia but more importantly to fulfill his own grand strategic objective "to bring China into the socialist bloc headed by the Soviet Union in order to control the situation in Asia and confront the Americans."[19] Even as the more powerful actor, Stalin yielded on specific issues for the sake of his broader mission. At this stage, the two sides' shared interests overrode their differences.

For the much weaker China, Mao's primary goal was party-state survival. Leaning to the Soviet side made sense ideologically as well

---

[16] Shen and Xia, *Mao and the Sino-Soviet Partnership*, 13.

[17] Alexander Lukin, *The Bear Watches the Dragon: Russia's Perceptions of China and the Evolution of Russian-Chinese Relations since the Eighteenth Century* (Armonk: M.E. Sharpe, 2003), 114–15; and Shen and Xia, *Mao and the Sino-Soviet Partnership*, 15.

[18] Vojtech Mastny, *The Cold War and Soviet Insecurity: The Stalin Years* (Oxford: Oxford University Press, 1998), 86–87.

[19] Shen and Xia, *Mao and the Sino-Soviet Partnership*, 58–59.

as practically.[20] Scholarship on Mao helps show the reinforcing roles that ideology and the requisites of authoritarian rule played. Mao is said to have subscribed to a rather voluntarist reading of Marxism, believing in the unlimited capacity of human beings to make things possible. Prudently exercising one's will meant distinguishing between antagonistic and non-antagonistic contradictions—the former being between enemies and requiring armed struggle, and the latter being between friends or among the people and requiring noncoercive methods. With the threat of the United States actively present within and beyond China's borders, there could be "no doubt as to what constituted the principal contradiction in the postwar international system."[21] "Imperialism" threatened in every way the existence—and leaders—of socialism.

## The Sino-Soviet Split

With twenty-twenty hindsight, one can trace the roots of the split between China and the Soviet Union back decades, well prior to World War II. Its first clear manifestation, however, was in the 20th Congress of the Communist Party of the Soviet Union (CPSU) in 1956, three years after Stalin's death.[22] It was then that the CPSU under Nikita Khrushchev proposed a new foreign policy of "peaceful coexistence, peaceful transition, and peaceful competition." Peaceful coexistence meant that capitalist and socialist countries could live together without fighting. Peaceful transition meant that the evolution of the world from capitalism to socialism could be nonviolent. And peaceful competition meant that the two systems vying peacefully with one another would facilitate that evolution.[23] On the last day of the congress, Khrushchev delivered his secret speech "On the Cult of Personality and Its Consequences," in which he criticized Stalin's

---

[20] A recent comprehensive assessment of Chinese grand strategy from Mao to Xi Jinping contends that protecting China has been the primary aim of every generation of PRC leaders, all of whom have viewed the country as a "brittle entity, in a world that was fundamentally dangerous." See Sulmaan Wasif Khan, *Haunted by Chaos: China's Grand Strategy from Mao Zedong to Xi Jinping* (Cambridge: Harvard University Press, 2018), ii.

[21] Samuel Kim, *China, the United Nations and World Order* (Princeton: Princeton University Press, 1979), 57, 60–62, 75.

[22] See Lorenz M. Lüthi, *The Sino-Soviet Split: Cold War in the Communist World* (Princeton: Princeton University Press, 2008).

[23] The CPSU's rationale may have been largely pragmatic. As Khrushchev would write in *Foreign Affairs* in 1959, "In our day there are only two ways: peaceful coexistence or the most destructive war in history. There is no third choice." Nikita S. Khrushchev, "On Peaceful Coexistence," *Foreign Affairs*, October 1959, 7.

mistakes in war and the 1930s Great Purge.[24] Importantly, he blamed Stalin's wrongdoings on personal and moral shortcomings rather than on features inherent to the Soviet apparat.

Chinese state media acknowledged the possibility of peaceful coexistence, and the three principles were endorsed at the CCP's 8th National Congress later that year.[25] More offensive to Mao was de-Stalinization. Mao countered that Stalin had been 30% wrong and 70% right. A *People's Daily* editorial asked, "How could it be conceivable that a socialist state which was the first in the world to put the dictatorship of the proletariat into practice, which did not have the benefit of any precedent, should make no mistakes of one kind or another?" The editorial affirmed, however, the "forever invincible, great camp of peace and socialism, headed by the Soviet Union."[26] Despite this show of support from Mao, de-Stalinization prompted unintended confusion and rebellion in other Communist states, notably Poland and Hungary in 1956. In a sign of insecurity, Khrushchev turned to Mao for advice on both European incidents, and at the Moscow Conference of Communist and Workers' Parties in 1957, Mao appeared to function "as the mentor and guide of the international Communist movement" by redefining "peaceful transition" and the acceptability of nuclear war.[27]

Between 1958 and 1960, Mao provoked disputes with the Soviet Union either to quell domestic opposition to his programs[28] or to push what he termed continuous revolution.[29] In 1958, he turned down Khrushchev's offer of military cooperation and fooled him into endorsing a crisis in the Taiwan Strait, which China started by shelling and launching air attacks

---

[24] An English translation of this speech is available from the digital archives of the Woodrow Wilson International Center for Scholars at http://digitalarchive.wilsoncenter.org/document/115995.

[25] *Renmin Ribao*, April 5, 1956. In his report before the 8th Party Congress, Liu Shaoqi repeatedly emphasized peaceful coexistence. He also said that China was "not afraid to engage in peaceful competition with capitalist countries" and would "achieve socialism through state capitalism, which is a peaceful means of transition." See Liu Shaoqi, "The Political Report of the Central Committee of the Communist Party of China to the Eighth National Congress of the Communist Party of China," 8th National Congress of the CCP, September 15, 1956. In 1963, Deng Xiaoping would disavow that China had agreed with these principles, telling CPSU delegates at a bilateral meeting in Moscow: "We have always considered and still consider that the 20th Congress of the CPSU put forward positions on the issues of war and peace, peaceful coexistence and peaceful transition which went against Marxism-Leninism. Especially serious are two issues: the issue of the so called 'peaceful transition' and the issue of the full, groundless denunciation of Stalin under the pretext of the so called 'struggle with the cult of personality.'" An English translation of Deng's speech is available from the digital archives of the Woodrow Wilson Center for International Scholars at http://digitalarchive.wilsoncenter.org/document/111237.

[26] *Renmin Ribao*, April 5, 1956.

[27] Shen and Xia, *Mao and the Sino-Soviet Partnership*, 255.

[28] Odd Arne Westad, ed., *Brothers in Arms: The Rise and Fall of the Sino-Soviet Alliance, 1945–1963* (Washington, D.C.: Woodrow Wilson Center Press, 1998).

[29] Chen Jian, *Mao's China and the Cold War* (Chapel Hill: University of North Carolina Press, 2001).

against islands controlled by the Republic of China (ROC) just twenty days after Khrushchev departed Beijing. Mao referred to Jinmen and Mazu, the bombarded islands, as "batons that keep Eisenhower and Khrushchev dancing, scurrying this way and that. Don't you see how wonderful they are?"[30] Unhappy now with peaceful coexistence, Mao was becoming bolder. Khrushchev sent Andrei Gromyko to Beijing to defuse the crisis, but there is no evidence that he was effective. Tit-for-tat exchanges strained bilateral ties during and after Mao's radical, economically devastating Great Leap Forward,[31] but the evidence suggests that leaders on both sides continued to invest in the relationship because they "keenly understood that by quarrelling, the brothers could only weaken their strategic position vis-à-vis the United States."[32]

It was in the wake of the 22nd CPSU Congress in 1961 that the relationship fully unraveled, culminating in the CCP's denunciation of Khrushchev in 1964.[33] The Soviets proposed the new concept of an "all people's state," meaning that before Communism was achieved, class would disappear in socialist societies—ending the dictatorship of the proletariat and leaving the state to manage only the administrative functions necessary to complete the evolution. The CCP vehemently disagreed, arguing that the dictatorship of the proletariat would endure until Communism's final stages, and that to say otherwise invited a new class to replace it.[34] Khrushchev also again criticized Stalin, along with Enver Hoxha, whose Albanian Labor Party had grown closer to China in recent years. Mao did not like having his personal authority and solidarity with the Albanians undermined, and Chinese media launched a wave of propaganda against the 22nd Congress.[35]

In 1962 the Soviet Union encouraged a mass exodus of ethnic minorities from Xinjiang (the Ita incident). During the Cuban Missile Crisis in October of that same year, China attacked India over their boundary dispute, Tibet,

---

[30] William Taubman, *Khrushchev: The Man and His Era* (New York: W.W. Norton, 2003), 392. See also Michael M. Sheng, "Mao and China's Relations with the Superpowers in the 1950s: A New Look at the Taiwan Strait Crises and the Sino-Soviet Split," *Modern China* 34, no. 4 (2008): 477–507.

[31] Vladislav M. Zubok, *A Failed Empire: The Soviet Union in the Cold War from Stalin to Gorbachev* (Chapel Hill: University of North Carolina Press, 2007), 137.

[32] Dong Wang, "The Quarrelling Brothers: New Chinese Archives and a Reappraisal of the Sino-Soviet Split, 1959–1962," Woodrow Wilson International Center for Scholars, Cold War International History Project, Working Paper Series, no. 49, 2005, 5, https://www.wilsoncenter.org/sites/default/files/WP49DW_rev.pdf.

[33] Ibid.; and Danhui Li and Yafeng Xia, "Jockeying for Leadership: Mao and the Sino-Soviet Split, October 1961–July 1964," *Journal of Cold War Studies* 16, no. 1 (2014): 24–60.

[34] See Roger E. Kanet, "The Rise and Fall of the 'All-People's State': Recent Changes in the Soviet Theory of the State," *Soviet Studies* 20, no. 1 (1968): 81–93.

[35] Li and Xia, "Jockeying for Leadership," 27–29.

and other issues. For years, Khrushchev had nurtured relations with India as well as China, and in the early days of the border war he portrayed Soviet policy as neutral. That changed in early November, two weeks into the war, when Soviet pronouncements began to side with India. U.S. policy was clearly on the side of India from the outset, and U.S. military forces were diverted toward India but not employed as China called a ceasefire. Khrushchev was playing a high-stakes long game to compete globally with the United States from the Caribbean to South Asia. At the same time, he and Mao were increasingly playing an interrelated high-stakes game, but 360 degrees around China's borders—in other words, where China's national interests (the threats to Mao and the CCP) were greatest. The CCP, not knowing that the United States had removed missiles from Turkey, criticized Khrushchev as weak for backing down in the missile crisis and railed at him for his explicit support for India.[36]

At the CCP's National Foreign Affairs Conference at the end of November, the Chinese leadership called the 22nd CPSU decisions "a comprehensive manifestation of revisionism" and formulated a new division of the world into three groupings: imperialism, led by the United States; revisionism, led by the Soviet Union; and Marxism-Leninism, led by China (and Mao in particular). In July 1963, to Mao's further chagrin, Khrushchev signed a nuclear test ban treaty with the United States.[37] The following year, Chinese state media attacked Khrushchev by name, calling the Soviet leader a "phony communist"—putting the final nail in the coffin of the alliance.[38] Khrushchev lost power on October 14, 1964, with his mishandling of foreign affairs, including relations with China, being a major reason. In a timely demonstration of pride and strength, China detonated its first atomic bomb just two days later.

While the new Soviet leadership was consolidating its power, China was both recovering from the disastrous Great Leap Forward and succeeding in testing ballistic missiles as well as nuclear weapons. The United States, for its part, was focused on thwarting the Soviet Union while deepening involvement in the Vietnam War. Washington and Taipei seemed to have no appetite for adding to the agenda an invasion of China. At this point, even with Khrushchev gone, neither the CPSU nor CCP would relent. The fresh Soviet leadership needed to appear strong, while Mao felt emboldened by

---

[36] Original diplomatic documents dating from 1959 to 1964 are available from the digital archives of the Woodrow Wilson Center for International Scholars at http://digitalarchive.wilsoncenter.org/collection/71/sino-indian-border-war-1962. See also Li and Xia, "Jockeying for Leadership," 43–49.

[37] Kim, *China, the United Nations and World Order*, 76–77.

[38] Li and Xia, "Jockeying for Leadership," 56.

China's weapons development, improved economy, and growing status in the Communist movement, together with the diminished prospect for U.S. intervention. He could strengthen his grip on the CCP through rejecting Soviet behavior and championing China and his "continuing revolution." The two leaderships' increasingly divergent Communist ideologies, which were grounded in their power struggles at home and fused with enduring national interests and international aspirations, drove bilateral relations toward confrontation.

## Sino-U.S. Rapprochement

In no position to accommodate Mao, Leonid Brezhnev and his colleagues ratcheted up pressure with a buildup of military forces on the Chinese border. In 1965, the Soviet Union had 15 divisions along the border, and in 1966 it signed a mutual defense treaty with Mongolia that justified the stationing of Soviet forces there. In 1967, the Soviet Union deployed tactical nuclear weapons, and by 1969 the number of Soviet divisions along the Chinese border had grown to between 27 and 34. They were heavily armored and motorized, with helicopters and advanced aircraft, juxtaposed to the lightly armed but massive Chinese forces—59 divisions—on the other side.[39] Mao's xenophobic Cultural Revolution continued its ideological assault on the CPSU and the legitimacy of the new Soviet leadership. The CCP also castigated the Soviet Union for building up forces on the borders. Meanwhile, China made strides in developing its nuclear forces, both weapons and medium-range missiles—some of which seem to have been targeted at the Soviet Union.[40] As Jonathan Pollack concludes, Brezhnev and his colleagues assessed that a long-term competition with China was developing out of a host of issues: conflicting national security interests, a troublesome history, difficult personalities, and Mao's ideology.[41]

In November 1968, China proposed resuming ambassadorial talks with the United States in Warsaw, an offer president-elect Richard Nixon immediately accepted (through then president Lyndon Johnson).[42]

---

[39] Michael S. Gerson, "The Sino-Soviet Border Conflict: Deterrence, Escalation, and the Threat of Nuclear War in 1969," CNA, November 2010, 16–17.

[40] Thomas W. Robinson, *The Sino-Soviet Border Dispute: Background, Development, and the March 1969 Clashes* (Santa Monica: RAND Corporation, 1970); and Thomas W. Robinson, "The Sino-Soviet Border Dispute: Background, Development, and the March 1969 Clashes," *American Political Science Review* 66, no. 4 (1972): 1175–1202.

[41] Jonathan D. Pollack, "China's Agonizing Reappraisal," in Ellison, *The Sino-Soviet Conflict*, 55.

[42] Li Jie, "Changes in China's Domestic Situation in the 1960s and Sino-U.S. Relations," in *Re-examining the Cold War: U.S.-China Diplomacy, 1954–1973*, Harvard East Asian Monographs 203, ed. Robert S. Ross and Jiang Changbin (Cambridge: Harvard University Press, 2001), 313.

One reason for this turn in CCP—and U.S.—policy, even amid the chaos of Mao's Cultural Revolution, was the Soviet invasion of Czechoslovakia in August 1968 and the Brezhnev Doctrine in September that subsequently attempted to justify the invasion.[43] Scholars dispute the extent of the invasion's impact on Mao's decision-making. Some suggest that the PLA was stronger and had less to fear from Soviet conventional forces than the received wisdom assumes,[44] but intelligence estimates at the time indicate that the Soviet Union held a substantial advantage.[45]

In March 1969, the former "brothers" came to blows. The border clash at Zhenbao Island lasted for months but did not escalate beyond skirmishes.[46] Evidence suggests that China, not the Soviet Union, initiated the fight—possibly to galvanize support for Mao's stalling domestic revolution.[47] Whatever each side's relative capabilities and intentions may have been, neither wanted to spark a full-scale war. To deter China, the Soviet Union indicated that if attacked by major forces it would use nuclear weapons.[48] Soviet leaders feared that a war would be exploited by their greatest foes, the United States and NATO, which could take advantage of the situation by supporting China and encouraging rebellious elements in Soviet satellites in Eastern Europe. Mao was also weighing the likelihood of war with the Soviet Union against that with the United States. His team of trusted marshals, faithfully employing Maoist terminology, concluded that the United States was genuine in its desire for closer relations with China, creating an opening for the CCP to exploit. As Marshal Chen Yi explained, "Because of the strategic need for dealing with the Soviet revisionists, Nixon hopes to win over China. It is necessary for us to utilize the contradiction

---

[43] Brezhnev sent 235,000 Soviet and Warsaw Pact troops into Czechoslovakia to suppress Alexander Dubček's Prague Spring and reorganize the Czech Communist Party and government.

[44] Lyle J. Goldstein, "Return to Zhenbao Island: Who Started Shooting and Why It Matters," *China Quarterly*, no. 168 (2001): 985–97.

[45] Letter from Allen S. Whiting to Henry Kissinger, August 16, 1969, enclosing report, "Sino-Soviet Hostilities and Implications for U.S. Policy," https://nsarchive2.gwu.edu/NSAEBB/NSAEBB49/sino.sov.9.pdf.

[46] A few years later the Soviet Union deployed as many as a million troops along the border.

[47] Goldstein, "Return to Zhenbao Island." Indeed, amid domestic chaos and the lurking influence of the CPSU—as evidenced later by Lin Biao's attempted escape to the Soviet Union in 1971—the split with Moscow provided Mao a rallying point to continue his revolution.

[48] William Burr, ed., "The Sino-Soviet Border Conflict, 1969: U.S. Reactions and Diplomatic Maneuvers," National Security Archive Electronic Briefing Book, no. 49, June 12, 2001, https://nsarchive2.gwu.edu/NSAEBB/NSAEBB49.

between the United States and the Soviet Union in a strategic sense, and pursue a breakthrough in Sino-American relations."⁴⁹

The fast-developing power of Japan was also a strategic issue for Mao and Zhou Enlai. In 1971, Nixon and Henry Kissinger "played on China's concern," Kenneth Pyle points out, by emphasizing that the United States' alliance with Japan assisted in containing the Soviet Union and prevented Japan from remilitarizing. China's concern then intensified with the "Nixon shocks" of 1971. Japan was taken aback by not being consulted by the United States in advance of U.S.-China rapprochement and by new U.S. foreign economic policies that seemed aimed at curbing the Japanese economy. Mao had so internalized the U.S. view by 1973 that he counseled Kissinger on how the United States needed to reassure Japan about the U.S. commitment to the alliance.⁵⁰

Mao was not thrilled about compromising with the "imperialists," but for the sake of survival, he held his nose.⁵¹ Specific outcomes of rapprochement pleased him; others brought disappointment. In 1971, China replaced Taiwan in the United Nations, and over a dozen states soon switched their recognition to the PRC. Taking advantage of Nixon's breakthrough with China, Japan normalized relations with the PRC in September 1972, and in spite of the "shocks" adhered to its moderate defense policy within the structure of the alliance. However, small Communist parties and countries, including Albania, were confused by what looked like an inexcusable abandonment of CCP principles.⁵² Most of all, U.S.-Soviet relations seemed to improve after the Sino-U.S. rapprochement, undermining the *raison d'être* of Mao's compromise. In the years following Nixon's visit to China, Washington and Moscow held many bilateral meetings and signed several

---

⁴⁹ Chen Yi, "Further Thoughts by Marshal Chen Yi on Sino-American Relations," Document No. 12, Bulletin 11, Cold War International History Project, September 17, 1969, 170–71. See also Chen Yi et al., "Report by Four Chinese Marshals—Chen Yi, Ye Jianying, Nie Rongzhen, and Xu Xiangqian—to the CCP Central Committee, 'Our Views about the Current Situation' (Excerpt)," Document No. 11, Bulletin 11, Cold War International History Project, September 17, 1969, 170.

⁵⁰ Kenneth Pyle, *Japan Rising: The Resurgence of Japanese Power and Purpose* (New York: PublicAffairs, 2008), 320–22.

⁵¹ Mao's ambivalence is evident in his repeated instructions to Zhou Enlai to include strong revolutionary language in the text of the Shanghai Communiqué. See Kuisong Yang and Yafeng Xia, "Vacillating between Revolution and Détente: Mao's Changing Psyche and Policy toward the United States, 1969–1976," *Diplomatic History* 34, no. 2 (2010): 395–423. John Garver, by contrast, argues that Mao willingly "leaned" toward the United States in order to sustain the Cultural Revolution, which he worried could be interrupted or derailed by collusion between the Soviet Union and Chinese domestic "reactionaries." John W. Garver, *China's Quest: The History of the Foreign Relations of the People's Republic of China* (New York: Oxford University Press, 2016).

⁵² China's Politburo and Foreign Ministry had to issue long and convoluted explanations for the sudden turn in policy. Yang and Xia, "Vacillating between Revolution and Détente," 405–6, 409–10.

important treaties. The lean toward the United States soon became a thorn in Mao's side.[53]

Mao's decisions on when and how to compromise—with respect to the international Communist movement, the Cultural Revolution, and China's national security—were informed by his self-interest and ideological views.[54] To properly understand Chinese policy at the outset of the rapprochement era, one must appreciate Mao's unique standing in the CCP, abiding insecurities, and radical notion of "permanent revolution." After Mao's death, the interests and ideas of Deng Xiaoping and other leaders filled the political vacuum. China's foreign and domestic policies underwent tremendous transformation. Without Mao's charismatic hold on the reins, Deng and his colleagues continued to wrestle with the Soviet challenge but toned down the ideological attacks. In the wake of the catastrophic Cultural Revolution, any claim to political legitimacy by the CCP had to come from economic performance, the party's role in building the nation's overall strength, and social stability. To their credit, Deng and colleagues were practical ideologues who chose a path, blazed by Japan and the "tigers" of Asia (Hong Kong, Singapore, South Korea, and Taiwan), that would prove successful economically almost beyond imagination. They introduced market forces, sought foreign capital and technology, opened the borders to carefully managed international trade, and sought foreign technical and business education. At the same time, they sustained the party's leadership by wielding ultimate control of the economy and its key state-owned enterprises and companies. They exerted political control, which became an acute issue in 1989, when the Soviet empire disintegrated and protests inside China culminated in the massacre at Tiananmen Square.

In comparison with the strong, economically savvy new Chinese leadership, Brezhnev and his successors overextended the Soviet Union's reach and failed to undertake economic reform through the remainder of the 1970s and the 1980s. The Soviet leaders underestimated the vitality and strategic leadership of the United States. They failed to appreciate the poverty of socialism in a wealth-producing, capitalist world.

---

[53] In 1973, Mao sought to protect himself by calling several meetings to criticize Zhou Enlai for the entire process, which he feared might fail, and began formulating a new kind of "united front" theory to resist the Soviet Union and United States simultaneously. Known as "the theory of the three worlds," this new foreign policy framework was emblematic of Mao's ideological ambivalence toward Sino-U.S. rapprochement—emerging within just a year or two of his meeting with Nixon—and his efforts to shore up power and enshrine his legacy as the revolutionary who brought greatness, internationally as well as nationally, back to China.

[54] Garver, *China's Quest*.

Several pertinent lessons can be drawn from this history. The international policies of the first and second generations of Communist leaders are explained by their struggles to retain power and by the ideologies—the fusion of historical and cultural legacies, national interests and aspirations, and variants of Communist ideology—that guided them. Second, authoritarians are always threatened by democratic ideals and the most powerful and committed purveyors of these ideals. Third, authoritarians are insecure generally and are constantly threatened by their domestic rivals, even cronies, and people who communicate and organize politically. Fourth, authoritarians are threatened by foreign authoritarians—including Communists being threatened by foreign Communists—when their legitimacy, national interests, and aspects of their ideologies are challenged. Fifth, authoritarians cooperate strategically even with hated and feared democracies when their regimes are sufficiently threatened—for example, Stalin with Franklin Roosevelt and Winston Churchill and Mao with Nixon. Sixth, some authoritarians, such as Deng and his successors, engage democracies in a carefully controlled, yet vigorous, fashion economically and diplomatically when they assess that such engagement will strengthen their power at home and abroad.

## The Contemporary Strategic Context

### The Distribution of Power

The Deng era's successes, in combination with the Soviet empire's collapse and Russia's economic failures since, define the core strategic reality today. Since Mao's death and Deng's reforms, over 500 million Chinese have escaped poverty, and China has largely urbanized.[55] The Chinese market has expanded exponentially to equal approximately that of the United States. China has gone from accounting for a tiny fraction of world trade to assuming the mantle of world leader, and its industrial sector has grown to over 1.5 times the output of the United States, which had led the world since the late nineteenth century. China has matched its economic growth with investments in its military, one of the "four modernizations." The PLA's progress has been extraordinary. U.S. fleets, bases, and allies in the region are increasingly vulnerable to Chinese attack, which has caused U.S. strategists

---

[55] See, generally, Barry J. Naughton, *The Chinese Economy: Adaptation and Growth*, 2nd ed. (Cambridge: MIT Press, 2018); and Loren Brandt and Thomas G. Rawski, eds., *China's Great Economic Transformation* (New York: Cambridge University Press, 2008).

to rethink military contingencies and responses and to call for expanded investments by the United States and its allies in new weapons systems.[56]

Depending on how one measures GDP (purchasing power parity versus current prices), China's economy ranks either first or second in the world and is, according to the latter measure, 8.5 times the size of Russia's. China also ranks second to only the United States in military expenditures. In terms of national GDP and military expenditures, there is not a close third, and given expected growth rates, the disparity between China and its regional competitors, with the exception of India, should widen. A glance at the distribution of global GDP and military expenditure, arrayed roughly geographically, reveals two poles (see **Figures 1** and **2**).

The integration of the major powers into the world economy is another structural factor affecting their calculations and behavior. Trade accounts for a significant portion of China's GDP—38% in 2017—giving the country a much greater stake in sustaining robust trade relations than was ever the case for the United States (for which trade accounts for 27% of GDP today).[57] China's export stake slightly exceeds that of Britain and Germany on the eve of World War I.[58]

Russia has also benefited from global trade—in its case, through energy sales to Europe and international flows of capital and goods—but it is not nearly as integrated as China into the world economy. Russian products do not flood world markets; in fact, an American is hard-pressed to name a single Russian-made item in one's possession, or for that matter ever purchased, except perhaps vodka. Russia is not critical in global supply chains. Nonetheless, trade makes up 47% of its economy.[59] Petroleum and natural gas constitute approximately 68% of Russian exports and even more

---

[56] See the debate over air-sea battle in Aaron L. Friedberg, *Beyond Air-Sea Battle: The Debate over U.S. Military Strategy in Asia*, Adelphi Book 444 (New York: Routledge, 2014); and U.S. Department of Defense, "Summary of the 2018 National Defense Strategy of the United States of America."

[57] "Trade (% of GDP)," World Bank, https://data.worldbank.org/indicator/NE.TRD.GNFS.ZS.

[58] China's merchandise exports were 18.4% of GDP in 2017, whereas Britain's and Germany's before World War I were 18% and 16% of GDP, respectively. "Trade (% of GDP)," World Bank; "Merchandise Exports (Current US$)," World Bank, https://data.worldbank.org/indicator/TX.VAL.MRCH.CD.WT?locations=CN; and "GDP (Current US$)," World Bank, https://data.worldbank.org/indicator/NY.GDP.MKTP.CD?locations=CN. See also Ana Swanson, "The World Today Looks Ominously Like It Did before World War I," *Washington Post*, December 29, 2016. For a chart comparing exports as a percentage of GDP for key countries between 1870 and 1913, see "Merchandise Exports as a % of GDP," Deutsche Asset Management, available at https://www.weforum.org/agenda/2017/01/why-the-world-looks-a-bit-like-it-did-before-world-war-i.

[59] "Trade (% of GDP)," World Bank, https://data.worldbank.org/indicator/NE.TRD.GNFS.ZS.

FIGURE 1  Share of global GDP (current prices, 2017)

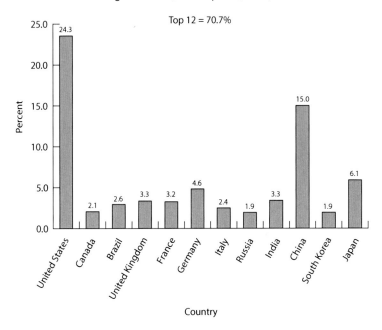

SOURCE: International Monetary Fund, World Economic Outlook Database, April 2018.

NOTE: Values are based on GDP in national currency converted to U.S. dollars using market exchange rates (yearly average). European nations are listed individually to reflect their separate political decision-making and defense and foreign policies.

importantly exceed 50% of Russian government revenues.[60] In short, the fortunes of the Russian economy and state rest on pipelines and the prices of oil and gas. In understanding the strategic environment of China-Russia relations, few facts stand out so remarkably.

The military balance between the two has changed no less. China spends far more on its defense today, and, like Russia, maintains substantial forces, including nuclear-capable missiles, to protect the border regions.[61]

---

[60] "Russia," Observatory of Economic Complexity, 2016, https://atlas.media.mit.edu/en/profile/country/rus.

[61] For analysis of the border defense, see Peter Wood, "Strategic Assessment: China's Northern Theater Command," Jamestown Foundation, May 15, 2017, https://jamestown.org/program/strategic-assessment-chinas-northern-theater-command.

FIGURE 2  Share of global defense expenditures

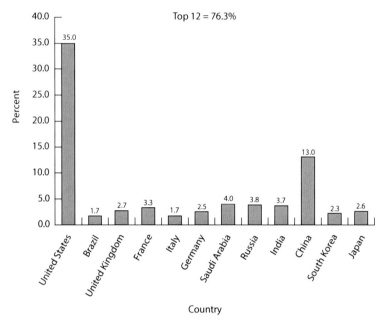

SOURCE: Stockholm International Peace Research Institute (SIPRI), SIPRI Military Expenditure Database, May 2, 2018, https://www.sipri.org/sites/default/files/styles/body_embedded/public/2018-05/fs_1805_figure_2_eps-01.jpg?itok=k-LE7TUK.

Figure 2 underreports Chinese—and probably Russian—spending.[62] In contrast with the Cold War, China's forces are now not only more numerous but also more powerful than Russia's. In 2015 the priority of China's Northern Theater Command was downgraded from first to fourth most important, presumably reflecting the diminution of the threat from Russia and higher priorities given to the Eastern, Southern,

---

[62] The Stockholm International Peace Research Institute (SIPRI) relies on official and open-source materials. According to SIPRI, "if extra- or off-budget sources of military spending exist…it is not possible to obtain figures or reasonable estimates for these." See "Frequently Asked Questions," SIPRI, https://www.sipri.org/databases/milex/frequently-asked-questions#5-where-does-your. In fact, both countries' official military expenditures are not credible in view of their known histories, interests in secrecy and underreporting, and lack of public accountability due to controlled presses and nondemocratic budgeting procedures.

and Western Theater Commands.⁶³ Russia has been upgrading recently its nuclear-capable missile forces along the border with China, but seemingly only for deterrence, as Russian conventional forces are now badly outgunned.

Given China's strides in defense technology, partly as a result of reverse engineering from Russian systems, Russia now sells China fewer items overall but more sophisticated systems, notably its premier jet fighter, the Su-35. Chinese imports of Russian arms are likely to continue to dwindle unless Russia somehow innovates faster than China.⁶⁴

In sum, today the economic and conventional military preponderance of China, combined with the growth trajectories of its economy and military power, constitutes the salient strategic feature of Asia. Xi and his colleagues, as well as their counterparts abroad, know this. At the same time, China benefits enormously from its trade with the world's commercial centers: East Asia, North America, and Europe, with its risks quite diversified. Worth noting are China's financial and broader economic fragilities, which, in a word, are complex. They stem from political and other nonmarket influences, with bad debt being the leading concern. These factors are difficult to gauge and are of strong concern to the regime, whose legitimacy depends on economic success.⁶⁵

Despite the PRC's advantages, Chinese leaders cannot act recklessly, given the proliferation of nuclear weapons throughout the region, their hostility-prone neighborhood, and domestic political and economic vulnerabilities. They need to avoid provoking the formation of new alliances against them and to continue encouraging Russia to lean toward China to divide U.S. strategic attention. Chinese leaders also have huge stakes in the international economy, but their country's structural advantages do give them the upper hand in their neighborhood. Putin needs Xi more than Xi needs Putin.

---

⁶³ As Richard Weitz underscores in his chapter, the border region today gives China and Russia "a de facto secure 'strategic rear'—a sphere where they do not perceive a threat from each other and that lies beyond the reach of the U.S. military." See also Artyom Lukin, "Why the Russian Far East Is So Important to China," *Huffington Post*, January 12, 2015, http://www.huffingtonpost.com/artyom-lukin/russian-far-east-china_b_6452618.html.

⁶⁴ Richard Weitz, "Sino-Russian Security Ties," in "Russia-China Relations."

⁶⁵ See Minzner, *End of an Era*. As Minxin Pei describes, corruption is systematically embedded into China's political economy, with officials and business leaders seizing state assets for the purpose of personal enrichment and political leverage. Minxin Pei, *China's Crony Capitalism: The Dynamics of Regime Decay* (Cambridge: Harvard University Press, 2016).

## Narratives (Ideologies) and Power

Another step in understanding the "drivers" and "brakes" in bilateral relations between China and Russia is examining the narratives that the leaders of these two states have constructed to capture their nations' international glory, grievances, and goals.[66] Ideology motivates both Xi and Putin, who draw on legacies of "greatness" and empire. They recast periods of "humiliation" to provide the foundation for resentment and point to current international circumstances that are tilted unfairly to their rivals' advantage. Because of the threat posed to their regimes, the two leaders mock and deride Western liberalism.[67] They portray themselves as embodying the virtues of their civilizations and as best equipped to fight their nations' foes and achieve national vindication and dreams.

*Russia.* Historical legacies pervade Russian international behavior. As Isabelle Facon shows in her penetrating assessment of Russian strategic culture, contemporary foreign and military policies reflect a deep-seated drive for status as an exceptional great power.[68] The elements of this culture go back centuries, were exacerbated by Communist ideology through the Soviet period, and persist today, heightened by the humiliation of the Soviet Union's collapse and by the re-emergence of authoritarian leadership under Putin.

A crucial element is Russia's dual identity of both greatness and vulnerability. The history of Russia is one of expansion and contraction, victory and defeat, international success and failure, resulting in extreme ambivalence about the country's relationship to the outside world. Tsarist empire-building was extraordinary, but it came to an ignominious conclusion, first at the hands of the Japanese navy in 1905 and then by the disaster of World War I and the Russian Revolution. From the ashes, Stalin built another empire in a world wracked by disorder, followed by World War II. Propelled by nationalism and ideological and imperial ambitions, all grounded in his paranoid, extreme dictatorship, he negotiated spheres

---

[66] For a discussion of these drivers and brakes, see Robert Sutter's chapter for this volume.

[67] Gilbert Rozman argues that Xi's and Putin's common "regime self-images" are a driving force behind their strategic cooperation. These images are a melding of ideology and nationalism, of leftover Communist ideas, especially "anti-imperialism," plus "Russocentrism" and "Sinocentrism," and the bilateral relationship is thus more resilient than if it were based on simple calculations of interests. See Gilbert Rozman, "Asia for the Asians: Why Chinese-Russian Friendship Is Here to Stay," *Foreign Affairs*, October 29, 2014; and Gilbert Rozman, "The Sino-Russia Partnership Is Stronger Than the West Thinks," Huffington Post, January 11, 2015. This thesis is not utilized here due to examples of autocrats with similar, shared self-images in the past parting strategic ways. In fact, many, if not most, wars have been fought between nations led by autocrats.

[68] Isabelle Facon, "Russian Strategic Culture in the 21st Century: Redefining the West-East Balance," in Tellis et al., *Strategic Asia 2016–17*, 63–89.

of domination at the Yalta Conference and inserted Soviet forces wherever he could to push the boundaries of his empire as far out from the core of the country as possible. In nearly all ways, the Soviet empire was more impressive than anything the tsars had assembled, but this period of "greatness" lasted less than three-quarters of a century, succumbing to a surge in competitive pressure from the United States in the context of Soviet economic malaise and political fragility.

The bases for feelings of humiliation in the wake of the Soviet collapse are stark. The Russia that is left over from the Soviet Union is roughly half the population (290 million in 1990 versus 144 million today) and three-quarters the area. At its peak, the Soviet economy was by a clear margin the world's second-largest; it fails to make even the top ten today. Except in nuclear military capacity, geography, and ambition, Russia is now a lesser, middle-sized power.

Despite the Soviet collapse and diminution of Russia by almost any measure, NATO not only persisted but expanded, incorporating key states that had been part of the Soviet empire and that feared Russian revanchism. NATO expansion was not universally endorsed in the United States. Fifty leading American specialists and practitioners, including scholars and former cabinet members, ambassadors, and senators, expressed their opposition from the outset in 1997 in an open letter to President Bill Clinton.[69] Since then other specialists have argued that NATO expansion did indeed play a role in Russia's efforts to reassert influence in its periphery.[70] In *The Clash of Civilizations*, published in 1996, Samuel Huntington reached a different conclusion, arguing that Russian revanchism was simply inevitable, a natural product of Russian civilization and historical national interest. As he put it, the country would seek to establish "a bloc with an Orthodox heartland under its leadership…from which it will attempt to exclude the influence of other powers. Russia expects the world to accept and to approve this system."[71]

A new Russian dictatorship eventually emerged out of the remnants of the Communist system and fragile experiments with democracy. The 1990s were wrenching for the Russians. In the uncertainty that swept the country

---

[69] "Opposition to NATO Expansion," Arms Control and Disarmament Agency, June 26, 1997, https://www.armscontrol.org/act/1997_06-07/natolet.

[70] See, for example, Stephen F. Cohen, "Have 20 Years of NATO Expansion Made Anyone Safer?" *Nation*, October 18, 2017; and J. Stapleton Roy, "Sino-Russian Relations in a Global Context: Implications for the United States," in "Russia-China Relations," 40.

[71] Huntington, *The Clash of Civilizations*, 164. Huntington noted that Ukraine would be a critical and difficult issue for Russia, which would want to reincorporate the country into its bloc. The major difficulty, he predicted, would stem from the strong national identity in western Ukraine.

as the Soviet system unraveled, Russians experienced residual statism, high unemployment, lawlessness, health crises, and the transition to a corrupt private economy dominated by monopoly capitalists known as the oligarchs. Putin, an ambitious, young KGB officer stationed in East Germany who observed the destruction of the Berlin Wall, came to power by political guile, charisma, nationalist fervor, and ruthlessness. He rose to control the military and its domestic component and successor to the KGB, the Federal Security Service (FSB). Through his command of Russia's organized means of violence, Putin manipulated the legal system as well as the media and civil organizations. He neutralized competitors and brought politically ambitious oligarchs to heel. It is an old recipe, but not one concocted of ingredients that give such leaders comfortable nights of sleep.

According to Michael McFaul, the factor that hardened Putin's harsh feelings and approach to the West was the palpable threat to his leadership.[72] The weak showing of his United Russia party in the December 2011 parliamentary elections and the associated massive demonstrations that began in December—the largest political demonstrations since 1991—shocked Putin. Already on edge due to the rapid demise of leaders from the Arab Spring revolutions and suspicious of U.S. meddling, he "needed to defuse these popular protests and restore his standing in time for the 2012 presidential election.... [H]e chose to repress and discredit his critics: He portrayed them as traitorous agents of the United States."[73] Putin blasted the United States for interfering in Russia's election, more than ever appealing to populism and nationalism to save his regime. By attacking the West, controlling the media, and manipulating the ballot count, Putin won the 2012 election with 64% of the popular vote.[74]

For additional reasons, he saw that the timing was right for extending his control of the periphery and confronting the West. Europe continued to present opportunities due to its disaggregated political organization, economic problems, weakening support for military investments and the use of force, and ambivalence toward Eastern Europe. Moreover, Europe's protector, the United States, was showing signs of overextension as it

---

[72] Michael McFaul, *From Cold War to Hot Peace: An American Ambassador in Putin's Russia* (New York: Houghton Mifflin Harcourt, 2018); and Michael McFaul, "The Smear That Killed the 'Reset,'" *Washington Post*, May 11, 2018.

[73] McFaul credits intelligence reports for the insight on Putin's shock at the fate of autocrats such as Hosni Mubarak and Muammar Gaddafi. See McFaul, "The Smear That Killed the 'Reset.'"

[74] "Russia's Presidential Election Marked by Unequal Campaign Conditions, Active Citizens' Engagement, International Observers Say," Organisation for Security and Co-operation in Europe, Office for Democratic Institutions and Human Rights, Press Release, March 5, 2012, https://www.osce.org/odihr/elections/88661.

struggled to recover from the Great Recession and to resolve the wars in Iraq and Afghanistan. President Barack Obama's commitment to restore the United States' image as a multilateralist may have also been a consideration. President Obama appeared to be far more cautious than his predecessor in operating unilaterally or applying military force, and he seemed earnest and committed to Washington resuming normal relations with Moscow.

Putin achieved his goal of acquiring Crimea quickly in winter 2014 and subsequently launched campaigns in eastern Ukraine and Syria. To further challenge U.S. and Western European influence, he mounted sustained, sophisticated propaganda campaigns and cyberattacks to disrupt American and European democratic institutions and processes.[75] According to U.S. director of national intelligence Dan Coats, Russia, China, Iran, and North Korea are the "worst offenders," but Russia is the "most aggressive foreign actor":

> [The Russians] are penetrating our digital infrastructure and conducting a range of cyber intrusions and attacks against targets in the United States.... These actions are persistent, they're pervasive, and they are meant to undermine America's democracy on a daily basis, regardless of whether it is election time or not. Russian actors and others are exploring vulnerabilities in our critical infrastructure as well.... What's serious about the Russians is their intent. They have capabilities, but it's their intent to undermine our basic values, undermine democracy, create wedges between us and our allies.[76]

Putin's popularity spiked in Russia with the annexation of Crimea, while support among Russians for a Western-style democratic government dropped significantly in the ensuing year.[77] Meanwhile, Putin backed right-wing opponents of immigration, same-sex marriage, abortion, and church-state separation and provided military assistance to sustain the Assad regime in Syria. Russian media demonized domestic protestors in authoritarian states as terrorists and radicals and labeled revolution

---

[75] According to Julia Ioffe, Putin's motivation was the personal affront that he and his inner circle perceived as a consequence of the publication of the Panama papers. For further discussion, see Julia Ioffe, "What Putin Really Wants," *Atlantic*, January/February 2018.

[76] Veronica Stracqualursi, "U.S. Intelligence Chief: 'The Warning Lights Are Blinking Red Again' on Cyber Attacks," CNN, July 14, 2018, https://www.msn.com/en-us/news/politics/us-intelligence-chief-the-warning-lights-are-blinking-red-again-on-cyber-attacks/ar-AAA3XY0?ocid=spartandhp. Chinese and Russian political interference is discussed at length by Peter Mattis in his chapter for this volume.

[77] See the extensive polling data collected by the Yuri Levada Analytical Center, available at http://www.levada.ru/en. The center is Russia's only independent polling agency and was labeled a "foreign agent" two weeks before the 2016 parliamentary elections.

seemingly everywhere as illicit and Western-sponsored.[78] The world needs a strong Russia, in this view:

> From the Kremlin's perspective, as Washington engages in stupid, hypocritical, and destabilizing global behavior, Moscow shoulders the burden of serving as a counterweight, thereby bringing sanity and balance to the international system....Putin's machismo posturing, additionally, is undergirded by a view of Russia as a country of real men opposing a pampered, gutless, and decadent West.[79]

"Civilization" thus became part and parcel of Putin's narrative, with the Russian Orthodox Church and Slavic ethnicity touted as key elements in making Russians culturally unique.[80] Putin seized on this message, understanding its meaning in national lore. Correspondingly, as Fiona Hill explains, "Putin wants respect in the old-fashioned, hard-power sense of the word" and "to turn the clock back seventy years to the old 'Yalta agreement' of 1945. He is pushing for a new division of spheres of influence." He claims that Russia "is the only country in this neighborhood with a unique civilization (rooted in Russian Orthodoxy and language), a long imperial history, a robust economy (based on energy and abundant natural resources) and the capacity to defend its territory and project power abroad."[81] Putin's vision, mirroring Russian history, is rooted in imperial notions of power and interests. Whether or not NATO expansion played a role, Putin exploited the "threat" NATO posed to these ambitions and Huntington's prediction was proved accurate.

Not part of the current narrative and just beneath the surface of Russian culture is a marked fear and lack of understanding of China that harkens to earlier periods. Chinese copying of Russian military technology, investments in the Russian Far East (RFE), and other activities in the border areas sound alarm bells in the press from time to time.[82] If history is any

---

[78] Dmitry Gorenburg, "Countering Color Revolutions: Russia's New Security Strategy and Its Implications for U.S. Policy," PONARS Eurasia, Policy Memo, no. 342, September 2014, 3–4, http://www.ponarseurasia.org/sites/default/files/policy-memos-pdf/Pepm342_Gorenburg_Sept2014.pdf.

[79] Stephen Kotkin, "The Resistible Rise of Vladimir Putin: Russia's Nightmare Dressed Like a Daydream," *Foreign Affairs*, March/April 2015, 150. See also Vladimir Putin, "Remarks at the Final Plenary Meeting of the Valdai International Discussion Club's XI Session" (Sochi, October 24, 2014), http://eng.news.kremlin.ru/news/23137.

[80] Michael Khodarkovsky, "Reviving Old Lies to Unite a New Russia," *New York Times*, January 11, 2018.

[81] Fiona Hill, "This Is What Putin Really Wants," *National Interest*, February 24, 2015. In an article almost identically titled, Julia Ioffe offers a different account of Putin's motives, arguing that he is less goal-oriented and is simply anti-West. See Ioffe, "What Putin Really Wants." The analysis in this chapter suggests that Russian interests may be subject to alteration and that Putin is probably capable of changing strategy when his and Russian interests change.

[82] For example, see Denis Abramov, "In Arms Trade, China Is Taking Advantage of Russia's Desperation," *Moscow Times*, November 16, 2017, https://themoscowtimes.com/articles/in-arms-trade-china-is-taking-advantage-of-russian-desperation-55965.

guide, fear of China could escalate in Russia should bilateral relations take a turn for the worse.

Putin's equating of himself with the Russian state and civilization is consistent with Xi's approach in China; it is what, in fact, dictators—Communist and former Communist alike—tend to do in their need for legitimacy and to survive in power. Putin's narrative portrays Russia as a great civilization now led by a strong, dynamic leader who personifies Russian virtues, is fighting Russia's enemies abroad (the West generally and the United States specifically), and is reasserting the country's rightful place as the preeminent power in Europe and establishing its dominance in new frontiers such as the Arctic.[83] It has no great vision of Russian international leadership or a system of values beyond "Russian" values. There is no sophisticated ideological underpinning. From national weakness, Putin has fashioned a traditional Russian, if personalized and opportunistic, nationalist ideology. His successors will inherit this—at most. They might also inherit chaos.

*China.* Historical legacies run even deeper in China. The CCP's narrative is of the country's singular greatness, enshrined in its name in Chinese (the central kingdom or country). Xi Jinping's strongest claim to legitimacy is showing progress in achieving what he calls the "China dream," which is no less than the return of China to its traditional position as the most powerful and respected country on earth with no peer competitors. Xi insists that only the CCP can realize this tectonic vision.

To be sure, China was the leading kingdom for most of the past two millennia. Its economy, innovations, and standard of living among the elite were mindboggling to the first European explorers who penetrated the Sinic world. Until the industrial revolution propelled Britain and then other European countries and the United States ahead, China was vastly wealthier, if not as inclined as some nations to extend influence far beyond its periphery. Except for a couple of recent centuries, China sustained a unique position of global wealth and regional hegemony.

As with Russia, this narrative may begin with greatness but quickly moves to bitterness—in China's case over mistreatment by European and Japanese imperial powers. The Japanese are singled out in a category of their own, frequently depicted in racist terms as evil and permanent enemies of China. Americans hold a special place in the narrative as well, as they were outright hostile to the Communist regime in China from 1949 until

---

[83] For a discussion of Russia's strategy to expand its sphere of influence, see Evelyn N. Farkas and James M. Ludes, "We Regret to Inform You That Russia Is (Probably) at It Again," *Atlantic*, August 16, 2018.

the early 1970s. According to the narrative, the United States persists today in "encircling" and "containing" China. Its naval bases and presence in the Pacific and Indian Oceans, support of Taiwan, and alliances with South Korea, Japan, and Australia are offered as proof. Added to these are the never-ending U.S. studies and policies regarding human rights violations. The "rebalance to Asia" undertaken by the Obama administration and most recently the "trade war" allegedly begun by the Trump administration are rankling to China. Unequal sharing of wealth and technology—claimed holdovers from colonialism and then the Cold War—is another recurrent gripe. Associated with these factors, Chinese leaders have held consistently that the post–World War II order is the creation of the United States and its allies for their own benefit.

Much more than Putin, Chinese leaders perceive enormous opportunities opening. The recession of 2008–9 (which China mostly dodged), the doldrums that have plagued the American heartland since then, and the terribly expensive and wearying wars with seemingly no end in the Middle East and Afghanistan engendered a great debate in China over just how soon it can replace U.S. international leadership with its own—and in so doing, bolster Xi's claims to CCP leadership for life and to an extraordinary place in Chinese and global history. Here several strands are interwoven into an ambitious narrative. Deng Xiaoping's admonition for China to "hide its strength and bide its time" has been supplanted by Xi's call to develop "a new type of great-power relationship" between the United States and China, one in which the two nations for some period stand alone as superpowers and the United States respects China's historic, preeminent interests and ways of asserting influence in the western Pacific. The latter expectation seems to include recognition of Chinese sovereignty in the South China Sea, exclusive air and naval rights extending far off China's coasts, incorporation of Taiwan into the PRC by 2049, and other unnamed privileges in the country's vicinity. Xi's intentions are similar to Putin's in terms of expanding Chinese influence and interests, but they are set on a much bigger stage. The Belt and Road Initiative (BRI), which comprises the Silk Road Economic Belt and 21st Century Maritime Silk Road, aims to position China into expansive regional—and eventually global—leadership by building a strategic network of infrastructure and economic hubs to increase Chinese influence across the Eurasian landscape, through Southeast Asia along the equatorial sea routes to the Middle East and Europe, and north to the Arctic.[84] The Made in China 2025 policy seeks to enable the country to leapfrog the United States in technology and innovation. The remarkable progress China has made in modernizing and building its military, already making it much more difficult for U.S. bases, operations, and contingency plans in the region, is a portent of what is to come. The progress the CCP anticipates in the decades ahead for the PLA would enable its forces to eclipse American superiority.[85]

Chinese military and quasi-military actions in the South China Sea and north to Japan have added substance to the narrative. China invoked an alleged historical claim for the great bulk of the South China Sea, the "nine-dash line" that was ironically contrived by the Republic of China after World War II and now is enshrined in a map in PRC passports. China embarked on constructing major island bases out of reefs and atolls across a wide sweep of these waters in 2014. The projects commenced after Russian aggression earlier that year in Crimea and eastern Ukraine had failed to provoke a military response from NATO or the United States; instead, the West only levied economic and diplomatic sanctions. China's base building met with an even weaker response: much international complaining, occasional and carefully nonconfrontational freedom of navigation operations by U.S. naval and air forces, and a case brought by the Philippines to the Permanent Court of Arbitration at The Hague. The court ruled against China, but there were simply no enforceable penalties, and China rejected and ridiculed the decision.

Past transgressions against China and ongoing efforts to keep the country down are invoked by the leadership to justify other actions to push the United States and its allies back and build the nation's wealth and power. On a daily basis, PLA Air Force planes harass the territorial airspace of Japan (as do Russian military aircraft) and frequently Taiwan as well, causing both to scramble their own fighters. Confrontations at sea are recurrent and dangerous, particularly because of China's use of fishing boats and heavily armed coast guard vessels. In addition, there are ubiquitous Chinese cyberattacks against the United States, Europe, Japan, South Korea, and Taiwan. Targets range from national labs and government computer systems to Congress, defense contractors, commercial businesses, think tanks, and utilities. Much of the hacking is

---

[84] Nadège Rolland, *China's Eurasian Century? Political and Strategic Implications of the Belt and Road Initiative* (Seattle: NBR, 2017).

[85] See, for example, Elizabeth Economy, "Xi Jinping's Superpower Plans," *Wall Street Journal*, July 19, 2018, https://www.wsj.com/articles/mr-xis-superpower-plans-1532013258.

government-sponsored, and much more is simply encouraged. A priority of these attacks is the theft of technologies and trade secrets—anything that is a priority to Chinese industrial policy and that can enrich an aggressive entrepreneur or benefit military development.[86] One of the more spectacular heists, based on different motives, was against the U.S. Office of Personnel Management. Chinese hackers obtained the dossiers, including Social Security numbers, of around 22 million Americans who work for or were associated with the U.S. government.[87]

The CCP has resurrected traditional symbols of Chinese civilization. Like his predecessor Hu Jintao, Xi has embraced Confucius and classic Chinese texts and art forms, seemingly for the purpose of justifying the need for "harmony" in society and more fully associating the CCP, and especially now Xi himself, with Chinese history and national pride. Chinese culture and interests are championed overseas to facilitate the acceptance of Chinese influence. Soft power is exercised around the globe through public affairs and nonprofit operations in important cities and through Confucius Institutes established at universities. Free copies of the *China Daily* deliver the CCP's messages at the world's newsstands. At the most recent party congress, Xi Jinping Thought was enshrined in the constitution. In today's version of Communist newspeak, Xi and the CCP espouse values such as freedom and the rule of law.[88] It is all pulled together in the "China dream," which Xi uses to inspire belief in his historic leadership of national "rejuvenation."[89]

If imperial Chinese hegemony and current ideology, foreign relations, industrial policies, and internal monitoring and repression are a guide to what Chinese hegemony will look like in the future, we should expect a hierarchical system directed by a regime whose first priority is maintaining control in order to protect its interests. In other words, we should not expect an open system of common seas and airspace, equal legal standing among nations, acceptance (let alone encouragement) of the rule of law

---

[86] Commission on the Theft of American Intellectual Property, "The Report on the Theft of American Intellectual Property," NBR, May 2013; Commission on the Theft of American Intellectual Property, "Update to the IP Commission Report—The Theft of American Intellectual Property: Reassessments of the Challenge and United States Policy," NBR, February 2017; Office of the U.S. Trade Representative, "2018 Special 301 Report," April 2018, https://ustr.gov/sites/default/files/files/Press/Reports/2018%20Special%20301.pdf; and William C. Hannas, James Mulvenon, and Anna B. Puglisi, *Chinese Industrial Espionage: Technology Acquisition and Military Modernisation* (New York: Routledge, 2013).

[87] A separate but related breach around the same time compromised the data of 4.2 million federal employees. Julie Hirschfeld Davis, "Hacking of Government Computers Exposed 21.5 Million People," *New York Times*, July 9, 2015.

[88] Javier C. Hernández, "The Propaganda I See on My Morning Commute," *New York Times*, January 28, 2018.

[89] Robert Lawrence Kuhn, "Xi Jinping's Chinese Dream," *New York Times*, June 4, 2013.

and democracy, or democratically run multilateral organizations, among other things. We might expect the extension of the CCP and its influence overseas—an economically corrupt, Leninist form of suzerainty.

To summarize, the external threats to the CCP (and according to the party, to China) and its international ambitions are democratic governments, notably the United States, which are accused of seeking to contain, encircle, and undermine China. Extraordinary efforts are justified for pushing back the democracies and depleting them, for they stand in China's path to its rightful preeminence. Despite the nation's success under the rules of the existing order, new or revised international arrangements are required to weaken the United States further and accommodate Chinese interests. Xi cites China's progress as proof that he and the CCP are winning the contest. Like Putin, Xi has a nationalist ideology, but his is less contrived, being built on nearly a century of evolving Communist doctrine and supporting party infrastructure.

Still weeding out potential rivals and attempting to refurbish the CCP's image through his anticorruption campaign, Xi appears to have amassed more political power in China than anyone since Mao. The CCP boasts around 90 million members, has a long history and tested procedures, and commands the military. Putin's United Russia party is relatively incoherent and still a work in progress. His power is grounded in personal control over his lieutenants and, with them, control of the military, secret police, media, and civilian components of the government. Compared with Putin, Xi commands vastly more impressive state bureaucracies and economic levers. Given his tightened grip on power, ideological sophistication, and the assets he wields internally, Xi would appear to be more secure, but even he has to be vigilant. The tariff war with the United States, the high expenses of BRI, his leadership cult, the new totalitarianism, continuing poverty in the country, a slowing economy, and environmental challenges, among other issues, reverberate among the elites and population as this volume goes to press.[90]

---

[90] See Xu Zhangrun, "Imminent Fears, Immediate Hopes—A Beijing Jeremiad," trans. by Geremie R. Barmé, *China Heritage*, July 2018, http://chinaheritage.net/journal/imminent-fears-immediate-hopes-a-beijing-jeremiad; Nectar Gan, "Chinese Intellectuals Urged to Toe the Party Line after Pushbacks on Policy," MSN, August 9, 2018, https://www.msn.com/en-sg/news/other/chinese-intellectuals-urged-to-toe-the-party-line-after-pushbacks-on-policy/ar-BBLDGka; Jerome A. Cohen, "Xi Jinping Sees Some Pushback against His Iron-Fisted Rule," *Washington Post*, August 2, 2018, https://www.washingtonpost.com/news/global-opinions/wp/2018/08/02/xi-jinping-sees-some-pushback-against-his-iron-fisted-rule; and Keith Bradsher and Steven Lee Myers, "Trump's Trade War Is Rattling China's Leaders," *New York Times*, August 14, 2018.

## Interests

*Shared and complementary interests.* There is an extraordinary level of strategic cooperation between the Russian and Chinese regimes, as the authors of this volume thoroughly document, and driving much of it is their shared interest in stopping Western influence, and that of the United States in particular, from undermining them. Ambassador J. Stapleton Roy describes the situation succinctly: "They are both opposed to a world dominated by a sole superpower. They both feel threatened by the United States' unilateralism, interventionism, and support for color revolutions."[91] Their strongest mutual fear is of democratic ideals, the Western policies that promote them, and the positions of influence held by the United States and other democracies around the world and in multilateral institutions. The authoritarians' nightmare is that Western policy could jump-start and then aid a new wave of "color revolutions" that flow into China and Russia, or even start there. Xi and Putin therefore have a common purpose in deterring, discrediting, weakening, destabilizing, and even defeating the democracies; breaking their coalitions; and checking and rolling back their overseas military bases and outposts of political influence. It is a global conflict, with the "battlegrounds" being Japan, the Korean Peninsula, Taiwan, and Southeast Asia in the East and the nascent democracies in Eastern Europe, the established ones in Western Europe, and most importantly the United States itself.

Besides sharing the threat posed by democracies in general and powerful ones in particular, and hence their common interest in defeating the threat, Russia and China share conventional strategic interests as ambitious nations. Aligned, they seek to pursue more effectively a number of strategic goals: (1) counterbalance the United States on a global level, stretch U.S. capabilities, complicate strategic planning, drive wedges between the United States and its allies and friends, and erode its will to lead, (2) broaden their militarily defended spheres of influence, overturning in these areas post–World War II rules such as freedom of navigation and skies and international rule of law, (3) check the United States and its allies in multilateral forums, blocking their decisions and actions and promoting those of China and Russia, (4) weaken the United States and its allies and friends at home through a withering array of cyberattacks and espionage aimed at their defense industries, economies, media, and political systems, (5) enhance their military capabilities through weapons and technology

---

[91] Roy, "Sino-Russian Relations in a Global Context," 39.

cooperation and sales, (6) repress ethnic, religious, and other movements that lead to terrorism and separatist challenges to their regimes, and (7) gain international legitimacy.

Accordingly, in contrast with the treatment they receive from the West, Xi and Putin support each other's political legitimacy and authoritarian values. Neither attacks the other for his monopoly on domestic political power, cyberattacks and espionage, human rights violations, lack of rule of law, extraordinary industrial and trade policies, or aggression overseas. Just the opposite, they honor and extol each other. Xi and Putin have a relationship constructed from expedient calculations. Learning from the past, they do not allow personal or ideological issues to undercut a useful strategic alignment against the United States and the West. In short, they seek to avoid the strategic mistake of their predecessors between the late 1950s and end of the Cold War.

Above all, they must avoid major conflict with one another. Both are nuclear powers possessing a second-strike capability. Even with a collapse in bilateral relations, one would expect no worse than a limited conflict on the scale of 1969—so long as neither perceived a vital interest such as regime survival or highly valued areas or populations to be threatened. At some time in the future, China might absorb parts or all of the lightly populated RFE if Russia were to falter. Today, their nuclear deterrents draw a strategic bottom line.

It is the combination of enduring complementary and expedient shared interests between China and Russia, more than any other factor, that should keep U.S. national security strategists up at night. Simply put, the complementary interests are their separate regional focuses; the expedient interest is dividing American power. With Russia's historical, enduring interests and ambition mainly in Europe, and China's in Asia and along the routes to Asia, memories of the first half of the twentieth century are rekindled. Beyond timing, literally no strategic cooperation between China and Russia need transpire for the United States' worst nightmare to be attempted—the conquering of East Asia and Eastern Europe by autocratic powers hostile to the United States. This is a plausible nightmare for three reasons. First, two decades ago, following the Cold War, Americans looked to cash in the so-called peace dividend. Without a peer competitor even on the horizon, the U.S. policy of maintaining the capacity to fight two major wars, one across the Pacific and one across the Atlantic, was abandoned.[92] Second, even if preserving that capacity had remained a policy, Chinese advancements eventually would challenge that capacity, should China sustain stronger economic growth than the United States and make commensurate military investments. Third, historically, wars have been waged when rising, ambitious powers threaten international and regional leaderships.

Scenarios for a collapse of the post–World War II order in Asia and Europe include ones short of war. International economic crisis and resulting political upheaval in the United States, Europe, and Japan might sap their capacity and will to resist new rounds of gray aggression in the two theaters, coupled with ultimatums.[93] Chinese strategy for achieving global political preeminence appears to be comprehensive, relying first and foremost on the accumulation of all the ingredients of raw power—economic, technological, and military—and then utilizing the leverage China can derive from these capacities to extend its influence regionally and globally; inserting power in strategic locations where it can do so without firing a shot, such as the South China Sea and base locations farther overseas; aligning with key actors such as Russia, Pakistan, and North Korea; establishing international alternatives to the Bretton Woods system and other international institutions; and harnessing soft power, such as propaganda and diplomatic tools. China is positioning itself for what it hopes will be as peaceful a transition to global leadership as possible, with sufficient advantage to deter violent contestation from the United States, and presumably, since Chinese policy does not reveal specific plans, to replace or heavily modify the post–World War II order.

Over 2,400 years of history should serve to caution Chinese leaders. Contemporary scenarios for the onset of war, and for a new two-front war, are hardly far-fetched. China was likely emboldened to embark on its island-building activities in the South China Sea and expand its harassment of Japanese airspace and territorial seas, as well as U.S. naval operations in the region, by the lack of a military response to Russia's aggression in Ukraine.

---

[92] See Richard J. Ellings, "Preface," in Tellis et al., *Strategic Asia: 2017–18*, vii–xv, xiii. As late as 2012, the Pentagon's 2012 Defense Strategic Guidance spoke of reducing the size of the force. The 2014 Quadrennial Defense Review (QDR), in a departure from preceding QDRs, noted that "a smaller force strains our ability to simultaneously respond to more than one major contingency at a time," suggesting the need to return to two-war preparedness. U.S. Department of Defense, *Sustaining U.S. Global Leadership: Priorities for 21st Century Defense* (Washington, D.C., January 2012), 7, http://archive.defense.gov/news/Defense_Strategic_Guidance.pdf; and U.S. Department of Defense, *Quadrennial Defense Review* (Washington, D.C., March 2014), 22, http://archive.defense.gov/pubs/2014_Quadrennial_Defense_Review.pdf.

[93] Gray aggression refers to planned actions by states to advance their influence, which are often taken without forewarning and lie between normal diplomacy and explicit military aggression.

Analysts should thus assume that there is already strategic interdependence between the Indo-Pacific and European theaters, if not formalized war planning between China and Russia. Signs of future allied weakness on one front—for example, a failure of U.S. resolve on the Korean Peninsula in the face of plausible Chinese and North Korean threats—would seem likely to encourage greater aggression on the other—for example, Russian aggressiveness in Europe. Big wars tend to break out in steps.

A host of developments might tip Asia into war. One can imagine scenarios. China might perpetrate incidents to achieve de facto control of some air or sea space—for example, by using Chinese coast guard destroyers against U.S. Navy ships in the South China Sea, believing that the United States would not respond forcefully. Or China might attack Taiwan following an independence referendum. In another scenario, war could break out on the Korean Peninsula because of an accidental missile launch or an attack ordered by a rogue officer. We should trust the United States to live up to its treaty obligations to Japan, South Korea, and Australia, and to very likely defend Taiwan out of a perceived need to sustain U.S. credibility and prevent the strategically located island from falling into hostile hands. If a Korean conflict erupts, for example, China might seek to divide U.S. forces by instigating crises in the South China Sea and involving Taiwan. These already dangerous circumstances, made ever more so by the uncertainties associated with the fast-changing balance of power in the region, produce an almost endless number of realistic conflict-producing scenarios.

With or without a war in Asia, Russia has proved in Georgia and Ukraine that it will invade its near abroad to extend its influence. If war breaks out in Asia first, with the bulk of U.S. forces being marshaled to fight there, it is hard to imagine Russia not taking advantage in Europe. How would Russia define its near abroad? Would it take one or more of the Baltic states, and perhaps the rest of Ukraine? If these fell rather easily, what would happen next? Would NATO respond before any of its members were attacked. If so, would it only attack advancing Russian forces in conquered territory or also forces in Russia? Would Russia threaten the nuclear annihilation of Western Europe to deter NATO from intervening or utilize enhanced radiation weapons if NATO did intervene? How many U.S. forces would be allotted to the European theater? Together, the enduring complementary and expedient shared interests of China and Russia form the principal challenge to U.S. strategy.

A sharply different category of shared interests is a complicated one and a source of concern to Russia as well as a source of profit. The economic relationship, which received a boost when Russia was hit by Western sanctions for its invasion of Ukraine, is growing. Russia is increasing energy exports and continues to sell military equipment to China, while China produces a wide array of goods purchased by Russia. Bilateral trade turnover in 2017 amounted to 5.5% of Russian GDP, compared with less than 0.7% of Chinese GDP.[94] Sino-Russian trade expanded by 21% in 2017 and may grow by another 20% in 2018 to $100 billion. The Power of Siberia gas pipeline, agreed to in 2014 following the sanctions against Russia, is reportedly 75% complete. The volume of Russian exports to China is thus expected to keep growing.[95] From the perspective of China, the gas is a boon to meeting the environmental aspiration of replacing coal use. Moreover, it enhances energy security by adding an overland supply from the north, safely far away from vulnerable sea lanes and coming from an adjacent supplier not likely to turn off the spigot, dwarfed as Russia is by Chinese power. In contrast, as Charles Ziegler shows in his chapter, Russia is sensitive to large-scale economic interchange due to the asymmetry in the relationship and the penchant by China to utilize economic leverage punitively when it sees fit, as it has recently done against South Korea, Japan, and Taiwan. Leverage in this instance comes from the market, not the supplier. The Russian interest here is to manage trade with China at a level that is profitable but does not provide Beijing with decisive leverage. Russia has similar concerns about selling military items to China. Profits aside, at what point does China no longer need Russian arms, and when might these weapons be pointed back at Russia?

*Coincident global interests.* The coincident global interests are the separate stakes that China and Russia have in the international economic system. Due to their very different stakes, the two countries' interests in the post–World War II economic system neither align nor conflict.

As noted earlier, China has prospered enormously from its integration with the world economy and the arrangements that support this order. It is a member of the World Trade Organization (WTO), has replaced the United States as the world's workshop, is vital to global supply chains, and pays great attention in industrial planning to the vertical and horizontal integration of its domestic economy—that is, in being the primary global supplier. Russia's stakes are comparatively idiosyncratic and consist mostly in supplying energy to Europe and China and to a lesser extent exporting arms. Individual energy contracts and arrangements are far more important

---

[94] "GDP Current Prices," International Monetary Fund, IMF DataMapper, http://www.imf.org/external/datamapper/NGDPD@WEO/RUS/CHN.

[95] "China-Russia Trade Volume Surges in 2018," BRICS Post, April 19, 2018, http://thebricspost.com/china-russia-trade-volume-surges-in-2018/#.W1nr71BKiUm.

than the global trading system and its rules. Russia is not a member of the WTO, and its stake in the international economic system is mainly indirect—the continued demand for energy and arms by its customers abroad, which derives in part from the customers' successful participation in international trade. Its other stake in the international economy is reliance on imports for some consumer goods, many of which come from China. Russia's direct stake in the global economic system is remarkably narrow and focused.[96]

China's astronomically greater integration into the global economy than Russia's may mean little for the prospects for peace. Economic integration—that is, globalization—fails to guarantee international stability. More often than not, it is the most economically integrated countries that go to war with one another. Like divorce, war rarely makes economic sense, but it happens every day. What is important here about Chinese-Russian coincident interests in the global economic system is not a comparative propensity for engaging in conflict; it is that they indicate relative vulnerability, investments in the status quo, and leverage short of war.

*Conflicting interests.* Geography and demography are destiny, at least to some extent. By far the world's largest nation by territory, Russia on maps looms over China, the world's most populous nation. The two countries are in fact each other's contiguous neighbor of greatest strategic importance, and that has been the case for centuries. The Chinese population has dwarfed Russia's for as long as the two have been identifiable as countries. Their border hostilities and worries have spanned from their first encounters during the Qing Dynasty in the mid-1600s to the depths of the Sino-Soviet split in the twentieth century to the present day. Even at the height of the Sino-Soviet alliance, as we discussed, the countries jockeyed diplomatically over their frontier.

The China-Russia border comprises two segments totaling nearly 2,700 miles. The major part is 2,607 miles in length and runs from just short of the Pacific Ocean, on the Tumen River across from North Korea, to Mongolia. The short segment, only 62 miles long, is far to the west, high in the Altai Mountains abutting Kazakhstan. As insecure, distrustful, authoritarian regimes, China and Russia remain natural competitors on their frontiers and in adjacent areas: Mongolia, Central Asia, and soon perhaps the Arctic. Today both countries have ambitious plans for the

---

[96] Russia aspires to join the WTO, perhaps wishing to emulate China in this regard. But as long as the country is saddled with Western economic sanctions, the prospects for Russia developing a compelling direct interest in the international trading system are bleak.

Arctic, including developing a significant naval presence.[97] In view of China's vastly superior economy and fast-developing conventional and nuclear military forces, Russia's nuclear deterrent and credibility are essential to its security. Russians are acutely aware of the vulnerability of the lightly populated RFE to China, historic Chinese claims to it, and ongoing Chinese actions with regard to its offshore Northeast and Southeast Asian claims—more than enough factors to give Russians serious pause. In short, alongside the ongoing, significant strategic coordination between China and Russia is latent competition deriving from their geostrategic proximity, exacerbated by the fearful nature of their regimes and the relative superiority of Chinese power.

BRI represents, according to Nadège Rolland, "the organizing foreign policy concept of the Xi Jinping era." It is, she shows, "not just a series of engineering and construction plans…to complete a fragmented Eurasian transportation system but a thoroughly considered and ambitious vision for China as the rising regional leader."[98] BRI's mainland route, known as the "economic belt," runs west from China through Kazakhstan, other former Soviet territories in Central Asia, Iran, and Turkey, branching into the Arab countries and Europe. Its plans include pipelines as well as transportation projects, communications and cyber links, university and other people-to-people exchanges, and financial services. By 2016, annual Chinese trade with the Central Asian states totaled $30 billion, far exceeding Russia's $18 billion.[99] Russia is maneuvering at the margins. In August 2018, it reached an agreement with Iran, Kazakhstan, Azerbaijan, and Turkmenistan to divide up the Caspian Sea, enabling it to better compete with China.[100] Should BRI be successful, Chinese economic ties and influence will predominate along the entire length of Russia's southern border and perhaps into its European neighborhood.

To date, Central Asian states have welcomed the Chinese initiative for the opportunity to boost their economies. According to Paul Stronski, Kazakhstan "is also using Chinese investment to signal to Russia that it

---

[97] Marc Lanteigne, "Northern Crossroads: Sino-Russian Cooperation in the Arctic," NBR, March 2018, http://www.nbr.org/downloads/pdfs/psa/lanteigne_brief_032718.pdf.

[98] Rolland, *China's Eurasian Century?* 1, 43.

[99] Paul Stronski, "China and Russia's Uneasy Partnership in Central Asia," East Asia Forum, March 29, 2018.

[100] The *New York Times* reports that "Russia may have agreed to finally resolve the sea's status now, after three decades of objections, not because of continued Western pressure but because of rising trade competition from China's 'One Belt One Road' policy, according to Shota Utiashvili." Andrew E. Kramer, "Russia and 4 Other Nations Settle Decades-Long Dispute over Caspian Sea," *New York Times*, August 12, 2018, https://www.nytimes.com/2018/08/12/world/europe/caspian-sea-russia-iran.html.

has options and that any attempt by the Kremlin to replicate a Ukraine scenario…a country with a large ethnic Russian population, could not go ahead without running into China." He notes that China may be building a military base on the border between Tajikistan and Afghanistan and is beginning to sell weapons and provide security assistance in the region.[101] Russia still leads the Collective Security Treaty Organization, whose other full members are Armenia, Belarus, Kazakhstan, Kyrgyzstan, and Tajikistan. Through this arrangement and its residual troops in the region, Russia may gain some leverage by supporting political leaderships. It also heads the Eurasian Economic Union, whose goal is a single market with Russia at its center, but lacks the capital to make the organization a significant competitor to BRI. In addition, Russia leads the Commonwealth of Independent States, its arrangement to sustain Russian political special interests in Central Asia. The organization appears more symbolic than real. Without the level of aid and investment funds wielded by China, Russia's artifices in the region are ineffectual and its efforts are frequently viewed suspiciously by regional states as aimed at undermining their sovereignty.[102] Russia's role as the region's hegemon is declining quickly.

As noted above, the expansive RFE is another region of competition. The RFE is bracketed by Siberia to the north and east, China to the south, and the Sea of Japan to the west. It anchors one of six corridors of China's long-term, geostrategic ambition to extend its hegemony through and beyond its Eurasian frontiers.[103] Consistent with BRI, China's current purposes in the RFE appear to be securing its borders and neighborhood, establishing transportation links, gaining privileged access to energy and natural resources, expanding its influence, and positioning itself for long-term dominance.

For the time being, China is pursuing these objectives peacefully to avoid raising fears in Russia and to enable it to concentrate strategically on the western Pacific, Central Asia, and other areas. China is making investments in the RFE and keeping its northern military forces away from the border. From its vulnerable position, Russia is currently pleased with this, as its interests are to maintain the RFE's security and bolster the region's Russian population and economic growth.

---

[101] Stronski, "China and Russia's Uneasy Partnership in Central Asia."

[102] Arkady Dubnov, "Reflecting on a Quarter Century of Russia's Relations with Central Asia," Carnegie Endowment for International Peace, April 19, 2018.

[103] Rolland, *China's Eurasian Century?* 72–73.

History haunts the region, however. While as formal policy the PRC accepts the current borders, it considers them to be illegitimate, the result of two of the many "unequal treaties" signed by the Qing Dynasty when it was feeble and defeated. The 1858 Treaty of Aigun and 1860 Convention of Peking allotted Russia what is today the RFE but to China is Outer Manchuria—large swaths on opposite sides of the Amur River, south to Khabarovsk in the middle of the area, and all the way southeast to Vladivostok on the coast of the Sea of Japan. It was along the Amur that the fighting between Soviet and PLA forces was most intense during the clashes of 1969. Although Beijing is quiet on its historic grievances in the current period of strategic alignment, memories of the Sino-Soviet border war and standoff are palpable in both China and Russia.

Day-to-day affairs reflect the comparative dynamism of China. The contrast in the populations and economies across the border is dramatic. Throughout the vastness of the RFE live only six million Russians, some of whom seek money, goods, and entertainment in the drastically more prosperous and urbanized China across the border. And that population is declining in numbers while experiencing miniscule growth in its standard of living. The Chinese population in Manchuria, in contrast, is growing and wealthier. According to one study, there are approximately five Chinese for every Russian between the ages of 15 and 64 living adjacent to the border. The ratio of Chinese to Russians is twenty to one when the distances from the border are widened to several hundred kilometers.[104] Estimates of how many Chinese are living inside Russia vary widely; the number is probably in the hundreds of thousands.[105]

The adjacent RFE's raw materials and land look attractive to Beijing. The RFE boasts oil and natural gas, minerals, large fish stocks in the Sea of Okhotsk, timber, and water. The scale of Chinese compared with Russian investments is astronomical. The most spectacular case is the $400 billion deal between Gazprom and the China National Petroleum Corporation to supply the RFE's natural gas to China for the next 30 years. Chinese companies have also invested in a giant copper mine, and Xi announced a $10 billion cross-border infrastructure fund in 2017. Agriculture is emerging as a vibrant business as well. Chinese farmers are growing a variety of crops on land that Russia is leasing at low rates to encourage production. Many of the timberlands near the border have been leased to

---

[104] Dragos Tirnoveanu, "Russia, China, and the Far East Question," *Diplomat*, January 20, 2016.

[105] See, for example, ibid.; and "Chinese in the Russian Far East: A Geopolitical Time Bomb?" *South China Morning Post*, July 8, 2017.

Chinese firms for harvesting.[106] In addition, since 2014, Russian and Chinese government-affiliated companies have been co-developing Zarubino Port, which is south of Vladivostok near the North Korean and Chinese borders and gives China direct access to the Sea of Japan.[107]

Russians have looked warily at all these developments, searching for signs that China is positioning itself to control the region. Not surprisingly, as Rolland observes, "Russia's initial reaction to BRI was cautious."[108] On balance, however, when viewed from the perspective of current Chinese and Russian priorities, the political and military status quo on the borders is likely to continue, albeit for a finite period. For China, the RFE is propagating fruit in need of regular irrigation. For Russia, the RFE is a profitable orchard seemingly perched near the edge of a cliff that is eroding. Russia needs internal migration to the region and other exceptional developments.

Making the situation even worse from the Russian perspective is the totality of China. The re-ascension of the historic Asian power is the new, long-term reality. There is near certainty that the towering asymmetry between them will endure and in all likelihood grow. Russian security and economic interests in the border and adjacent regions are increasingly vulnerable. What could divide their alignment down the road is the prospect of China continuing to expand more rapidly than Russia, making the relationship even more lopsided and ending Russian dreams of recapturing hegemony in its historic, southern "near abroad" and perhaps into Eastern Europe. Another possibility is a victory by China and Russia over the West, leading, for example, to the dismantling of NATO, the United States' withdrawal from the western Pacific, and the end of the U.S. alliances in Asia. These would be a short-lived boon to Russia, perhaps, but winning coalitions tend to fall apart. Moreover, if the Soviet experience is any guide, even if they were to achieve victory against the United States either peacefully or in a two-front war, Russia and China would presumably position themselves for maximum advantage over each other for the post-victory era.

In either scenario—faster growth or victory over the West—there would be little cause for China to continue to give a comparatively impotent Russia special consideration. Putin and Xi (or probably their successors) share no universalist, democratic ideology, such as the one that anchors the liberal post–World War II order, to temper raw power politics. What would be

---

[106] "Chinese in the Russian Far East."

[107] "China, Russia to Co-develop Zarubino Port," IHS Maritime 360, July 3, 2014; and Artyom Lukin, "Why the Russian Far East Is So Important to China," Huffington Post, March 14, 2015.

[108] Rolland, *China's Eurasian Century?* 80.

China's incentive to share hegemony in any part of Central Asia, or elsewhere on the new Silk Road for that matter, or to be satisfied with Mongolian neutrality or even sovereignty, let alone Russia-Mongolia strategic alignment? Why would China permit Russia to retain sovereignty in the RFE, which the tsars wrested unfairly from the Qing Dynasty? Why would China permit Russia to exercise influence on the Korean Peninsula, or with Japan, or to play a decisive role in any important market or supply source around the world, including Western Europe? China could conceivably make exceptions, allowing Russia a small empire in Eastern Europe and carving out for it a special mercenary role as China's enforcer in unstable areas of Central Asia.

In the meantime, reflecting its acute need for markets and investment, Russia nurtures foreign trade opportunities that are out of sync with Chinese foreign policy. It did not, for example, join China in sanctioning South Korea over the deployment of the Terminal High Altitude Area Defense (THAAD) system in 2017 and is instead pursuing the growth of a Russian-Korean partnership.[109] Another interesting example is Russia's special relationship with China's competitor, India. Russia continues to rank as India's top foreign supplier of military equipment and has plans for much stronger economic ties. The biggest energy market it might tap down the road is Japan, which could also serve as a strategic partner someday, providing Russia with leverage against China as well as the United States.

## Strategic Questions

The chapter's opening quotations by Xi and Putin were taken from their remarks made on June 8, 2018, on the occasion of Xi awarding Putin China's first friendship medal. The lavish, highly publicized ceremony was held in the Great Hall of the People, where the CCP and PRC convene their grandest meetings. There could hardly have been a clearer symbol of the Chinese regime's sense of its power and interests. There could hardly have been a clearer demonstration that China is the "big brother" to Russia today and that authoritarian fidelity with Putin is currently important to the CCP.

Indeed, the modern history of China-Russia relations underscores the point that the two countries' authoritarian leaders have acted on the basis of their interests, interests shaped by the balance of power and historically

---

[109] Anthony V. Rinna, "Russia's Strategic Partnerships with China and South Korea: The Impact of THAAD," *Asia Policy* 13, no. 3 (2018): 79–99.

based, nationalist ideologies that they have championed in their quests to survive, achieve popular legitimacy, and enhance their influence. In view of the trends in the distribution of power and seeming decline of U.S. global and regional leadership, Xi and Putin assess their shared and complementary interests to exceed their conflicting ones. Both have a fundamental interest in undermining and dividing the influence of the United States and other democracies as means to protect their power at home and extend their influence abroad.

How susceptible are China and Russia to reassessing their interests and alignment? Scholars cannot answer that question with certainty, but it stretches credulity to accept that Xi and Putin are immune to reconsidering their cooperation in view of changing international strategic and domestic circumstances. As we have seen, history provides precedents for strategic recalculations by once-collaborating Chinese and Russian authoritarians. The real questions involve identifying the circumstances that would most likely weaken the China-Russia alignment and conducting a full cost-benefit analysis of the policies designed to produce those circumstances.

Policymaking in the United States and its allies is in flux. The rise of China, aggressive actions by Russia, the strategic coordination between the two countries, and the fast-changing balance of power are driving Western and East Asian nations to question their domestic as well as foreign policies. Many are struggling over how to respond to Russian actions and policies that are based on interests shared with or complementary to China's—for example, assassinations in Europe, efforts to undermine democratic elections in the United States and Europe, aggression in Ukraine, and support of the Assad regime in Syria. Similarly, many democracies are struggling with how to coordinate responses to a wide range of Chinese actions. These actions start with predatory industrial policies such as intellectual property acquisition and subsidies causing overcapacity in various industrial sectors. The United States and its allies and partners are struggling to respond to China asserting territorial claims in the South China Sea, conspiring with Russia to circumvent UN and U.S. economic sanctions against North Korea, and intimidating Japan, Taiwan, the Philippines, and Vietnam militarily. Democracies are struggling with how to reorganize their multilateral cooperation. How can they more effectively assemble as coalitions in Europe and Asia to bolster their trade and economic growth and protect sectors of their economies? How can they better balance and deter Russia through NATO and respond to China's stated goal of exerting preeminent influence in Asia and more ambiguous goal of reaching global preeminence? At a minimum, the balance of power in Asia and Europe must be more stable than in recent years, grounded in the United States' and its allies' improved economic vitality, military strength, and credibility to defend core interests. The United States and its allies need to agree on what those core interests are and to bolster deterrence in both theaters appropriately.

The question of values, as the world learned in the Cold War, is not inconsiderable. No attempt by the United States and its allies to downplay values such as individual freedom, rule of law, and democracy is likely to change the threat perceived by Xi and Putin to their reigns. On the contrary, such attempts could serve to reduce the leverage, credibility, and legitimacy of U.S. and Western leadership. In this regard, the strategic advantage the United States obtained through its championing Western values over the decades of the Cold War serves as a guidepost.

From the West's perspective, how might the interests of these two powers be exploited without, as Angela Stent warns in her foreword to this volume, driving the two closer together? According to Robert Sutter in his chapter, China now occupies the advantageous "hinge" position in China-Russia-U.S. relations. That dynamic may be ending with the Trump administration's tougher policies toward China and efforts to reach out to Putin. U.S. policy matters. Can a full Sino-Russian alliance be prevented, for example, by helping Russia contend with the far more powerful China over the longer term and giving it a greater stake in peaceful relations with European countries, the United States, and Japan, thereby bringing Russian interests into greater alignment with the democracies? Was the rapprochement between the United States and China in the last quarter of the 20th century, ironically, a model of what might portend for U.S.-Russian relations in the second quarter of the 21st century? Are the interests of the Russian dictatorship simply incompatible with such a realignment? And can today's Chinese strategists revert to "biding their time" and downplaying China's overwhelming advantages to calm Russian leaders' fears and avoid pushing them into the West's camp?

As the drastically weaker of the two countries, Russia may be more susceptible to Western policies that seek to change its alignment interests. On his own, Putin (or his successor) is in no position to pressure, let alone pick a fight with, Xi. From the West's perspective, Russia's weak economy is one source of leverage, and specifically the government's dependence on oil and gas sales abroad for revenue. How might stronger sanctions over Ukraine and cyberattacks on democracies affect Putin's calculations? Might there be counter-cyberattack options to signify resolve and the capability to weaken critical components of the Russian economy on which Putin depends? Other points of leverage are the Russian military operations and aid in eastern Ukraine, which are expensive and dangerous. What if those burdens became heavier through stronger Western military support for Ukraine, to be lifted with Russia's withdrawal? How might Putin respond to accelerated arms budgets and investments by Europeans, budgets and investments that the vastly smaller Russian economy could not match? How vulnerable to influence is Putin if the West were to expand its own cyberstrategy against Russia and more forthrightly champion democratic values? Russia does not share enduring interests with China in their border areas now, and in the longer term the two countries would seem to share no significant interests other than avoiding nuclear conflict. Without credible partners with which to balance China, Russia's long-term prospects appear bleak, to the point that the country risks declining into a vassal of China. Once Russia's aggressive behavior abates, would the United States and its allies consider adding the carrot of additional markets—for example, the long-proposed pipeline to Japan—to diversify Russian interests?[110] Would not Japan make an attractive strategic partner to balance China? Would the prospect of Western, Japanese, and international acceptance, should Russia cease aggressive, anti-democracy behavior, assist in Russia's tilting toward the West?

In sum, is there a new strategic equilibrium, a stabilizing grand bargain that the West could construct carefully and methodically over time with Putin and his successors, communicating clearly the methods and goals from the outset and that verifiable Russian behavior is the measure of success or failure?[111] The analysis here suggests that Putin's and Russia's interests may be subject to alteration. Like his Soviet forebears, Putin has changed strategy in the past when he perceived that his and Russian interests warranted change. His successors, whoever they may be, will assume

---

[110] Shoichi Itoh, "Sino-Russian Energy Relations in Northeast Asia and Beyond: Oil, Natural Gas, and Nuclear Power," in "Japan and the Sino-Russian Entente: The Future of Major-Power Relations in Northeast Asia," NBR, NBR Special Report, no. 64, April 2017, 29–41.

[111] Because there appears to be zero basis for trusting Russia's leadership, letting up on sanctions without proven progress on key issues is a poor option. Russia needs to know U.S. strategy, just as the Soviet Union knew from day one Ronald Reagan's zero-zero option for getting rid of the SS-20s. Relief from sanctions and progress on a gas pipeline to Japan must come after, or be (incrementally) consonant with, Russia's withdrawing from eastern Ukraine and ending cyberattacks. Indeed, akin to the deployment of Pershing II and Tomahawk missiles, the initial step for the United States and its allies would be to increase support of Ukraine, the Baltic states, and other regional countries, holding in abeyance the carrots until good faith has been shown. Simultaneously, the other NATO members have to raise their defense budgets and act with greater cohesion. The United States likewise must continue to increase its defense spending and show resolve in backing NATO. This requires, in other words, a comprehensive melding of U.S. and multilateral commitments over an extended period of time for the purpose of changing Russia's calculations for aligning with China. In adopting this approach, the United States will be better prepared to deter, and if deterrence fails, to fight, a two-theater war.

responsibility for Russia's interests from the same position of national weakness and could be even more insecure politically.

Xi and the CCP are another story. Strengthened by continuing economic growth and military progress, and with Chinese nationalism surging, they sense that trends are on their side. They are more secure and far more powerful internationally than Putin. They believe that their closer relations with both Russia and the United States and decent relations in Europe give them still fuller advantage. Through his public statements and policies, Xi is committed to bold international accomplishments leading to China's global preeminence. The construction of island bases in the South China Sea and the rollout of BRI provide the most conspicuous evidence of growing Chinese power and the relevance of the current narrative. Barring a major national stumble and presuming continued autocracy, Xi's successors doubtlessly will continue down this path, seeking to fuse national interests, Chinese traditions, and contemporary ideology to legitimize their leadership, protect themselves, and attain greatness.

Xi's and the CCP's vulnerabilities are fewer than Putin's, but still worth considering, as are policies that aim for no more than balancing and containing Chinese power. How dependent on trade is the Chinese people's prosperity? What would be the effects on China and the West of a reduction of that trade through expulsion from the WTO, export or import controls, or long-term tariffs to discourage trade? What would be the effects of reductions in China's ability to invest overseas? Over time, can a coalition of like-minded nations, such as that imagined in the Trans-Pacific Partnership, outcompete China economically? Can enhanced investments in defense and cooperation in the Indo-Pacific successfully balance the fast-growing power of the PLA? Can enhanced ideological confrontation and successful resistance overseas to Chinese power and influence stir resistance to the CCP's totalitarianism domestically and infiltrations elsewhere?

The details of China-Russia strategic cooperation matter enormously. What are the two sides choosing to do together? Which of their cooperative efforts are working? Which are not? What specifically is motivating each effort? Where are their strengths and vulnerabilities? Reducing ambiguity is an important step in assessing threats and opportunities soberly and promoting good policymaking. In the subsequent chapters, this volume will delve deeper into the China-Russia alignment and then weigh options available to the United States.

## EXECUTIVE SUMMARY

This chapter analyzes Sino-Russian economic relations by exploring trade, energy, and finance in bilateral ties; assessing the strategic import of economic projects; and discussing the strategic implications for U.S. policy in the region.

MAIN ARGUMENT
The strategic partnership between China and Russia is vital for both sides as U.S.-Russia relations have deteriorated and U.S.-China trade ties have frayed. Beijing and Moscow oppose U.S. hegemony and share an authoritarian, neomercantilist vision that seeks to reshape the liberal international order. Russia, however, does not support China unconditionally; it is following a complex policy of aligning politically with Beijing to balance the U.S., while hedging in pursuit of its economic interests. China-Russia economic relations are complementary but unbalanced, with Beijing holding a dominant position in most dimensions. U.S.-China economic interdependence provides Washington with considerable leverage, but this advantage could be squandered through ill-considered policies that drive Beijing and Moscow closer together. China's leverage over the U.S. is augmented by its economic relations with Russia. This influence will grow as the U.S. government pursues a trade war with China while shunning multilateral forums like the World Trade Organization and the Trans-Pacific Partnership.

POLICY IMPLICATIONS
- The U.S. should recognize the competitive dimension in Sino-Russian relations and avoid actions that encourage further cooperation against U.S. interests.

- Confrontational economic policies toward U.S. allies and partners in the Asia-Pacific will likely create openings for China, with Russian backing, to develop new economic mechanisms and promote an illiberal order that reduces U.S. influence.

- Russia's energy turn away from Europe toward the Pacific enhances China's energy security, but also diversifies supply for U.S. allies and so does not negatively affect U.S. interests.

Chapter 2

# China-Russia Relations in Energy, Trade, and Finance: Strategic Implications and Opportunities for U.S. Policy

*Charles E. Ziegler*

This chapter analyzes the economic dimension of Sino-Russian relations—trade, energy, and finance—and considers the strategic implications for U.S. policy in the Asia-Pacific. Eurasia, with Russia at its center, is key to China's massive Belt and Road Initiative (BRI). Ramping up energy exports and seeking new investments, particularly from China, are crucial in Russia's pivot toward the Pacific. There are significant complementarities in the Russian and Chinese economies, and a commitment on both sides to deepen ties, but the evolving economic relationship is asymmetrical. This chapter explores the role of trade, energy, and finance in China-Russia relations; assesses the strategic import of economic ties; and assesses the implications for U.S. policy in the region.

The Asia-Pacific regional order and indeed the global power structure are at a critical inflection point. Russia has benefitted only marginally from the liberal international order and resists the United States' hegemonic position in the global economy. China has benefitted greatly from and largely accepts this rules-based system, but it stands accused by the United States and others of engaging in unfair trade practices to achieve economic dominance, including excessive tariffs, dumping, nontariff trade barriers, forced technology transfers, and bans on certain products, making it

---

**CHARLES E. ZIEGLER** is Professor of Political Science and University Scholar at the University of Louisville. He can be reached at <charles.ziegler@louisville.edu>.

The author is grateful to Robert Sutter, Brian Franchell, and NBR's anonymous reviewers for their helpful comments on an earlier version of the manuscript. He also wishes to thank NBR intern Ian McManus for providing research assistance on trade data.

difficult or impossible for foreign firms to compete.[1] Clearly, Beijing wishes to reshape existing global economic institutions to its advantage through a new set of trade and financial mechanisms, and Russia could prove useful in this endeavor. Russia's economic power lags far behind that of China and the United States, and Moscow consequently has little ability to shape this order. The Kremlin, however, prefers Beijing's geopolitical and geoeconomic visions over Washington's. The implications for China-Russia relations are central to this study.

The "new balance of power" in the Pacific focuses not only on military capabilities but also on economic leverage.[2] China dominates the region's economy as the primary or secondary trading partner of virtually every country in Asia and the Pacific. Its economic power is also evident by its success in getting 57 countries, including major U.S. allies in Asia and Europe, to sign on to the Asian Infrastructure Investment Bank (AIIB). More importantly, BRI—China's initiative to build a complex of rail, port, road, and pipeline infrastructure connecting Asia and Europe—is "one of the main instruments of China's grand strategy, coordinating and giving direction to an extensive array of natural resources in pursuit of an overarching political objective."[3]

Policies that combine geopolitical and economic objectives are not unique to Russia and China, but these two countries have become especially adept at utilizing geoeconomic strategies to promote and defend their national interests. As Robert Blackwill and Jennifer Harris observe, geoeconomic approaches are frequently more effective than the militarily dominant geopolitical strategies preferred by the United States. Moreover, Washington's long-standing commitment to neoliberal economics has led it to eschew blending state power and control with economic instruments to project power.[4] By contrast, Russia and China employ state-owned or state-supported national champions to achieve national goals domestically and abroad, and their leaders are often willing to sacrifice purely commercial considerations in order to realize geopolitical goals. The geoeconomic

---

[1] See "President Donald J. Trump Is Confronting China's Unfair Trade Policies," White House, Fact Sheet, May 29, 2018, https://www.whitehouse.gov/briefings-statements/president-donald-j-trump-confronting-chinas-unfair-trade-policies.

[2] Graham Allison, *Destined for War: Can America and China Escape Thucydides's Trap?* (New York: Houghton Mifflin Harcourt, 2017), 20–24.

[3] Nadège Rolland, "China's 'Belt and Road Initiative': Underwhelming or Game-Changer?" *Washington Quarterly* 40, no. 1 (2017): 136. See also Nadège Rolland, *China's Eurasian Century? Political and Strategic Implications of the Belt and Road Initiative* (Seattle: National Bureau of Asian Research [NBR], 2017).

[4] Robert D. Blackwill and Jennifer M. Harris, *War by Other Means: Geoeconomics and Statecraft* (Cambridge: Harvard University Press, 2016).

policies pursued by Moscow and Beijing at times reinforce their strategic partnership (as when Western sanctions led Russia to finalize new energy deals with China), but they may also strain relations (as in the competition for influence in the Middle East through nuclear power programs).[5]

Of the seven main geoeconomic instruments described by Blackwill and Harris, China has the clear advantage in five: trade, investment, sanctions, economic assistance, and financial/monetary policy. Russia has the advantage in energy and commodities, and the two are roughly equal in cyber capabilities.[6] In 2016, China was the world's leading exporter (nearly $2 trillion), while Russia ranked seventeenth at just under $282 billion.[7] Moreover, China has a highly diversified trade structure, which makes its economy far more robust than Russia's hydrocarbon-dominated economy. Regarding investment potential, China's foreign exchange reserves in April 2018 were roughly nine times as large as Russia's.[8] China's diversified economy and its dominant position in the world ($11.2 trillion GDP in 2016) make it far less vulnerable to sanctions than Russia ($1.3 trillion GDP in 2016). This wealth makes it possible for China to provide more foreign assistance than can Russia, and Beijing does so without the neoliberal conditionality provisions generally attached to Western aid.[9] Although the yuan is a long way from replacing the dollar for most international transactions, it is considerably stronger than the Russian ruble and in 2015 was included in the International Monetary Fund's basket of currencies comprising special drawing rights.

On the cyber dimension of geoeconomic power, China and Russia are global leaders. China's cyber capabilities, however, have been oriented more toward achieving economic objectives, whereas Russia has focused on political or security issues. Regarding energy and commodities, Russia would immediately appear to have an advantage over China, given its huge reserves of oil and gas, vast stores of minerals and timber, and long history of exporting nuclear power technologies. But even here, Russia's apparent strength has limitations. A volatile global oil market and the dynamics of

---

[5] Shoichi Itoh, "Sino-Russian Energy Relations in Northeast Asia and Beyond: Oil, Natural Gas, and Nuclear Power," in "Japan and the Sino-Russian Entente: The Future of Major Power Relations in Northeast Asia," NBR, NBR Special Report, no. 64, April 2017.

[6] Blackwill and Harris, *War by Other Means*.

[7] "The World's 20 Largest Exporting Countries," WorldAtlas, https://www.worldatlas.com/articles/exports-by-country-20-largest-exporting-countries.html.

[8] "Russia Foreign Exchange Reserves," Trading Economics, https://tradingeconomics.com/russia/foreign-exchange-reserves.

[9] China does, however, use trade, investment, and finance to leverage access to markets, secure port facilities, or pressure recipients into supporting its one-China policy.

the oil curse constrain Russia's economic performance, though the Russian economy is less distorted than that of Nigeria or Venezuela. Prime Minister Dmitri Medvedev has observed that the fuel and energy complex accounts for nearly 30% of Russia's national budget and over two-thirds of its export revenues.[10] In the wake of the Crimea conflict and 2015 drop in oil prices, GDP growth slowed and the state budget deficit worsened.

A complex of eastern-oriented oil and natural gas pipelines will link Russia with the Chinese energy market for some three decades or more. China, for its part, is intent on maintaining diversified sources of energy and can choose from various oil and gas suppliers. Russian firms are competing with Middle Eastern, Central Asian, and African oil exporters; Central Asian pipeline gas; and liquefied natural gas (LNG) from Indonesia, Australia, Qatar, Malaysia, and the United States. Finally, China is rapidly developing its nuclear power industry and is already competing with Russia for projects across the globe.

This brief overview demonstrates that while Russia is positioned to exercise significant economic leverage against the former Soviet republics and European countries, its capabilities pale by comparison with China's. As strategic partners, Moscow and Beijing have largely renounced the use of military or coercive diplomatic measures in their relationship—power dimensions where Russia is China's equal or superior. The realm of economics is quite different. Russia may try to hold its own with China economically, but it simply cannot surmount these asymmetries. China is more favorably positioned than Russia to achieve its regional (and global) objectives, which may result in a less than harmonious relationship.

The following section addresses trade, finance, and infrastructure in the Sino-Russian relationship, with observations on investment trends, regional cooperation, and international economic institutions. Energy ties between the two powers constitute the focus of the subsequent section, followed by an assessment of bilateral economic cooperation and a brief discussion of possible future directions. Implications for U.S. policy are then presented, while the conclusion ties together the various threads of the argument.

---

[10] Michael Bradshaw and Richard Connolly, "Barrels and Bullets: The Geostrategic Significance of Russia's Oil and Gas Exports," *Bulletin of the Atomic Scientists* 72, no. 3 (2016): 158.

## Trade, Finance, and Infrastructure

### An Asymmetric Trade Relationship

The China-Russia relationship in trade and finance is complementary, but it is not one of equals. China is the world's largest trading nation, ranking 1st in exports and 2nd in imports, with total trade turnover of $4.1 trillion in 2017.[11] By contrast, Russia ranked 16th in exports and 24th in imports in 2016, and its total trade in 2017 was far below China's at $606 billion.[12] China's foreign exchange reserves at the end of 2017 were the world's largest at $3.14 trillion, while Russia's reserves were $356 billion, according to the Central Bank of Russia.[13] This asymmetry confers a distinct advantage on China in dealing with Russia.

The 2014 crisis in Ukraine and sanctions regime imposed by the United States and its European allies accelerated a trend toward greater economic cooperation between Russia and China, though ties had been developing throughout the 2000s and 2010s. For Russia, the denial of Western technologies and finance, compounded by lower oil prices after 2014 and flat demand in Europe, made the Chinese market for hydrocarbons even more attractive than before. China also can provide much of the investment and technology Russia needs to develop its vulnerable Far East and Eastern Siberian territories.[14] For China, the crisis strengthened Beijing's hand in dealing with Moscow. One prominent example is the Power of Siberia natural gas deal. Held up for nearly a decade over pricing disagreements, President Vladimir Putin stepped in to broker a 30-year, $400 billion agreement between Gazprom and China National Petroleum Corporation (CNPC) in May 2014. Although specific details of the Power of Siberia pipeline were not released, China reportedly secured a favorable price.[15]

Sino-Russian trade relations reflect the classical notion of comparative advantage. China's export strengths are in manufactures—94.3% of total

---

[11] "Economic and Trade Information on China," HKTDC Research, June 26, 2018, http://china-trade-research.hktdc.com/business-news/article/Facts-and-Figures/Economic-and-Trade-Information-on-China/ff/en/1/1X000000/1X09PHBA.htm.

[12] Directorate-General for Trade, "European Union, Trade in Goods with Russia," European Commission, April 16, 2018, http://trade.ec.europa.eu/doclib/docs/2006/september/tradoc_113440.pdf.

[13] "China December Forex Reserves Rise of $3.14 Trillion, Highest since September 2016," Reuters, January 7, 2018, https://www.reuters.com/article/us-china-economy-forex-reserves/china-december-forex-reserves-rise-to-3-14-trillion-highest-since-september-2016-idUSKBN1EW061; and Russian Federation Central Bank, "International Reserves of the Russian Federation (End of Period)," https://www.cbr.ru/eng/hd_base/mrrf/mrrf_m.

[14] Ironically, China is the country most likely to encroach on the Russian Far East.

[15] Morena Skalamera, "Sino-Russian Energy Relations Reversed: A New Little Brother," *Energy Strategy Reviews* 13–14 (2016): 103–4.

exports in 2015, according to the World Trade Organization (WTO)—while 75.5% of Russia's imports are manufactures. Russia's exports are dominated by the fuels and mining products (67.4%) that China needs to keep its economy running (fuels constituted 21.3% of China's imports). European plans to reduce dependence on Russian hydrocarbons after the supply interruptions of 2006 and 2009 only marginally affected Russia's export structure. In 2016 the EU-28 still accounted for 45.8% of Russia's exports (largely oil and gas), while China took just 9.8% of Russian exports. China did provide a somewhat greater share of Russia's imports after the Ukraine crisis—20.9% in 2016 compared with 16.9% in 2014—but 38.2% of Russia's total imports originated in the European Union.[16]

The data in **Table 1** illustrates the rapid expansion of trade between Russia and China. According to UN estimates, total trade was a mere $15.4 billion in 2004, increased to $83.5 billion in 2014, and then declined in the wake of the economic slowdown and drop in oil prices. According to Russian estimates, bilateral trade slipped to $63.6 in 2015 before rebounding to $86.9 in 2017. Still, this figure is well below the optimistic $200 billion that the leaderships on both sides have touted as a goal for 2020.[17]

More importantly, the structure of Sino-Russian trade has shifted dramatically. In 2001 the share of machinery and equipment in Russia's exports to China was 28.7%, while the share of mineral exports to China (mostly oil and gas) was 10.3%. The share of machinery and equipment in China's exports to Russia was 9.3%. In that year, Russia accounted for just over 2% of China's total trade, while China accounted for just over 5% of Russia's.[18]

By 2011 the share of machinery and equipment in Russia's exports had declined to just 0.7%, though it had rebounded slightly to 2.7% by 2016. Minerals constituted three-fourths of Russian exports to China in 2014, though this figure declined to around 59% in 2016. The share of machinery and equipment exported by China to Russia reached nearly 39% in 2016. China had become Russia's chief trading partner at just under 15% of total foreign trade, whereas Russia accounted for less than 2% of China's total foreign trade. This data suggests that

---

[16] "Trade Profiles," World Trade Organization, http://stat.wto.org/CountryProfile/WSDBCountryPFReporter.aspx?Language=E.

[17] Catherine Putz, "China and Russia Aim to Increase Trade Turnover to $200 Billion by 2020," *Diplomat*, November 8, 2016, https://thediplomat.com/2016/11/china-and-russia-aim-to-increase-trade-turnover-to-200-billion-by-2020.

[18] Alexander Korolev, "Neblagopriatnaia vzaimodopolniaemost' v Rossiisko-Kitaiskikh ekonommicheskikh otnosheniiakh i ee posledstviia" [Unfavorable Complementarity in Russian-Chinese Economic Relations and Its Consequences], *Mezhdunarodnyi neftegazovyi biznes* 1 (2018): 44.

TABLE 1   Total China-Russia trade (in billions of dollars)

| Year | Russian estimates | UN estimates |
|---|---|---|
| 2000 | – | 6.7 |
| 2001 | – | 8.7 |
| 2002 | – | 9.8 |
| 2003 | – | 11.9 |
| 2004 | – | 15.4 |
| 2005 | – | 21.1 |
| 2006 | 28.7 | 27.7 |
| 2007 | 40.3 | 39.6 |
| 2008 | 55.9 | 52.7 |
| 2009 | 39.5 | 39.8 |
| 2010 | 59.3 | 57.7 |
| 2011 | 83.2 | 76.8 |
| 2012 | 87.5 | 82.5 |
| 2013 | 88.8 | 83.4 |
| 2014 | 88.4 | 83.5 |
| 2015 | 63.6 | 60.0 |
| 2016 | 66.1 | 63.2 |
| 2017 | 86.9 | – |

SOURCE: Russian estimates are taken from the Federal Customs Service of Russia. Foreign trade reports are provided from 2007 onward in the Customs Service archive (in Russian) at http://www.customs.ru/index.php?option=com_newsfts&view=category&id=125&Itemid=1976. UN estimates are based on the UN Statistics Division's SITC Database and were accessed through the Observatory for Economic Complexity project at the Massachusetts Institute of Technology, https://atlas.media.mit.edu/en/resources/data.

NOTE: Figures are rounded. UN data available to 2016. Dash indicates estimate is not available.

Russia's industrial base has eroded and the country has become largely a raw materials supplier to China, while China's rapid modernization has increased the proportion of high-tech exports, including personal computers and automobiles.[19] National and regional officials regularly stress the importance of promoting value-added exports to China, but this imbalance will not likely be corrected in the near future.

---

[19] Korolev, "Neblagopriatnaia vzaimodopolniaemost' v Rossiisko-Kitaiskikh ekonommicheskikh otnosheniiakh i ee posledstviia," 43–49.

In the 1990s, arms sales accounted for a significant share of Russian machinery exports to China. Sophisticated weapons constituted one of Russia's few viable exports (other than raw materials), while China needed arms suppliers in the wake of Western sanctions following the Tiananmen Square massacre. In Putin's first presidential term, Russia exported well over $2 billion per year in weapons to China, with sales peaking at $3.12 billion in 2005 and accounting for 60% of all Russian arms exports. Sales then declined in the following years, as Moscow became wary of transferring top-of-the-line systems to a potential competitor and China developed advanced manufacturing capabilities, in part through reverse engineering Russian systems.[20] In 2010, Russian arms sales declined to $744 million and stayed below the billion-dollar mark through 2017, according to the Stockholm International Peace Research Institute.[21] As China modernized its weapons systems, it shifted from importing Russian weapons to competing with Russia for a share of the international arms market, most notably in fighter aircraft, submarines, tanks, air defense systems, and ballistic missiles.[22]

Political tensions between the United States and both Russia and China have affected the Sino-Russian economic relationship. Although Russia's economic pivot toward Asia predated the Ukraine crisis and imposition of Western sanctions, heightened tensions with the United States and Europe have accelerated this process. Politically, Asia—especially China—has been far less confrontational, as the Asian states are generally willing to overlook Russia's annexation of Crimea and military involvement in Syria and southeast Ukraine. Moscow is aware that the Asia-Pacific will shape global economic trends well into the 21st century, and the Kremlin is seeking to position Russia within this emerging framework. Development of the sparsely populated Russian Far East is a declared national priority, which requires trade and investment from the country's Asia-Pacific neighbors. At the same time, the vulnerability of this resource-rich territory has shaped Russian security policy toward the region.

Since the early 2000s, China has been developing a comprehensive and skillful economic diplomacy that advances Chinese commercial,

---

[20] Siemon T. Wezeman, "China, Russia, and the Shifting Landscape of Arms Sales," Stockholm International Peace Research Institute (SIPRI), July 5, 2017, https://www.sipri.org/commentary/topical-backgrounder/2017/china-russia-and-shifting-landscape-arms-sales.

[21] Ibid.

[22] Robert Farley, "Russia vs. China: The Race to Dominate the Defense Market," *National Interest*, July 13, 2015, http://nationalinterest.org/feature/russia-vs-china-the-race-dominate-the-defense-market-13316.

strategic, and foreign policy goals, and ostensibly seeks to build a more "just" international order—that is, one that better represents the interests of non-Western nations.[23] China's economic power has made possible a multifaceted and effective trade policy. By contrast, Russia's lack of economic diversification and relatively low level of trade puts the country at a disadvantage in economic relations with China.

## Investment

Russia's approach to investment is highly personalistic and lacks strategic direction. Close friends and associates of President Putin occupy key positions in the oil and gas industries and are influential in shaping negotiated deals. Igor Sechin (deputy prime minister and head of Rosneft), Gennady Timchenko (director of the Russian-Chinese Business Council), and Alexei Miller (CEO of Gazprom) are some of the most prominent examples. Weak institutionalization on the Russian side results in poor coordination among various energy firms, excludes participation by local governments in the Russian Far East, reduces the effectiveness of Russian energy diplomacy, and gives Chinese companies (especially the powerful state-owned enterprises) an advantage in energy negotiations.[24] Putin's promotion of national champions has constrained foreign investment, especially in the energy sector, but in recent years Moscow has revised its position on Chinese firms acquiring equity in the oil and gas industries. In 2016, for example, Sinopec acquired a 10% share in SIBUR, China's Silk Road Fund acquired a 9.9% stake in the Yamal LNG project, and CNPC acquired 20% interest in the Yamal project.

Chinese officials are well aware of the personalistic nature of doing business with Russia and have deliberately targeted the executives of Russia's national champions as a means of influencing Putin.[25] Chinese investment in Russia greatly exceeds Russian investment in China, though reliable figures are difficult to find. Alexander Lukin notes the wildly differing figures advanced by the respective governments. Official Chinese data shows around $9 billion invested by the end of 2015, while Bank of Russia data records just under $1.7 billion. The Russian figures are obviously far too

---

[23] Timothy R. Heath, "China's Evolving Approach to Economic Diplomacy," *Asia Policy*, no. 22 (2016): 157–91.

[24] Bo Xu and William M. Reisinger, "Russia's Energy Diplomacy with China: Personalism and Institutionalism in Its Policy-Making Process," *Pacific Review* 31 (2018).

[25] Alexander Gabuev, "China's Pivot to Putin's Friends," *Foreign Policy*, June 25, 2016, http://foreignpolicy.com/2016/06/25/chinas-pivot-to-putin-friends-xi-russia-gazprom-timchenko-sinopec.

low, while the higher Chinese figures may omit offshore investments.[26] Large Chinese firms are attracted by Russia's abundant natural resources and are better able to deal with the challenges of doing business in Russia, which include a murky legal system, questionable guarantees for investors, and an overall weak economy.

Chinese projects in Russia (and elsewhere) do not consistently receive official state support, as the recent deal between CEFC China Energy and Rosneft illustrates. In September 2017, CEFC, a private firm, agreed to purchase a 14.6% stake in Rosneft for $9.1 billion from Glencore and the Qatar Investment Authority. The Russian government would have retained a controlling interest in Rosneft, and the deal was widely publicized as signaling a new level of Russian-Chinese energy cooperation. However, in May 2018 the deal fell apart after CEFC's chairman Ye Jianming was detained for questioning in a criminal investigation and the company's debts ballooned.[27] Although the Rosneft deal and other CEFC projects appeared to support BRI, no Chinese state-run investment company stepped in to assume CEFC's share. Chinese national oil companies are looking for opportunities to partner with international firms, but they will likely be more careful about acquiring foreign assets given President Xi Jinping's anticorruption campaign and relatively low oil prices.[28] Since strategic Chinese investments are proceeding in other countries, Rosneft simply may have been deemed too risky an investment.[29]

Russia's ability to attract FDI dropped off significantly in the wake of the Ukraine crisis, as oil prices declined and Western firms suspended projects. The number of greenfield projects declined by 39% to 134, lower than in Poland. In the past, Russia has ranked low in Chinese FDI, often not making the top ten destinations. However, Chinese companies took advantage of the post-Ukraine situation to conclude over $5 billion in deals, led by automotive groups Hawtai and Chongqing Lifan Industry. This investment

---

[26] Alexander Lukin, *China and Russia: The New Rapprochement* (Cambridge: Polity, 2018), 145–48.

[27] Aibing Guo, Elena Mazneva, and Judy Chen, "China's Russian Oil Marriage Nixed Amid Fall of Suitor CEFC," Bloomberg, May 6, 2018, https://www.bloomberg.com/news/articles/2018-05-06/china-s-russian-oil-marriage-nixed-amid-collapse-of-suitor-cefc.

[28] See Erica Downs, "China's National Oil Companies Return to the World Stage: Navigating Anticorruption, Low Oil Prices, and the Belt and Road Initiative," in "Asia's Energy Security and China's Belt and Road Initiative," NBR, NBR Special Report, no. 68, November 2017.

[29] Michael Lelyveld, "China Bows Out of Russian Oil Deal," Radio Free Asia, May 14, 2018, https://www.rfa.org/english/commentaries/energy_watch/china-bows-out-of-russian-oil-deal-05142018103852.html; and Maximilian Hess, "China Has Decided Russia Is Too Risky an Investment," *Foreign Policy*, May 16, 2018, http://foreignpolicy.com/2018/05/16/china-has-decided-russia-is-too-risky-an-investment.

was desperately needed—Russia saw capital outflows of $151 billion in 2014, well above the $133.6 billion during the 2008 crisis.[30]

Official Chinese policy prioritizes investments in projects related to BRI, high-tech manufacturing, overseas R&D, agriculture, and in general projects that enhance China's national security. Strategic considerations are important, but China targets investments based on expected return. For example, Chinese FDI in Russia during 2017 increased significantly, to $10 billion, but that same year the United Kingdom received $19 billion in Chinese FDI, while ChemChina's purchase of the Swiss-based Syngenta (agribusiness) put Switzerland at the top with $45.4 billion. China's emphasis on investment in the energy and commodities sectors, which accounted for nearly half of all Chinese FDI in 2017, extends well beyond Russia.[31]

## *The Regional Dimension of Economic Relations*

Globalization notwithstanding, geographic proximity remains a critical dimension of trade. China's three northeast provinces and the Russian Far East historically have had close economic relations. Though suspended during the Soviet era, these relations resumed after the collapse of the Soviet Union. Both governments are committed to developing cross-border trade and investment to promote development in these remote and less affluent regions.[32]

For Moscow, expansion and diversification of Russian exports are closely linked to development of Eastern Siberia and the Russian Far East. At present, the population drain has stabilized, albeit at a very low level. Infrastructure is inadequate, and the Russian government has not allocated sufficient funds to modernize the Far East, a key goal of the Kremlin's plan for social and economic development of the region by 2025. The system of airports is critical to this remote region, but since 1991 the number of airports has declined from 470 to 82, and only half of those have paved runways that can accommodate large aircraft. Although Russia's Ministry of Transport is planning to spend more than 100 billion rubles over six years on renovating 61 of the region's airfields, the Ministry of Finance has

---

[30] Courtney Fingar, "FDI to Russia Slumps but Chinese Investors Step In as Others Pull Back," *Financial Times*, May 6, 2015, https://www.ft.com/content/99ff3bc8-f338-11e4-8141-00144feab7de.

[31] Betty Huang and Le Xia, "ODI from the Middle Kingdom: What's Next after the Big Turnaround?" BBVA Research, February 2018, https://www.bbvaresearch.com/wp-content/uploads/2018/02/201802_ChinaWatch_China-Outward-Investment_EDI.pdf.

[32] See Rensselaer Lee and Artyom Lukin, *Russia's Far East: New Dynamics in Asia Pacific and Beyond* (Boulder and London: Lynne Rienner, 2015), 153–78.

yet to approve the program.³³ Moreover, in 2013 the government allocated 106.1 billion rubles for airport renovation and new construction, but 64 billion "went missing," according to Yury Trutnev.³⁴

By shifting the geopolitical axis toward central Eurasia, and hyping Russia's position as a bridge between Europe and Asia, Moscow can enhance its claim to regional great-power status. Russia is also seeking to reassert its presence along the Pacific littoral, yet without incurring the potential costs of formal alliances. Concrete steps toward reclaiming a place in the Asia-Pacific include strengthening the Pacific Fleet and closer political ties with key partners in the region.³⁵

As envisioned by government officials, the plan is to integrate the Russian Far East into Asia's dynamic economies, drawing on the technology and demographic resources of Russia's Asian neighbors. In particular, Moscow is looking to China for investment and anticipates that the AIIB and BRI will inject significant funding into Russia's eastern regions. This expectation may be misplaced, however, as BRI prioritizes more westerly and southerly routes, while Russia's proposed projects for the Far East tend to be unprofitable or plagued by pervasive corruption. Nonetheless, China does support the development of cross-border infrastructure with the goal of enhancing access to Russia's raw materials in the Far East region, including as a component of BRI. In 2009 the two sides signed an investment cooperation framework supporting a wide range of projects that would coordinate development strategies and accelerate economic growth on both sides of the border.³⁶ In July 2017 the China Development Bank agreed to create a joint investment fund with the Russian Direct Investment Fund valued at 68 billion renminbi ($11 billion) to invest in energy, transportation, and industry in Siberia and the Russian Far East, as well as in projects through the Eurasian Economic Union (EEU).

---

[33] Vasilii Marinin and Valeriia Komarova, "100 mlrd na posadku: Kak Mintrans postroit 61 aeroport na Dal'nem Vostoke" [100 Billion for Runways: How the Ministry of Transport Built 61 Airports in the Far East], *RBK*, April 27, 2018, https://www.rbc.ru/business/27/04/2018/5ae049689a79471da0a51a20?from=center_1.

[34] Mariya Kokoreva and Sergei Vit'ko, "Trutnev rasskazal o propazhe 64 mlrd. rub. dlya aeroportov Dal'nego Vostoka" [Trutnev Discusses Missing 64 Billion Rubles for Far Eastern Airports], *RBK*, November 28, 2017, https://www.rbc.ru/society/28/11/2017/5a1d60659a79476f830b3add?from=materials_on_subject.

[35] Lee and Lukin, *Russia's Far East*.

[36] "Joint Statement of the Moscow Meeting between Heads of State of China and Russia," June 18, 2009, http://www.fmprc.gov.cn/mfa_eng/wjdt_665385/2649_665393/t573751.shtml.

The deal allows Vnesheconombank (Russia's foreign development bank) to raise capital in the face of Western sanctions.[37]

Russia's maritime strategy incorporates protecting the Far East's colossal resources—especially on the continental shelf and within the country's exclusive economic zone—which supposedly other nations seek to exploit. Russian naval forces off the Pacific coast are tasked with defending these natural resources, while deploying a survivable nuclear deterrent capability. An important component of Russian national maritime strategy is developing friendly relations with China and maintaining positive interactions with other states in the region, while modernizing military forces deployed in the Far East. Other key tasks of Russia's navy include defending hydrocarbon resources along the shelf; securing underwater pipelines around Sakhalin; protecting shipping, fishing, and tourism; combatting piracy and narcotics trafficking; and developing ports and links to the Trans-Siberian Railway.[38]

For more than a decade, China has sought to reinvigorate the rust belt industries in its northeast provinces through its "Rejuvenate the Northeast" program. The State Council has developed plans to improve economic growth by restructuring the region's state-owned enterprises, modernizing traditional manufacturing industries, and introducing more private enterprise.[39] The reforms also include measures to strengthen trade with neighboring countries, including Russia, Mongolia, Japan, and South and North Korea.[40] China's northeast suffers from overcapacity, and the country's largest oil field at Daqing is in decline, so enhancing ties with Russia's resource-rich Far East makes economic sense. But an influx of Russian raw materials, such as oil from the Daqing spur of the Eastern Siberia–Pacific Ocean (ESPO) pipeline, which provides crude for the region's oil-processing industries and transportation sector, can only marginally address the structural problems—the inefficient state firms—of these provinces.[41]

Despite the close economic relations between China and the Russian Far East, there is ongoing tension between Moscow and Beijing over

---

[37] Max Seddon and Kathrin Hille, "China and Russia Strike $11BN Funding Deal," *Financial Times*, July 4, 2017, https://www.ft.com/content/323f8254-60d2-11e7-8814-0ac7eb84e5f1.

[38] "Morskaia doktrina Rossisskoi Federatsii" [Maritime Doctrine of the Russian Federation], 2015, 27–30, http://kremlin.ru/events/president/news/50060.

[39] "China to Revitalize the Northeast," Xinhua, April 27, 2016, available at http://english.gov.cn/policies/latest_releases/2016/04/27/content_281475336315607.htm.

[40] "China Steps Up Support for Lagging Northeast Rustbelt Region," Reuters, August 19, 2014, https://www.reuters.com/article/us-china-economy-northeast/china-steps-up-support-for-lagging-northeast-rustbelt-region-idUSKBN0GJ08C20140819.

[41] "China Economy: Learning from Daqing," *Economist*, September 30, 2013, available at http://www.businessinsider.com/china-economy-learning-from-daqing-2013-9.

this region. Inhabitants of the region are suspicious of Chinese intentions and fear that they will be swamped by a wave of immigrants. China's three northern provinces alone (Heilongjiang, Liaoning, and Jilin) have nearly 110 million inhabitants compared with a population of just over 6 million in the Russian Far East. Chinese farmers have been acquiring long-term leases on agricultural land in Eastern Siberia and the Russian Far East, often at preferential rates. Although long-standing border disputes were officially settled in 2008, fears remain that Beijing may at some point in the distant future decide to revisit the "unequal treaties" of 1858 (Aigun) and 1860 (Beijing), by which Russia gained Primorsky Krai.

However, fears of massive Chinese migration seem exaggerated. Salaries in eastern Russia are relatively low, while prices are high. There are also language and cultural barriers that make life in Russia difficult. For most Chinese, opportunities are greater in China than in eastern Russia. Still, Russian nationalists periodically sound alarm bells about potential Chinese aggression.[42] Russia shares a long border with China, and while official relations are warm, Moscow is justifiably concerned about the relative weakness of Russia's eastern regions compared to the economic dynamism and immense population just across the border.[43]

To summarize, the partnership between Russia and China has directed greater attention toward developing their Far East and northeast regions, respectively. China benefits from the flow of natural resources and limited opportunities for farmers and traders. But Russia's poor business environment and inadequate infrastructure have frustrated expectations of massive inflows of Chinese investment.

## *International Economic Institutions*

Although China has generally accepted the rules of Western economic institutions, its dominant position in global commerce places it in a position where it could eventually reshape the liberal economic order established by the United States after World War II. The Kremlin resents Russia's far weaker position as a rule taker in the Western order. Following Putin's first term as president, Russia adopted a more skeptical position on such multilateral economic institutions as the WTO,

---

[42] One extreme example is the 2015 conspiracy video "Smertel'nyi Drug: Kitai" [Deadly Friend: China] about China's plan for subtle expansion into Russia, available at https://www.youtube.com/watch?v=oZZN0Kr4yDo.

[43] Malin Østevik and Natasha Kuhrt, "The Russian Far East and Russian Security Policy in the Asia-Pacific Region," in *Russia's Turn to the East*, ed. Helge Blakkisrud and Elana Wilson Rowe (London: Palgrave Macmillan, 2018), 78–81.

International Monetary Fund, and World Bank, a trend that accelerated after the Ukraine crisis.[44] However, Russia has put forth no alternative global model but rather has chosen to support China's efforts to erode U.S. hegemony. While China has worked constructively through multilateral economic institutions and is compliant with most rules, it carefully guards its sovereignty and seeks to reshape the global order to more fully reflect its interests as a rising global power.[45]

Alternative economic institutions being promoted by Beijing—the AIIB, the Shanghai Cooperation Organisation (SCO), and the New Development Bank established by the BRICS countries (Brazil, Russia, India, China, and South Africa)—are for the most part supported enthusiastically by Moscow, though in some instances (primarily the SCO) Russian and Chinese interests are not fully in harmony. On balance, Russia prefers China's version of the global economic order to the United States'. For example, Moscow supports China's critical position on U.S. dollar hegemony in the global economy, enables China to evade Western restrictions on arms technology through weapons exports, and enhances Chinese energy security through piped supplies of oil and gas. In short, Russia's weak economic position favors Chinese economic statecraft and aligns the two countries against the United States and Europe.[46]

Yet Russia does not want to become too reliant on China. Sergey Karaganov, one of Russia's foremost foreign policy experts and a strong supporter of developing ties with Asia, has warned against the very real possibility of the Russian Far East, and Russia more broadly, being transformed into a "raw materials appendage" and political satellite of China.[47] The following section examines their energy relationship in greater detail.

---

[44] Andrew Radin and Clint Bruce Reach, *Russian Views of the International Order* (Santa Monica: RAND Corporation, 2017), 54–58.

[45] Michael J. Mazarr, Timothy R. Heath, and Astrid Stuth Cevallos, *China and the International Order* (Santa Monica: RAND Corporation, 2018), 48–55, 77–84.

[46] Zhang Xiaotong and James Keith identify five main areas of a more active Chinese economic statecraft pursued under Xi Jinping: trade, finance, energy, technology, and structure of the international order. See Zhang Xiaotong and James Keith, "From Wealth to Power: China's New Economic Statecraft," *Washington Quarterly* 40, no. 1 (2017): 185–203.

[47] Sergey Karaganov, "Russia's Asian Strategy," *Russia in Global Affairs*, July 2, 2011, http://eng.globalaffairs.ru/pubcol/Russias-Asian-Strategy-15254.

## Energy

### Sino-Russian Energy Cooperation

Energy is the one bright spot in Russia's export potential, though limitations exist here as well. The International Energy Agency (IEA) projects that about 62% of global primary energy demand growth from 2016 to 2040 will come from India, China, and Southeast Asia. India is projected to be the largest contributor to demand growth, while China is expected to move toward a cleaner energy mix, including using more natural gas. Oil consumption will continue to grow, though at a slower pace.[48] Renewables, and additional oil and gas from the fracking industry will meet part of Asia's energy needs, but the market for Russian hydrocarbons should remain strong.

Russian pipelines provide a more secure alternative to vulnerable Middle Eastern and African oil transiting the narrow Strait of Malacca, which could be interdicted in the event of a conflict with the United States. But China already imports significant quantities of oil and gas by pipeline from its Central Asian partners, and Central Asian energy resources are frequently cited as a possible arena of Sino-Russian competition. China is investing heavily in Central Asia's energy potential. At present, the entirety of Turkmenistan's natural gas exports (31.7 billion cubic meters in 2017) go to China.[49] In 2017, Kazakhstan delivered 12.3 million tons of crude oil to China via the Atyrau-Alashankou pipeline, and late that year Kazakhstan agreed to begin pumping natural gas to China to meet growing demand.[50] While the competitive dimension may be overstated, China clearly has a range of options for energy imports beyond Russia.

For the Kremlin, energy cooperation with China, the world's largest energy consumer, is a top priority. According to the *China Statistical Yearbook*, coal accounted for 62% of China's primary energy consumption in 2016, while oil accounted for 18.3%, and natural gas 6.4%, with nuclear and renewables making up the remainder.[51] In 2016, China produced about 4 million barrels per day (bpd) of crude and imported an additional

---

[48] International Energy Agency (IEA), *World Energy Outlook 2017* (Paris: IEA, 2017).

[49] Fabio Indeo, "Settling the Caspian Issue and Realizing the Trans-Caspian Energy Corridor," *Diplomat*, July 10, 2018, https://thediplomat.com/2018/07/settling-the-caspian-issue-and-realizing-the-trans-caspian-energy-corridor.

[50] Aygerim Sarymbetova, "Kazakhstan to Start Gas Deliveries to China," *Caspian News*, October 10, 2017, https://caspiannews.com/news-detail/kazakhstan-to-start-gas-deliveries-to-china-2017-10-10-17.

[51] National Bureau of Statistics of the People's Republic of China (PRC), *China Statistical Yearbook* (Beijing, 2017), http://www.stats.gov.cn/tjsj/ndsj/2017/indexeh.htm.

7.59 million bpd, of which 11% came from Russia. Increasing access to natural gas is a priority for China to reduce reliance on coal and address its severe air pollution problem. Domestic Chinese production of natural gas is growing (150 billion cubic meters in 2016), leaving about 75 billion cubic meters of imports, mostly in the form of LNG from Qatar, Australia, Malaysia, and Indonesia.[52] Russia's ability to provide oil and dry gas via pipelines and its developing capacity to export LNG provide an important alternative source for these key commodities.

Russian analysts also point to the potential for cooperation on nuclear energy. State agency Rosatom, for example, provided technology for construction of the Tianwan nuclear power station in Jiangsu Province. But the potential for cooperation is limited because China and Russia compete with each other and with the United States to supply nuclear technology globally. Not only is China better positioned than Russia to finance major export projects, but its rapidly developing nuclear industry will make future Russian nuclear deals with China less likely.

Despite energy cooperation between Russia and China (as well as other Asian countries), the opportunities for Russia to play a leading role in Pacific affairs through energy deals are limited. In 2016, Russia exported 1.37 million bpd of oil and condensate to Asia and Oceania, or 26% of its total oil exports. In contrast, 70% of Russian oil exports went to Europe.[53] China is gradually taking a larger share of Russian oil exports, but it is unlikely to overtake Europe as Russia's largest export market, even though growth in energy demand is flat in Europe and European countries, with U.S. support, are developing alternative sources to Russian natural gas.[54] Russia's hydrocarbon economy also remains heavily dependent on natural gas exports westward. In 2016, Europe took fully 90% of Russian gas exports.[55] Although LNG from Sakhalin projects supplied Japan and other Asian countries, the Power of Siberia pipeline to China and the Pacific coast is not scheduled to come

---

[52] "China—Oil and Gas," Export.gov, https://www.export.gov/article?id=China-Oil-and-Gas; and Energy Information Administration (EIA), "China," https://www.eia.gov/beta/international/analysis.php?iso=CHN.

[53] EIA, "Russia," https://www.eia.gov/beta/international/analysis.php?iso=RUS.

[54] At their July 2018 meeting, President Donald Trump and European Commission president Jean-Claude Juncker agreed that the United States would provide more LNG to Europe. Overall, U.S. exports of LNG quadrupled in 2017 over the previous year, though 54% of exports went to Mexico, South Korea, and China. Countries in Europe (primarily Portugal, Spain, and Turkey) accounted for the third-largest share of exports after North America and Asia. See EIA, "U.S. Liquefied Natural Gas Exports Quadrupled in 2017," March 27, 2018, https://www.eia.gov/todayinenergy/detail.php?id=35512.

[55] EIA, "Russia."

onstream until the end of 2019 at the earliest.[56] In short, Europe will remain Russia's largest natural gas market in the foreseeable future.

Russia's pipeline infrastructure in the eastern regions has expanded in recent years with the construction of the ESPO pipeline and the planned Power of Siberia pipeline. At the beginning of January 2018, the ESPO project opened the second pipeline spur to Daqing, doubling Chinese imports of Russian crude to 600,000 bpd, or roughly 45% of all Russian oil supplied to China.[57] However, production levels in the east are far lower than those in the western fields (which are linked to European markets), as are proven reserves. In 2016, Western Siberia and the Ural-Volga regions accounted for 81% of Russia's total oil production, while Eastern Siberia and the Russian Far East provided just over 12%. The situation is much the same with natural gas—the U.S. Energy Information Administration reports that Western Siberian and Ural-Volga production is 90% of Russia's total, with Eastern Siberian and Far East production accounting for just 7.5%.[58] In short, there are distinct limits to Russia's capacity to supply China (and other Asia-Pacific countries) with hydrocarbons without a shift in increased production and in the development of new infrastructure—conditions that may not make economic sense.

## *The Arctic*

A mix of competitive and cooperative elements in Chinese-Russian energy relations is evident in the Arctic, which holds an estimated 13% of undiscovered conventional oil reserves and 30% of conventional natural gas resources, according to the U.S. Geological Survey.[59] Russia has the world's longest Arctic border at over 24,000 kilometers and controls approximately 40% of territory within the Arctic Circle. Putin has declared the Arctic a strategic priority for Russia, and in 2011 the government announced plans to invest over 21 billion rubles to develop the Northern Sea Route.[60] Russian leaders are keen to develop northern ports, reap profits from Russian

---

[56] EIA, "Russia."

[57] "Russia Tightens Oil Grip with China's Second Pipeline," Bloomberg, January 1, 2018, https://www.bloomberg.com/news/articles/2018-01-01/second-chinese-crude-oil-pipeline-linked-to-russia-s-espo-opens.

[58] EIA, "Russia."

[59] "Circum-Arctic Resource Appraisal: Estimates of Undiscovered Oil and Gas North of the Arctic Circle," U.S. Geological Survey, https://pubs.usgs.gov/fs/2008/3049/fs2008-3049.pdf.

[60] Heather A. Conley and Matthew Melino, *Maritime Futures: The Arctic and the Bering Strait Region* (Washington, D.C.: Center for Strategic and International Studies, 2017), 3, https://csis-prod.s3.amazonaws.com/s3fs-public/publication/171027_Conley_MaritimeFutures_Web.pdf?mHPGy0uKqRMcek0zw6av5jI332MeELk5.

icebreakers accompanying Chinese shipping, and securitize the region. China is interested in the potential of the route to reduce transportation costs to northern Europe.

Yet as Elizabeth Wishnick observes, although Moscow and Beijing share many international norms, "Russia's Arctic identity and China's emerging identity as a great power drive them apart on Arctic affairs."[61] Russia views the region as a privileged sphere of interest that it will defend militarily and is keen on exploiting the Arctic's vast stores of minerals, particularly oil and gas. China, by contrast, is not technically an Arctic state, and Russian officials in the past have complained of non-Arctic states that "obstinately strive" for access to the region.[62]

Chinese leaders refer to their country as a "near-Arctic state" and an important Arctic stakeholder with key interests in fishing, climate change, scientific research, exploitation of natural resources, and shipping routes (the Polar Silk Road). China has declared a commitment to protection of the region's natural environment and expects to participate in the governance of the Arctic in its role as an observer in the Arctic Council.[63] Statements by high-level Chinese officials describing the Arctic as a global commons where China should play an "indispensable role" led Russia and Canada to press for rules changes to the Arctic Council that would protect the sovereign rights of Arctic states.[64] Subsequently, China's Arctic Policy of 2018 acknowledged that states outside the Arctic do not have territorial sovereign rights, while asserting rights in scientific research, navigation, fishing, resource exploration and exploitation, the laying of submarine cables, and other relevant areas based on the United Nations Convention on the Law of the Sea (UNCLOS) and the Spitsbergen Treaty (which China signed in 1925).[65]

Although Moscow is wary of allowing non-Arctic states like China to have an equal voice on Arctic issues, Western sanctions have pushed Russia and China closer together on Arctic exploration. China can provide financing and technological expertise for oil and gas exploration and development, which are subject to U.S. and EU sanctions. Cooperation with Russia to

---

[61] Elizabeth Wishnick, *China's Interests and Goals in the Arctic: Implications for the United States* (Carlisle: U.S. Army War College, 2017), 36–39.

[62] "Russia Could Protect Interests in Arctic via Military Means—Defense Minister," RT, February 26, 2015, https://www.rt.com/news/235615-arctic-defense-arms-resources.

[63] "Full Text: China's Arctic Policy," Xinhua, January 26, 2018, available at http://english.gov.cn/archive/white_paper/2018/01/26/content_281476026660336.htm.

[64] Wishnick, *China's Interests and Goals in the Arctic*, 42–43.

[65] "Full Text: China's Arctic Policy."

develop Arctic energy resources is a priority for Beijing as well.[66] The Yamal LNG agreement is one example of Sino-Russian cooperation in the region. CNPC acquired a 20% stake in the Novatek project in 2014, and following the imposition of sanctions on Russia, China's Silk Road Fund acquired an additional 9.9%. The China Development Bank and the Export-Import Bank of China later provided a $12 billion loan for the project in April 2016, raising Chinese capital investment to 60% of total funding.[67] In addition, a Chinese company recently signed an agreement to develop a deepwater port in the northwestern city of Arkhangelsk that would connect to the Belkomur railway line. But Chinese companies have also been working with Arctic countries other than Russia, including Canada, Iceland, Norway, Finland, and the United States, which have more favorable investment climates and better infrastructure.[68]

## *Summary*

The expanding network of oil and gas pipelines eastward will create a long-term energy partnership between Russia and China, just as the pipeline network linking Russia and Europe has made them interdependent. The European experience, however, has both positive and negative dimensions. Moscow's tendency to use gas supplies as a geoeconomic instrument against Ukraine, and contentious disputes over EU rules on ownership unbundling, created deep mistrust in the relationship.[69] Common Chinese-Russian strategic interests may dampen tensions over energy issues, but neither nation is willing to fully trust the other on energy. China has expressed firm support for joint projects, such as the ESPO and Power of Siberia pipelines, while limiting dependence on Russian energy supplies. Moscow in turn seeks to diversify its markets in the Asia-Pacific so as not to be overly dependent on Chinese demand.

---

[66] Wishnick, *China's Interests and Goals in the Arctic*, 44.

[67] Ekaterina Klimenko, "Patterns of and Incentives for Entry into the Arctic and South East Asia," in *China-Russia Relations and Regional Dynamics: From Pivots to Peripheral Diplomacy*, ed. Lora Saalman (Solna: SIPRI, 2017), https://www.sipri.org/sites/default/files/China-Russia-relations-regional-dynamics.pdf.

[68] Paul Stronski and Nicole Ng, "Cooperation and Competition: Russia and China in Central Asia, the Russian Far East, and the Arctic," Carnegie Endowment for International Peace, February 2018, 25–31, https://carnegieendowment.org/files/CP_331_Stronski_Ng_Final1.pdf.

[69] Charles E. Ziegler, "Energy Pipeline Networks and Trust: The European Union and Russia in Comparative Perspective," *International Relations* 27, no. 1 (2013): 3–29.

## Implications

### Sino-Russian Cooperation in the Region

While Russia remains dependent on Europe for much of its trade (particularly natural gas exports), rising tensions over Ukraine, Western sanctions that affect the energy technology sector, and the attraction of Asian markets have accelerated the country's pivot eastward. Russia is seeking to capitalize on its geographic and cultural position between Asia and Europe. In 2011, then prime minister Putin sketched out the Kremlin's reasoning for a common economic space in Eurasia, claiming that Russia could serve as a bridge or connector (*sviazka*) between Europe and the Asia-Pacific.[70] Toward this end, in 2015 Putin and Xi agreed to coordinate development between the EEU and BRI.

Officially, China and Russia tout the potential for coordination between their respective programs. Of the six economic corridors of BRI, three transit EEU member states. The countries are rich in natural resources, and China already has major energy and infrastructure projects underway in the region. Beijing has been careful to leave security issues to Russia, but China's increasingly dominant economic presence and the large number of ethnic Chinese in Central Asia, together with its BRI connections in Eastern Europe, generate unease within Moscow about the loss of influence in the former Soviet republics.[71]

Realistically, Russia simply cannot compete with China economically in Central Asia, and so BRI will very likely overshadow Putin's EEU in the near future. Beijing's more open model of integration and its stronger attachment to liberal economic mechanisms gives BRI an advantage over the highly politicized and statist EEU. Some analysts, however, downplay the potential for tension in the relationship.[72] They believe that Russia and China have reached a division of labor whereby Moscow provides security guarantees for the region while China supplies much-needed investment and infrastructure. In addition, Moscow and Beijing agree on the need to maintain authoritarian governments to preserve

---

[70] Vladimir Putin, "Novyi integratsionnyi proekt dlia Evrazii—Budushchee, kotoroe rozhdaetsia segodnia" [New Integration Project for Eurasia—The Future That Is Being Born Today], *Izvestiia*, October 3, 2011, https://iz.ru/news/502761.

[71] One example is the China-Belarus Great Stone industrial park outside Minsk, which is planned as an important link in BRI. See also Paul Stronski, "China and Russia's Uneasy Partnership in Central Asia," East Asia Forum, March 29, 2018, http://www.eastasiaforum.org/2018/03/29/china-and-russias-uneasy-partnership-in-central-asia.

[72] See, for example, Marcin Kaczmarski, *Russia-China Relations in the Post-Crisis International Order* (London: Routledge, 2015); and Lukin, *China and Russia*.

regional stability. This interpretation has a more positive long-term evaluation of the bilateral relationship.

Yet, as discussed in the first section, China is far more important for Russia than Russia is for China. The economic disparity between the two, and a trade structure that favors China, places Russia at a significant disadvantage in the relationship. Post-Ukraine sanctions merely accelerated Russia's pivot eastward, but ill-advised policies from Washington (e.g., starting a trade war with China) could drive the two countries even closer together in an effort to resist U.S. economic pressure. Their national interests, however, are not fully compatible. Over the long term, China's growing power is likely to erode Russian influence in Central Asia and limit Moscow's ability to realize its plans for an expanded role in the Asia-Pacific.

Russian and Chinese leaders do have common interests in quashing separatism, extremism, and terrorism in Central Asia. To date, China has been careful not to infringe on Russia's position in the region. As BRI develops and China's economic interests become entrenched in Central Asia, however, Beijing may be expected to expand its security footprint. Beijing is deeply concerned about the potential for extremist violence by ethnic Uighurs in Xinjiang, the connections of the Islamic State of Iraq and Syria (ISIS) to post-Soviet Central Asia, and instability in Afghanistan. Chinese forces have conducted counterterrorism exercises with Tajik and Kyrgyz forces, and China has sold weapons systems to Turkmenistan and Kazakhstan. Chinese leaders are reportedly in discussions with Afghan officials to build a military base in the Wakhan Corridor bordering Xinjiang.[73] In the near future, however, China will likely continue to defer to Russia on regional security issues through the SCO and the Collective Security Treaty Organization.

Tensions are less apparent farther eastward. Russia does not make much of a contribution to Asia-Pacific security, either positively or negatively. The one area where Russia could make a positive contribution is energy security. Economic development and intraregional trade are key elements of interdependence in this East Asian regional security complex. East Asia is the world's largest energy-importing region, and future growth in hydrocarbon consumption will be concentrated here. Although Russia is less capable of guaranteeing the security of the sea routes than either the United States or China, it is uniquely positioned to supply hydrocarbons via pipelines to the Chinese mainland or to ports along the Pacific coast.

---

[73] "China in Talks over Military Base in Remote Afghanistan: Officials," *Straits Times*, February 2, 2018, https://www.straitstimes.com/world/middle-east/china-in-talks-over-military-base-in-remote-afghanistan-officials.

Russia's energy plans also involve the Korean Peninsula. Discussions about a trans-Korea gas pipeline that would supply South Korea date to the early 2000s, and the potential for rapprochement between North Korea and the United States has improved the prospects for this project. Greater Russian involvement on the peninsula could lessen North Korean dependence on China, generate lucrative transit fees for North Korea, provide South Korea with a more diverse supply of natural gas, and lower the possibility of Moscow acting as a spoiler.[74]

In South Asia, Russia and China are finding common ground in Pakistan. As the Trump administration recasts its Asia policy to focus on the Indo-Pacific and continues to improve ties with India, tensions have ratcheted up with Pakistan. In 2018 the United States urged the Financial Action Task Force to place Pakistan on a watch list of countries with inadequate terrorism financing controls, further angering Islamabad. Both Beijing and Moscow quickly praised Islamabad for its significant contributions to fighting terrorism and provided assurances of their continued support. Pakistan's defense minister subsequently stated that his government had decided to "recalibrate" its defense and security policy by purchasing weapons and supplies from Russia and China, reducing intelligence-sharing activities with the United States, and possibly enacting restrictions on U.S. land and air routes into Afghanistan.[75]

Pakistan is critical for BRI, and China is planning some $60 billion in infrastructure investments. Russia is exploring the possibility of increasing trade with Pakistan in energy and weapons, including helicopters and jet engines. Energy deals worth $10 billion are under discussion, as Gazprom is looking to export LNG to Pakistan, which would be routed through the 1,100-kilometer North-South pipeline from Karachi to Lahore. China may finance this pipeline through the Silk Road Fund, as Western sanctions on RT Global Resources, the Russian state company constructing the pipeline, have made it difficult to secure financing.[76]

---

[74] Liudmila Zakharova, "Economic Cooperation between Russia and North Korea: New Goals and Approaches," *Journal of Eurasian Studies* 7, no. 2 (2016): 151–61; and Ariel Cohen, "Putin Uses North Korea Summit to Make Energy Moves," *Forbes*, June 25, 2018, https://www.forbes.com/sites/arielcohen/2018/06/25/putin-uses-north-korea-summit-to-make-energy-moves/#26b3a72d71d3.

[75] Michael Peel and Kiran Stacey, "Pakistan Turns to Russia and China after U.S. Military Aid Freeze," *Financial Times*, January 28, 2018, https://www.ft.com/content/81aea830-0238-11e8-9650-9c0ad2d7c5b5.

[76] Drazen Jorgic, "With Gas and Diplomacy, Russia Embraces Cold War Foe Pakistan," Reuters, March 5, 2018, https://www.reuters.com/article/us-pakistan-russia/with-gas-and-diplomacy-russia-embraces-cold-war-foe-pakistan-idUSKBN1GH27P; and Zafar Bhutta, "China's Silk Road Fund to Finance North-South Pipeline," *Express Tribune*, December 20, 2017, https://tribune.com.pk/story/1588223/2-chinas-silk-road-fund-finance-north-south-pipeline.

## *Future Outlook for Sino-Russian Trade, Energy, and Finance*

On trade, the overall volume can be expected to increase gradually as China consumes more Russian gas and Russian agricultural products replace U.S. goods that fall victim to a U.S.-China trade war. But bilateral trade levels are likely to fall short of the optimistic scenarios envisioned at summit meetings. The structure of trade will not change dramatically, though Russia is making an effort to export more value-added products and to reduce the share of energy and raw materials. Russian agricultural products may take a larger share of exports, particularly if China lowers its imports of U.S. produce. Russia is not likely to fill many gaps that might arise in the event of a U.S.-China trade war. The same, however, cannot be said for Brazil, Japan, Australia, South Korea, and the major European countries that trade extensively with China.

On energy, Russia will continue to serve as a key supplier of oil and natural gas (both dry and LNG), with deliveries of gas ramping up if the Power of Siberia pipeline comes onstream as planned at the end of 2019. Joint exploration of the Arctic is more problematic, as expensive projects are unlikely to be commercially viable in the absence of high oil prices. China will continue to diversify its energy imports, reduce consumption, increase domestic production of hydrocarbons, and seek renewable energy sources, all of which will limit demand for Russian oil and gas. Oil and natural gas from the Middle East, Africa, Australia, and Indonesia, and even LNG from the United States, will provide much of Chinese energy imports. The United States should welcome China's efforts to diversify energy imports and reduce dependence on nonrenewable hydrocarbons, given the positive effects on climate change.

In finance, China has become an important investor in key sectors of the Russian economy, though other countries surpass Russia in terms of total Chinese investment. The Chinese renminbi is not likely to replace the U.S. dollar as the world's reserve currency in the near future.[77] China and Russia may agree to conclude certain deals in Chinese rather than U.S. currency, and both will seek to constrain American financial and monetary hegemony through the BRICS, G-20, and other mechanisms. Yet, barring the complete meltdown of the U.S. economy, these actions are unlikely to have much impact.

---

[77] See Daniel W. Drezner, "Perception, Misperception, and Sensitivity: Chinese Economic Power and Preferences after the 2008 Financial Crisis," in *Strategic Adjustment and the Rise of China: Power and Politics in East Asia*, ed. Robert S. Ross and Øystein Tunsjø (Ithaca: Cornell University Press, 2017), 95–96.

The Sino-Russian partnership is real and is likely to see further progress in the near future. The main threat to the United States' global economic position, however, does not come from Chinese-Russian cooperation but rather from Washington's confrontational and counterproductive approach to international trade. Should the United States create an economic vacuum by weakening or abandoning the Bretton Woods system that has served U.S. interests since the end of World War II, Russia and China will benefit.

## *Implications for U.S. Policy*

Russia's need for foreign investment, technology, and energy markets cannot (or will not) be met entirely by China. This fact will encourage flexibility in its relations with other Asian states, many of which have tense relations with China. This hedging behavior is evident in Northeast Asia, where Russia maintains good commercial relations with Japan and South Korea, both formal allies of the United States. Its hedging is also observable with members of the Association of Southeast Asian Nations (ASEAN) and with India.[78] Yet although Russia has options in trade, investment, and energy beyond China, China will remain its chief strategic partner in the near future.

U.S. sanctions on Russia and the Trump administration's threatened trade war with China are driving the two countries closer together. One example may be found in Chinese imports of Russian soybeans, which spiked dramatically in 2017–18 as the Trump administration debated imposing punitive tariffs on Chinese imports (though Russia still provided less than 1% of Chinese soy imports in 2017).[79] Russia's agricultural sector has improved in recent years, and food security and food exports was one of four priority issues promoted at the 2012 Asia-Pacific Economic Cooperation (APEC) summit in Vladivostok. By 2016, cumulative Chinese investment in agriculture, forestry, and

---

[78] See Alexander Korolev, "Russia in the South China Sea: Balancing and Hedging," *Foreign Policy Analysis*, February 15, 2018, https://doi.org/10.1093/fpa/orx015.

[79] See Anatoly Medetsky, "China Buys Record Amount of Russian Soy as It Shuns U.S. Growers," Bloomberg, May 17, 2018, https://www.bloomberg.com/news/articles/2018-05-17/china-buys-record-amount-of-russian-soy-as-it-shuns-u-s-growers. Russia is still far behind other suppliers when it comes to soybeans. In 2017, Brazil accounted for 53.3% of Chinese imports, while the United States provided 34.4%, the lowest share since 2006. Brazil surpassed the United States as China's largest supplier in 2012. See Hallie Gu and Naveen Thukral, "Soy Source: Brazil's Share of Soybean Exports to China Hits Record," Reuters, January 25, 2018, https://www.reuters.com/article/us-china-economy-trade-soybeans/soy-source-brazils-share-of-soybean-exports-to-china-hits-record-idUSKBN1FE111.

fisheries in Russia, largely in the Far East, was over $3 billion.[80] Given Russia's "food wars" with its European neighbors, China can provide a more reliable source of foodstuffs and serve as a more reliable importer of Russian agricultural products.

The emergence of a Russia-China-Pakistan axis would complicate the Trump administration's strategy in Afghanistan and weaken U.S. influence in Central Asia. Russia seeks to take advantage of Pakistan's tensions with the United States but also does not want to jeopardize its long-standing defense relationship with India. New Delhi has urged its former patron not to sell weapons to its rival and in mid-2018 announced plans to purchase S-400 SAM platforms from Russia to preserve military ties.[81] Still, Russia concluded an agreement with Pakistan in 2015 to sell 20 Mi-35M helicopters, and the two countries are negotiating terms of the sale of Su-35 and Su-37 fighter aircraft. Their first joint military exercises were held in September 2016, and naval exercises were held in the Arabian Sea in 2017. In addition to the commercial benefits, Russia and China see Pakistan as playing an important role in helping stabilize Afghanistan.[82] U.S. arms exports to Pakistan decreased from $1 billion in 2010 to a mere $21 million in 2017, as Washington became increasingly critical of Islamabad's inability to deal with extremism. Chinese weapons exports fell during the same period (from $747 million to $514 million), but this decrease still left China as Pakistan's largest military supplier.[83] Although China and Russia may have different reasons for supporting Pakistan, their role is likely to complicate U.S. policy in South Asia regardless.

Several policy implications follow from this study. First, the United States should recognize that Chinese-Russian relations are both cooperative and competitive. Washington should thus avoid actions that encourage further cooperation against U.S. interests, while capitalizing on tensions in the relationship (as in the Arctic). Second, China has a stronger commitment to the liberal international order than does Russia. By undermining the structure of rules and institutions established after World War II and

---

[80] Elizabeth Gooch and Fred Gale, "China's Foreign Agricultural Investments," U.S. Department of Agriculture, Economic Research Service, EIB-192, April 26, 2018.

[81] Ankit Panda, "India to Press On with Purchase of Russian S-400 Surface-to-Air Missile System," *Diplomat*, July 16, 2018, https://thediplomat.com/2018/07/india-to-press-on-with-purchase-of-russian-s-400-surface-to-air-missile-system.

[82] Kashif Hussein, "What Russia's Changing Role in South Asia Means for Pakistan," *Diplomat*, January 20, 2018, https://thediplomat.com/2018/01/what-russias-changing-role-in-south-asia-means-for-pakistan.

[83] Kiran Stacey, "Pakistan Shuns U.S. for Chinese High-Tech Weapons," *Financial Times*, April 17, 2018, https://www.ft.com/content/8dbce0a0-3713-11e8-8b98-2f31af407cc8.

confronting U.S. allies and partners in the Asia-Pacific on trade issues, the United States creates openings for China, with Russian backing, to reduce U.S. influence in the region. Washington must reassert its commitment to the postwar order that has served the United States so well. Third, Russia's turn away from Europe and toward the Pacific as a market for energy exports enhances China's energy security; however, poor infrastructure and small reserves in Eastern Siberia limit Russia's potential to serve as China's dominant energy provider. It is worth recognizing that Russian energy projects in Asia also diversify supply for U.S. allies and so do not negatively affect U.S. interests.

## Conclusion

The strategic partnership between Beijing and Moscow is vital for both sides, and has become even more so as U.S.-Russia relations have deteriorated and U.S.-China trade ties have frayed. Sino-Russian economic relations are complementary but unbalanced, with China in a dominant position. At present, U.S.-China economic interdependence provides Washington with considerable leverage, but this advantage could be squandered through ill-considered policies that might drive Beijing and Moscow closer together. China's leverage over the United States is augmented by its economic relations with Russia, and this influence will only grow if the U.S. government pursues a trade war with China while shunning multilateral forums like the WTO and the Trans-Pacific Partnership (TPP).

Oil and gas deals concluded in the past few years between Russia and China involve the construction of pipelines and long-term contracts, the scale of which ensures that China and Russia will be energy partners for the next three decades or so. To diversify regional economic ties, Russia is trying to expand economic relations with other Asia-Pacific countries. Many of these countries—Japan, South Korea, Vietnam, India, and Malaysia—are wary of China's increasingly aggressive behavior. Likewise, China views Russia as just one, albeit a very important, source of oil, natural gas, and other commodities necessary for its industrial machine. Political considerations occasionally influence economic projects, yet neither side is willing to sacrifice national interests for the strategic partnership.

The United States should not assume that energy interdependence implies a close, amicable relationship—the Russian-European experience proves otherwise. Piped oil and gas from Russia make China more energy secure, but overland supplies will not significantly reduce China's security concerns regarding ocean routes through the western Pacific. In short, U.S. interests are not threatened by developing China-Russia energy ties.

Russia's regional hedging strategy in the Pacific may bring the country into competition with China, as in Russian energy development projects with Vietnam.[84] Similar conflicts may arise as Russia pursues arms sales and trade deals with other Southeast Asian nations. Russia, then, is not supporting China unconditionally. Instead, it is following a more complex pattern of aligning with China to balance the United States, while hedging in pursuit of its economic interests.[85]

U.S. interests are served by preserving economic cooperation through bilateral ties and multilateral forums. The Trump administration's decision to withdraw from the TPP was extremely shortsighted and in effect concedes political influence to China and, to a lesser extent, Russia, as each country pursues trade, sells weapons, and participates in regional institutions. The United States must remain engaged in the region economically rather than relying heavily on military instruments of power.

While Japan and South Korea are not likely to abandon their formal alliances with the United States, Washington's confrontational posture on trade has weakened its position in the Asia-Pacific. Both countries rely heavily on imports to meet their energy needs, and oil and gas connections provide an incentive for them to maintain good relations with Russia. This dependence could frustrate U.S. efforts to pressure the Kremlin over its aggressive behavior in Ukraine, Georgia, and Europe. At the same time, Japan and South Korea understand that Russia is a potential balancer against a rising China, an alignment that serves U.S. strategic interests.

In sum, the Russian-Chinese partnership has made substantial progress over the past two decades based on economic ties and will continue to develop in the near to medium term, though results have fallen short of official expectations. China's overwhelming economic power relegates Russia to a distinctly secondary position in trade, and while Russia is an energy superpower, the constraints of geography and competition also limit Russian influence in this key area. The challenge posed by the economic partnership is real and merits Washington's attention, but it should not be unmanageable as long as the United States effectively cultivates its allies and partners and avoids a destructive trade war with China.

---

[84] China's Foreign Ministry, for example, pointedly warned Rosneft and PetroVietnam against continuing oil exploration in disputed waters off the Vietnamese coast. See Nicholas Trickett, "Working with Vietnam, Russia's Rosneft Draws China's Ire," *Diplomat*, May 19, 2018, https://thediplomat.com/2018/05/working-with-vietnam-russias-rosneft-draws-chinas-ire.

[85] Korolev, "Russia in the South China Sea," 10.

# EXECUTIVE SUMMARY

This chapter assesses the main dimensions of the Sino-Russian defense relationship and discusses the outlook for further cooperation on security issues.

## MAIN ARGUMENT

Military ties between China and Russia have increased dramatically in recent years and look set to deepen in key dimensions, including regional security cooperation, arms sales, military exercises, and defense dialogues. Sino-Russian security cooperation presents challenges to U.S. interests, including to regional security balances, U.S.-led sanctions, and U.S. military freedom of action and access. These challenges would grow if China and Russia were to form a full-fledged defense alliance. Fortunately, this scenario is unlikely to develop, especially if U.S. policymakers prudently look for opportunities to constrain their defense ties, or at least to avoid strengthening them. Most likely, the future will bring expanded Sino-Russian defense industrial cooperation, joint exercises, and the deepening of regional security collaboration in select areas.

## POLICY IMPLICATIONS

- In the short term, arms control issues give Washington a tool to divide China from Russia, given that U.S. and Russian officials share concerns about China's growing nuclear power and strategic opaqueness.

- In the long term, the U.S. should apply more resources to evaluating Sino-Russian defense ties and ensure that U.S. defense dialogues with allies and friends comprehensively address this issue. Strengthening U.S. alliances and security partnerships with other countries is imperative since these networks provide the U.S. unique strategic advantages over China and Russia.

- Washington should discourage technology transfers and other exchanges that can enhance Chinese and Russian military cooperation by warning third parties that contributing to either country's military power could decrease their access to U.S. defense technology and subject them to other security-related sanctions.

Chapter 3

# Growing China-Russia Military Relations: Implications and Opportunities for U.S. Policy

*Richard Weitz*

Sino-Russian defense and security collaboration has continued to grow in many areas, including arms sales, defense dialogues, joint exercises, and other bilateral and multilateral activities. Since the Cold War, the People's Republic of China (PRC) has acquired more weapons from Russia than from all other countries combined. Beijing and Moscow have signed several confidence-building measures that constrain their military actions regarding the other, including limits on military deployments near their shared borders. More recently, the two countries have expanded their national security dialogues, military exchanges, and strategic consultations, within both bilateral and multilateral frameworks, notably the Shanghai Cooperation Organisation (SCO). China's and Russia's shared security objectives encompass averting bilateral conflicts, maintaining border security, promoting arms transfers, and influencing third parties such as the United States.

The leaders of both countries view their defense relationship as a major policy success that they desire to sustain. Most importantly, neither side views the other's military as a near-term threat. One reason that the Russian government has encouraged its defense companies to supply sophisticated maritime and air defense platforms to the People's Liberation Army (PLA), though Russia rarely exports a leading-edge system to any country until its decision-makers are confident that a more advanced system is or will soon enter service with the Russian armed forces, is

---

**RICHARD WEITZ** is Senior Fellow and Director of the Center for Political-Military Analysis at the Hudson Institute. He can be reached at <weitz@hudson.org>.

This chapter draws on Richard Weitz, "Sino-Russian Security Ties," in "Russia-China Relations: Assessing Common Ground and Strategic Fault Lines," National Bureau of Asian Research (NBR), NBR Special Report, no. 66, July 2017, 27–36.

Moscow's confidence that the PLA would employ these systems only against other countries. Another driver of their defense relationship is that Beijing's and Moscow's contentious ties with Western countries leave each as the most crucial security partner of the other. Until recently, Chinese and Russian representatives routinely denied that their cooperation is directed against the United States or any other country. However, at the time of his April 2018 visit to Moscow, China's new defense minister General Wei Fenghe said that his visit, which included a keynote speech at the Moscow Conference on International Security, aimed to signal to Washington and others the growing closeness of Sino-Russian military ties.[1] Furthermore, at the time of the July 2018 NATO summit, Russian defense minister Sergei Shoigu stated that "Russia and China are rigorously improving strategic ties to be better prepared for the challenges of today's world, as the U.S. resorts to deception, hybrid wars, and controlled chaos."[2] Whatever they say, the wide-ranging ties between China and Russia challenge important U.S. national security interests and make both countries more formidable rivals of the United States. For instance, Russian arms deliveries to China have enhanced the anti-access/area-denial (A2/AD) capabilities that the PLA would employ against the United States and its Asian allies.

Nonetheless, Sino-Russian mutual defense commitments and engagements remain significantly weaker than those between the United States and its principal allies in Asia or Europe. Though military collaboration between Beijing and Moscow is growing broader, along most dimensions it is not deep. In particular, there is little indication that China and Russia will soon build a formal mutual defense alliance.

This chapter first assesses the main dimensions of the Chinese-Russian defense relationship, beginning with regional security cooperation in Central Asia, East Asia, and the Middle East. The next section then analyzes Sino-Russian functional security cooperation, including Russian arms sales to China, military exercises, joint security statements, and political-military tactics. The third section covers possible future scenarios for security cooperation and discusses several possible alternatives that could drive China and Russia closer together or farther apart. The last section assesses policy implications for the United States and offers several recommendations for responding to growing Sino-Russian security ties.

---

[1] "Chinese Defence Chief Says His Visit to Moscow Is a Signal to the U.S.," *South China Morning Post*, April 4, 2018, https://www.scmp.com/news/china/diplomacy-defence/article/2140182/chinas-defence-chief-calls-his-moscow-trip-signal-us.

[2] "Uncertainty, Tension in World Affairs Push Moscow & Beijing Together—Russian Defense Minister," RT, July 12, 2018, https://www.rt.com/news/432629-russia-china-military-shoigu.

## Regional Security

### Central Asia

In Central Asia, Beijing and Moscow share concerns over Islamic extremism, migrating militants, and transnational narcotics trafficking. Their overlapping interests lie in limiting the Western military presence in Eurasia, cultivating regional security structures under their control, and averting wars, forced regime change, and other sources of local instability that would threaten their economic and security priorities. Their cooperation within Central Asia is embodied in the SCO, which now includes India, Kazakhstan, Kyrgyzstan, Pakistan, Tajikistan, and Uzbekistan as full members. Unlike NATO or the Russia-dominated Collective Security Treaty Organization, however, the SCO has no joint command or standing military structures or functions. Its counterterrorism center focuses on exchanging information about terrorist threats and harmonizing member countries' terrorism-related laws and regulations but lacks an independent operational capacity.

Due to its proximity and protracted instability, Afghanistan has long been a major area of concern for Beijing and Moscow. China and Russia have at times sharply criticized the U.S.-led military campaign in Afghanistan, especially its inability to suppress narcotics trafficking, and clearly do not want to see a long-term military presence in their backyard. Yet they also worry about a Western military drawdown that could worsen instability in Central Asia and undermine their regional integration projects. Both China's Belt and Road Initiative and Russia's Eurasian Economic Union traverse Central Asia. The two countries have expressed alarm at the recent spread of the Islamic State of Iraq and Syria (ISIS) in Eurasia and launched a controversial trilateral peace initiative involving the Afghan Taliban, which now encompasses the Afghan government, India, Iran, and other parties.[3]

Even so, the future could see a greater rivalry between China and Russia over Central Asia and Afghanistan given the proximity of this region to both countries and potentially competing economic and security interests. Chinese and Russian national companies have already competed for the exploration, development, and transit of energy reserves out of the

---

[3] Cristina Burack, Mikhail Bushuev, and Masood Saifullah, "U.S. Skips Out on Afghanistan-Taliban Conference in Moscow," Deutsche Welle, April 14, 2017, http://www.dw.com/en/us-skips-out-on-afghanistan-taliban-conference-in-moscow/a-38426486.

region and into the global economy.[4] As a long-time guarantor of security and economic linkage in the region, Russia has retained sizeable influence throughout these post-Soviet republics. One of its principal goals since has been to preserve its preeminent position as a major oil and gas supplier and transit route, specifically to Europe but increasingly to China and the rapidly developing nations in Asia as well. For instance, this consideration has encouraged Moscow to pursue the recently announced Caspian Sea agreement. Meanwhile, China, under its Belt and Road Initiative, values Central Asia for transit, moving not only energy but also other goods from western Chinese provinces through Central Asia and into Europe. Though Russia would prefer that Central Asia remain within its sphere of influence, it has tolerated the rise of Chinese influence as preferable to Western influence, given how the relationships between Russia and Western countries are at their lowest point since the Cold War. However, Russian leaders may come to regret this accommodation because China's presence is likely to become more pervasive and powerful than any plausible Western role. At some point, China might exploit its superior economic position in Central Asia to secure a military presence in a region hitherto dominated by the Russian armed forces.

## East Asia

Another important region of Sino-Russian security interaction is East Asia. Unlike in Central Asia, where Russia retains major economic interests and assets, in East Asia China's economic primacy is nearly absolute. Russia's military presence in the Russian Far East is limited largely to fortifying some of the islands that it disputes with Japan and providing its strategic submarines a bastion against U.S. antisubmarine warfare capabilities. Meanwhile, Chinese military capabilities and ambitions have been growing to the point where the PLA can largely ignore Russian military activities in the region. Yet, due to historical divergences as well as neither side making the issue a priority, Russia has not fully endorsed China's territorial claims in the South or East China Seas, while China has not unreservedly backed Russia's occupation of the Southern Kuril Islands (known as the Northern Territories in Japan). Russia also sells substantial quantities of arms to Vietnam. Beijing's self-confidence could continue to expand to the point where Chinese leaders feel more (or even overly) confident about pressing

---

[4] Hu Bin, "Oil and Gas Cooperation between China and Central Asia in an Environment of Political and Resource Competition," *Petroleum Science* 11, no. 4 (2014): 596–605, https://link.springer.com/content/pdf/10.1007%2Fs12182-014-0377-7.pdf.

Russia to curtail its defense cooperation with Vietnam and remove other impediments to China's regional security hegemony.

Regarding the Korean Peninsula, Beijing and Moscow perceive benefits from recent developments at the expense of the United States. Chinese and Russian analysts do not think that the Democratic People's Republic of Korea (DPRK) would deliberately attack either of their countries, or even the United States or its allies. Both Beijing and Moscow view Pyongyang's pursuit of nuclear weapons as partly justified as a quest for a robust deterrent and defensive instrument against the Pentagon. For example, they find it hard to imagine North Korea giving up its nuclear option without the United States and other countries' guaranteeing protection of the regime.[5] Instead, they want South Korea to be included in any nuclear-weapons-free zone.[6] Russian scholars also doubt the current North Korean government would ever surrender its nuclear arsenal given concerns about U.S. threats.[7] Furthermore, they continue to be more concerned about the regional chaos that would result from the DPRK's abrupt collapse, as well as the U.S. military presence on the Korean Peninsula, than about the adverse impact of Pyongyang's nuclear and missile development programs. This leads them to challenge U.S.-proposed coercive measures against Pyongyang.

In the past, China and Russia have joined forces in the UN Security Council to block severe sanctions on North Korea and criticize U.S. missile defenses in the Asia-Pacific. On the Korean Peninsula, as elsewhere, China and Russia profess to perceive U.S. missile defenses as threatening their missile forces. Their military representatives have been making joint presentations at various regional security conferences. Their objections have encompassed U.S. missile defense collaboration with close allies like South Korea, Japan, and NATO countries as well as the national missile defenses in North America. Although China and Russia acknowledge the currently limited capabilities of U.S. missile defenses, they argue that the United States is positioning itself to establish an interlinked global defensive network that would invariably degrade the effectiveness of their strategic missiles. In a joint statement issued on June 8, 2018, Beijing and

---

[5] *Hankyoreh*, March 8, 2018, http://www.hani.co.kr/arti/international/china/835218.html.

[6] *Segye Daily*, August 16, 2018, http://www.sedaily.com/NewsView/1S3DUHM176; and "U.S., North Korea May Return to Confrontation before Year-End—Russian Expert," TASS, August 6, 2018, http://tass.com/politics/1016207.

[7] "U.S., North Korea May Return to Confrontation before Year-End."

Moscow described U.S. missile defenses as disrupting regional strategic balances and global stability.[8]

In the future, China and Russia will likely strive to expand the current détente between Pyongyang and Washington to encourage the removal of all sanctions on North Korea and the withdrawal of all U.S. military forces, including missile defenses, from South Korea. Still, even here it is not impossible to envisage major Sino-Russian competition for influence in a future, more valuable North Korea (one retaining nuclear weapons and largely freed from most sanctions, exporting strategic minerals, and providing Russia with opportunities to reach Chinese economic competitors through new trans-Korean rail lines, pipelines, and other conduits). South as well as North Koreans want to reduce their economic dependence on China and are therefore aiming to build pipelines, railways, and other infrastructure developmental projects to deepen their Russian ties. The two Koreas and Russia have tried to develop trilateral commercial cooperation as well.[9] Russia also wants to reduce its economic dependence on China and sees the Korean Peninsula as a bridge to deeper East Asian ties.[10] However, bilateral and trilateral cooperation between the Koreas and Russia could arouse Chinese concern since many Chinese believe they warrant security primacy over the Korean Peninsula.[11]

## *The Middle East*

Although China and Russia are both heavily involved in the Middle East, China has focused mostly on economic and energy issues, though it sometimes sells weapons to Middle Eastern countries, such as Syria and Iran.[12] In May 2018, the Chinese special envoy for Syria, Xie Xiaoyan, stated that Moscow and Beijing are cooperating efficiently on the Syrian issue, adding that there remains a "huge space" for expanding their collaboration.[13]

---

[8] "Zhonghua Renmin Gongheguo he Eluosi Lianbang lianheshengming (quan wen)" [Joint Statement of the People's Republic of China and the Russian Federation (Full Text)], June 8, 2018, https://www.fmprc.gov.cn/web/zyxw/t1567243.shtml.

[9] The trade volume of North Korea with China was approximately $5,300 million, or 94.8% of North Korea's national foreign trade. See Korea Trade-Investment Promotion Agency (KOTRA), *2017 North Korea Foreign Trade Trends* (Seoul: KOTRA, 2018).

[10] Heung-ho Moon, "The Sino-Russian Strategic Partnership and a Peace Regime on the Korean Peninsula," *Sino-Soviet Affairs* 41, no. 4 (2018): 69–97, http://www.riss.kr/search/detail/DetailView.do?p_mat_type=1a0202e37d52c72d&control_no=645b52eef2fe59614884a65323211ff0.

[11] Ibid., 88.

[12] Stockholm International Peace Research Institute (SIPRI), SIPRI Arms Transfers Database, August 1, 2018, https://www.sipri.org/databases/armstransfers.

[13] "China, Russia Have Potential to Expand Cooperation Regarding Syrian Crisis—Envoy," TASS, May 13, 2018, http://tass.com/world/1004011.

Thus far, the Chinese and Russian governments have consulted mostly to promote a political solution in Syria. Beijing has echoed Moscow's call for the international community to respect Syria's territorial integrity.[14] In addition, they have jointly cast a string of vetoes in the UN Security Council to block U.S.-backed measures against the Assad government. In particular, they have shielded the regime from Western accusations that it has employed chemical weapons, instead blaming the insurgents for the alleged attacks. In April 2018, Shoigu praised Beijing for joining with Moscow against "the irresponsible behavior of some Western countries that, under a false pretext, attacked a sovereign state."[15] China has offered to assist in Syria's postwar reconstruction, without demanding the same kinds of prior political reforms as Western countries.

In addition to objecting to U.S. military strikes and U.S.-backed regime change in general, another motivating factor for Sino-Russian cooperation has been their joint concern about the thousands of Chinese and Russian citizens who have traveled to Syria to fight with various terrorist organizations.[16] Beijing sent military advisers to Syria in 2017 to help train the government forces to use their Chinese-purchased weapons and possibly to study the war, but it has not been very active in the Russian-led military campaign. Still, China "supports Russia's intervention in Syria but does not consider Syria a strategic priority."[17] Russia has been much more active in the Middle Eastern security domain. Not only has the Russian military made a decisive contribution to reversing the course of the Syrian civil war and keeping Bashar al-Assad in power, but Moscow has offered major arms packages to Egypt, Iraq, and other countries. One of the interesting features of Russia's intervention in Syria is how its military has partnered with Iran. Not only have Russian pilots provided air support for the Iranian and pro-Iran Lebanese Hezbollah forces in the region, but Iran has allowed Russian planes to use its airfields on some Syrian-bound missions.

Thus far, Chinese and Russian regional security policies in the Middle East, though generally compatible, have not been that closely linked. However, the U.S. decision to withdraw from the Iran nuclear

---

[14] "Special Envoy of the Chinese Government on the Syrian Issue Xie Xiaoyan Attends International Symposium on the Syrian Issue," Ministry of Foreign Affairs of the People's Republic of China (PRC), May 14, 2018, http://www.fmprc.gov.cn/mfa_eng/wjbxw/t1559820.shtml.

[15] Tom O'Connor, "Russia and China Militaries Reach 'New Heights' Together, Agree to Challenge U.S. in Middle East," *Newsweek*, April 24, 2018, http://www.newsweek.com/china-russia-military-reach-new-heights-together-agree-challenge-us-middle-899689.

[16] Yixiang Xu, "Evolving Sino-Russian Cooperation in Syria," U.S. Institute of Peace, October 3, 2017, https://www.usip.org/publications/2017/10/evolving-sino-russian-cooperation-syria.

[17] Ibid.

deal may change this dynamic. Chinese and Russian officials have jointly criticized the U.S. decision and affirmed their intent to work with Iran to sustain the deal. They might pursue joint measures to circumvent U.S. extraterritorial sanctions designed to limit their commercial dealings with Iran, such as designing mechanisms to allow Chinese and Russian firms to circumvent the U.S.-controlled or -influenced financial system when conducting business with Iran. The SCO might also expand to include Iran now that India and Pakistan have become its first new members since the organization's formation in 2001. Turkey is already a dialogue partner, and given its importance in the Belt and Road Initiative, it could eventually consider membership as well. Such moves could spark interest among Arab states to apply to the SCO, especially if they perceive that the United States is disengaging from regional leadership and decide to pursue China and Russia as potential security partners.[18]

The distance of the Middle East from China and the asymmetry of interests, given Beijing's economic orientation toward the region, means that the Middle East is unlikely to generate major Sino-Russian competition in the near term. However, Chinese interest in securing better control over the main source of its imported oil, which comes primarily from Sunni regimes alienated from Russia, and China's growing economy each may stimulate longer-term divergences. China has been far more successful than Russia (or the United States) in maintaining good ties with regional rivals, including Iran and its allies as well as the anti-Iranian Sunni powers. If the Russian-U.S. military competition in the Middle East escalates, Chinese policymakers may seek to distance themselves more from Russian policies in the region.

## Functional Security Cooperation

Cooperation between China and Russia is growing in many areas. The two countries have signed several arms control and confidence-building measures, expanded contacts between their national security establishments, and institutionalized their defense and regional security dialogues, military exchanges, and strategic consultations, within both bilateral and multilateral frameworks. China and Russia's extensive security ties

---

[18] Jonathan Fulton, "Could the SCO Expand into the Middle East?" *Diplomat*, February 24, 2018, https://thediplomat.com/2018/02/could-the-sco-expand-into-the-middle-east; and Jonathan Fulton, "China Is Trying to Pull Middle East Countries into Its Version of NATO," *Washington Post*, June 21, 2017, https://www.washingtonpost.com/news/monkey-cage/wp/2017/06/21/how-china-is-shifting-toward-the-middle-east.

encompass bilateral and multilateral agreements; formal and informal mutual consultations; pledges of cooperation against separatism, terrorism, and religious extremism; and public declarations of mutual nonaggression, noninterference, peaceful coexistence, antiterrorism, international law, and respect for national sovereignty, equal security, and territorial integrity.

## Arms Sales

Russia's voluminous arms sales to China have enhanced the PLA's effectiveness in several areas, especially in terms of air defense and maritime aviation. In recent years, China has resumed purchasing complete Russian weapons systems rather than, as before 2014, just specific subsystems, components, licensed production, or spare parts. Indeed, Moscow has offered the PLA some of its most sophisticated weapons—the Su-35S Flanker-E high-performance fighter jet and the S-400 Triumf (NATO designation: SA-21 Growler) air defense system are two prominent examples. The Su-35S will provide Chinese engineers with the ability to learn more about the jet's AL-41F1S engine, Irbis-E radar, and electronic warfare suite. China became the first foreign country to buy the Su-400 in late 2014, even before India, which until recently was Moscow's most privileged buyer. India typically was the first foreign country to buy Russia's most advanced weapons, occasionally even being allowed to purchase systems that Moscow refused to offer the PRC. China received delivery of the air defense system, which can target aircraft and short-range ballistic missiles, in April 2018. Compared with the S-300 that China bought from Russia earlier, the new S-400 has better sensors, software, and missiles.[19] The two countries have also agreed to coproduce new weapons systems, including reconnaissance drones and dual-use systems with military as well as civilian applications, such as helicopters.[20] Progress, however, has been modest.

As noted earlier, Russian decision-makers prudently avoid selling China their most advanced weapons until an even more advanced system has entered, or is about to enter, service with the Russian armed forces. For example, Russia is acquiring the more advanced S-500 to replace the Su-400, and the Russian air force has an even more advanced version of

---

[19] Franz-Stefan Gady, "Russia Delivers 1st S-400 Missile Defense Regiment to China," *Diplomat*, April 3, 2018, https://thediplomat.com/2018/04/russia-delivers-1st-s-400-missile-defense-regiment-to-china; and Christopher Woody, "China Now Reportedly Has a Full Set of Russia's Advanced S-400 Air-Defense Missile System," *Business Insider*, May 11, 2018, http://www.businessinsider.com/china-has-russian-s-400-air-defense-system-2018-5.

[20] "Rostec and China to Sign Contract for Heavy Helicopter Production at the End of 2016," Rostec, July 11, 2016, http://rostec.ru/en/news/4518543; and "China Teams Up with Russia to Develop Rocket-Launched Reconnaissance Drone," TASS, March 30, 2018, http://tass.com/defense/996974.

the Su-35 and is beginning to acquire fifth-generation planes. However, blatant cases of Chinese reverse engineering continue, even following the recently adopted rigorous intellectual property agreements between the two countries. This could lead Moscow to renew export curbs on protected Russian-supplied defense technology to counter knockoff production.

Despite Russian concerns over reverse engineering and the improving capacity of China's own military-industrial complex, this partnership will likely continue because the PLA cannot acquire most weapons from Western countries due to sanctions and export controls. Meanwhile, Russia seeks arms sales to support its military modernization program through export revenue and larger production runs. They also provide an opportunity for Moscow to gain a deeper understanding of, and ideally influence over, future Chinese defense activities. In addition, high-tech arms sales help dilute the perception, which neither partner wants to further, that Russia is becoming a raw materials appendage to China. The PRC has limited arms sales to Russian allies in Central Asia out of deference to Russia's preeminent defense position in the region. Beijing has also disclaimed any intention of pursuing military alliances or bases in Central Asia. Furthermore, Russian strategists perceive the PLA's growing capabilities as distracting Pentagon planners from concentrating on Russia. Arms sales also enhance Moscow's influence with other potential Chinese adversaries such as Japan. Japanese leaders want to limit Sino-Russian defense cooperation while reducing security tensions with Moscow to gain leverage over Beijing.

## *Military Exercises*

Regular military exercises have also become a well-established feature of the Sino-Russian defense relationship. Chinese and Russian multilateral and bilateral war games have increasingly varied in size, format, and location. In September 2016, the two countries held naval drills in the South China Sea for the first time. In June 2017, the Russian and Chinese navies participated in the first stage of the Joint Sea 2017 naval exercises in St. Petersburg and Kaliningrad. Chinese state media claimed that the objective of the drills was to ensure coordination in maritime joint rescue missions and economic activities.[21] The naval drills took place in novel locations. In July of that year, maneuvers occurred in the Baltic Sea, whereas the second phase in September took place in the Sea of Japan and, for the

---

[21] Prashanth Parameswaran, "Military Drills Put Russia-China Ties in the Spotlight," *Diplomat*, June 20, 2017, https://thediplomat.com/2017/06/military-drills-put-russia-china-ties-in-the-spotlight.

first time, in the Okhotsk Sea.[22] In the Baltic, the Russian fleet consisted of "one frigate, fixed-wing aircraft, helicopters, and marines"; the Chinese deployed "one destroyer, one frigate, one supply ship, ship-borne helicopters, and marines." The joint drills simulated the following on a map: "ship-to-sea firing by secondary cannons, air defense, joint landing and inspection, maritime search and rescue, and underway replenishment."[23] In the second stage of Joint Sea 2017, the drills focused on joint submarine rescue and antisubmarine warfare techniques.[24]

In April 2018, Chinese and Russian officials announced that the 2018 Joint Sea exercises would take place in the fall in the Yellow Sea, off the eastern coastal city of Qingdao—near the security-sensitive Korean Peninsula. In August, moreover, the SCO states conducted the Peace Mission 2018 counterterrorism drills in the Ural Mountains, with a combined force of some three thousand troops as well as five hundred weapons systems. These ground exercises have been held every one or two years since 2005. The 2018 drills were the most inclusive drills in the organization's history, including China, Kazakhstan, Kyrgyzstan, Russia, and Tajikistan, as well as, for the first time, India and Pakistan. The SCO aspires to reduce tensions between these South Asian rivals, which impede Chinese and Russian regional security and economic ambitions. The PLA also regularly joins Russian-led multinational showcase events, such as the International Army Games (which include an Aviadarts military aviation contest and other elements that sometimes occur on Chinese territory) and tank biathlons.[25] The May 2016 aerospace security drill in Moscow represented the first joint command air-and-missile defense exercise between the two countries. In December 2017, Russia and China held the joint Aerospace Security 2017 exercises in Beijing. According to the Russian state media, the six days of drills prepared their militaries for "combat operations when organizing air missile defenses, operation and mutual fire support, as well as responding to sporadic and incendiary ballistic and cruise missile strikes."[26]

---

[22] Ankit Panda, "Chinese, Russian Navies Hold Exercises in Sea of Japan, Okhotsk Sea," *Diplomat*, September 21, 2017, https://thediplomat.com/2017/09/chinese-russian-navies-hold-exercises-in-sea-of-japan-okhotsk-sea.

[23] "China, Russia Conduct Simulation Exercise for Joint Naval Drills," Xinhua, July 24, 2018, http://www.xinhuanet.com/english/2017-07/24/c_136466432.htm; and Prashanth Parameswaran, "China, Russia Launch First Military Drills in Baltic Sea," *Diplomat*, July 26, 2017, http://thediplomat.com/2017/07/china-russia-launch-first-military-drills-in-baltic-sea.

[24] Panda, "Chinese, Russian Navies Hold Exercises."

[25] "First Stage of Aviadarts—2018 Military Aviation Contest Kicks Off in Russia," TASS, March 2, 2018, http://tass.com/defense/992456.

[26] "Russian-Chinese Joint Air Defense Drills Kick Off in Beijing," TASS, December 11, 2017, http://tass.com/defense/980318.

In their ground exercises, China and Russia rehearse skills such as fighting insurgent movements, interdicting guerrillas, liberating hostages, providing close air support, and preparing for airborne and other special forces assaults. They also have conducted naval exercises that cover maritime search and rescue, antisubmarine warfare, combined air defense, freeing of seized ships, escorting of civilian vessels, and amphibious assaults on Pacific islands. These bilateral drills serve several purposes, including enhancing interoperability between the two armed forces through the development of joint tactics, techniques, and procedures. They also encourage arms sales and other defense industrial collaboration and send signals to third parties—reassuring partners while deterring adversaries. Finally, the joint drills enable China and Russia to stay informed on each other's military capabilities as a means of mutual confidence building.

## Defense Dialogues and Meetings

Chinese and Russian leaders have described the two countries' military ties as a critical dimension of their broader strategic partnership. Over the course of the 1990s, both sides established confidence- and security-building measures, developed processes to avoid future incidents, placed constraints on conventional military activities within one hundred kilometers of their border, constructed rapid communication networks, and arranged regular consultations between their general staffs and defense ministries. Chinese and Russian leaders frequently meet bilaterally and at gatherings of major regional security institutions. For example, at the Russian-Chinese Intergovernmental Commission on Military-Technical Cooperation, the deputy chiefs of staff and other national security officials have met regularly.[27] From 2013 to 2018, Lieutenant General Xu Qiliang, the vice chairman of the Chinese Central Military Commission, and Russian defense minister Sergei Shoigu co-chaired its sessions. In April 2018, Xu told Shoigu that "every one of our sessions is a great success. We have achieved a uniform understanding on aspects of military-technical cooperation."[28] General Zhang Youxia, the other vice chairman of the Chinese Central Military Commission, recently replaced Xu as the Chinese co-chair at these intergovernmental commission sessions. Moscow has also arranged for instructors from the International

---

[27] "Foreign Ministry Spokesperson Hua Chunying's Regular Press Conference on September 13, 2016," Ministry of Foreign Affairs (PRC), http://www.fmprc.gov.cn/mfa_eng/xwfw_665399/s2510_665401/2511_665403/t1397276.shtml.

[28] "Russian-Chinese Military-Technical Cooperation Has Never Been Better—Chinese Central Military Commission Vice Chairman (Part 2)," Interfax, April 24, 2018, http://www.interfax.com/newsinf.asp?pg=3&id=828002.

Special Forces Training Center in Chechnya to provide antiterrorism training for Chinese special police forces in Xinjiang, which borders Central Asia.[29] On June 29, 2017, China and Russia signed a roadmap on military cooperation for 2017–20 that focuses on top-level planning for military cooperation through the end of the decade. The agenda includes paying more attention to cooperation between Chinese and Russian border regions.[30]

The last year has seen a number of important Sino-Russian meetings. In December 2017, Shoigu met with the vice chairman of the Central Military Commission, Zhang Youxia, in Moscow and affirmed that comprehensive cooperation is a priority of Russian defense policy.[31] In April 2018, Chinese defense minister Wei Fenghe met with Shoigu in Moscow while attending the seventh Moscow Conference on International Security. During the meeting, Wei stressed China's desire to demonstrate solidarity with Russia against the United States, advocated stronger bilateral security relations, and spoke of both countries forming a "united position" on the international stage. Wei maintained that "the two countries' comprehensive strategic partnership of coordination is 'as stable as Mount Tai,' adding that strengthened cooperation between Chinese and Russian militaries has contributed to regional and global peace and stability."[32] On May 31, 2018, Major General Shao Yuanming, deputy chief of the Joint Staff Department of China's Central Military Commission, and Colonel General Sergei Rudskoy, chief of the Main Operational Directorate of the General Staff of the Russian Armed Forces, co-hosted the twentieth round of bilateral strategic consultations.[33] The two countries reached broad consensus on important international and regional issues and agreed to further deepen bilateral military cooperation and strategic coordination. Much of their discussion was bolstered by shared concern about the United States, with both sides criticizing the new U.S. sanctions against Russian

---

[29] Yixiang Xu, "Evolving Sino-Russian Cooperation in Syria," U.S. Institute of Peace, Brief, October 3, 2017, https://www.usip.org/publications/2017/10/evolving-sino-russian-cooperation-syria.

[30] D.D. Wu, "China and Russia Sign Military Cooperation Roadmap," *Diplomat*, June 30, 2017, https://thediplomat.com/2017/06/china-and-russia-sign-military-cooperation-roadmap.

[31] "Russia, China to Boost Defense Cooperation," TASS, December 8, 2017, http://www.tass.com/defense/979852.

[32] "Chinese Defense Minister Comments on Moscow International Security Conference," TASS, April 3, 2018, http://www.tass.com/world/997455; Alice Scarsi, "China Sent Delegation to Russia to Show 'Russo-Chinese Unity' against the U.S.," *Express*, April 3, 2018, https://www.express.co.uk/news/world/940792/china-news-russia-alliance-military-ties-usa-trade-war-salisbury-attack; and Hong Yu, "China Ready to Strengthen International Defense Cooperation: Defense Minister," Xinhua, April 5, 2018, available at http://en.people.cn/n3/2018/0405/c90000-9445912.html.

[33] "China, Russia Hold 20th Round of Strategic Consultations in Beijing," China Military Online, May 30, 2018, http://eng.chinamil.com.cn/view/2018-05/30/content_8045918.htm.

and Chinese defense industries.³⁴ Later in July, Chinese defense minister Wei Fenghe and Russian ground forces commander-in-chief General Oleg Salyukov met in Beijing. They emphasized expanding and deepening cooperation in all military areas and pushed for greater development of China-Russia relations.³⁵

### Joint Statements

In joint defense and security statements, Chinese and Russian representatives advocate nonaggression, antiterrorism, noninterference in internal affairs, adherence to international law, and respect for national sovereignty, equal security, and territorial integrity. Representatives from both sides deny that they view one another as military threats. Previous evidence of the contrary, such as statements by prominent Russians expressing alarm about China's long-run ambitions to recover lost Chinese territory in Siberia, is no longer being updated. Each government prudently avoids publicly expressing concern about the other's military activities, while jointly (if typically indirectly and implicitly) criticizing the United States and its allies. For example, in a joint statement on strategic stability issued during President Vladimir Putin's visit to Beijing in June 2016, the Chinese and Russian leaders warned against the threat to international stability from "some countries and military-political alliances" that "seek decisive advantage in military and relevant technology." They also expressed concern about the adverse strategic impact of "long distance [conventional] precision attack weapons" as well as "the unilateral deployment of anti-missile systems all over the world," which their statement claimed "has negatively affected global and regional strategic balance, stability, and security." In their joint declaration, China and Russia called for "fair and balanced disarmament and arms control," new measures to keep terrorists from using biological and chemical weapons, respect for the UN Security Council and international law, noninterference in countries' internal affairs, refraining from enlarging military alliances, and a wider conception of the concept of "strategic stability." The two governments also released other declarations during

---

[34] Tom O'Connor, "Russia and China Declare Closer Military Ties in 'New Stage' as They Resist U.S.," *Newsweek*, May 30, 2018, http:// www.newsweek.com/russia-china-declare-closer-military-ties-new-stage-they-resist-us-949847; and "China, Russia Hold 20th Round of Strategic Consultations in Beijing."

[35] Tom O'Connor, "China Military Tells Russia They Will 'Jointly Deal with Threats and Challenges' as Tensions with U.S. Rise," *Newsweek*, July 3, 2018, http://www.newsweek.com/china-military-tells-russia-they-will-jointly-deal-threats-challenges-us-1007451.

Putin's visit supporting their views on international law and cybersecurity.[36] In their most recent joint statement, issued in June 2018, Chinese and Russian leaders declared their intention to "enhance existing mechanisms of military cooperation, broaden practical military and military-technical collaboration, and jointly counter regional and global security challenges."[37]

Under President Xi Jinping, the PRC's policies and rhetoric on nuclear issues have moved much closer to Russia's. For example, both Chinese and Russian official discourse present a similar anti-American narrative regarding many security issues. In the Sino-Russian narrative, Washington compelled Moscow and Beijing into accepting security agreements and practices that codified initial but fleeting U.S. advantages, pursued "absolute" rather than "equal" security that disregards Russian-Chinese interests, applied sanctions selectively to promote U.S. commercial rather than security interests, and encouraged "terrorists" that are seeking to subvert anti-American regimes aligned with Beijing and Moscow. Previous differences between Russian and Chinese approaches to arms control with the United States and its allies are narrowing. In particular, Chinese defense officials now express much more concern about U.S. missile defense, echoing Russian concerns about these systems. Meanwhile, the previous comprehensive network of Russian-U.S. arms control has collapsed under the weight of bilateral tensions. The only difference in the Russian and Chinese perspectives, which may become more important, is that Moscow wants Beijing to participate in the next round of strategic arms control talks, which Chinese officials show no enthusiasm for doing.

### Other Activities

Since the PLA has not fought a major conflict in decades, the Chinese defense community studies foreign militaries and their operations closely. Such learning is one reason for the PLA's enthusiasm about participating in joint exercises with the advanced military of Russia. Chinese national security decision-makers are likely studying Russian tactics in Ukraine and Syria for lessons on how Russia has been making major territorial gains with limited expenditure of conventional military power. Russia's annexation of Crimea and military consolidation in the area are considered the precedent of the current embrace of hybrid tactics, with the invasion of Georgia in

---

[36] "China, Russia Sign Joint Statement on Strengthening Global Strategic Stability," China.org.cn, June 27, 2016, http://www.china.org.cn/world/2016-06/27/content_38751766.htm.

[37] "Zhonghua Renmin Gongheguo he Eluosi Lianbang lianheshengming (quan wen)."

2008 being the precursor of this current adoption of hybrid warfare.[38] China meanwhile has been utilizing hybrid tactics in its pacification policies in Xinjiang, Taiwan, and Tibet, as well as in its behavior in the East and South China Seas—for example, the installation of artificial islands and air-denial systems.[39] It is possible that Chinese perceptions of Russian techniques have contributed to China's changing tactics regarding the East and South China Sea disputes. For example, like Russia in Crimea, China has presented the world with a *fait accompli* by declaring an air defense identification zone and more recently constructing artificial islands around these territories. Like Russia in Ukraine, China has consolidated its recent gains by reinforcing its military potential in the area. Their mutual learning has manifested not only in the like-for-like application of the same tactical actions but in the construction of an underlying narrative for these actions and the adaptation of such tactics in different circumstances. Russia's actions established a narrative that has demonstrably been co-opted by China.[40] The notion of the "dark hand" of Washington, one that among its other actions manipulates dangerous "extreme nationalism" with hybrid tactics, was applied in the case of Crimea and Ukraine and has been readily adopted by China.[41] The presence of the "little green men," the irregular forces involved in the annexation of Crimea, equally has been used and adapted for Chinese purposes. A former admiral in the U.S. Navy, James Stavridis, claimed in December 2016 that China had established its own "little blue sailors," the "maritime militia."[42] The maritime militia "is a civilian force posing as fishing boats and other noncombatants, but is clearly under the operational control of the government."[43] This itself created a discernable precedent for maritime hybrid warfare, which some claim has in turn been co-opted by Russia in the Arctic.[44]

---

[38] Richard Weitz, "China, Russia, and the Challenge to the Global Commons," *Pacific Focus* 24, no. 3 (2009): 271–97, https://onlinelibrary.wiley.com/doi/full/10.1111/j.1976-5118.2009.01026.x.

[39] Lora Saalman, "Little Grey Men: China and the Ukraine Crisis," *Survival* 58, no. 6 (2016): 135–56, https://www.tandfonline.com/doi/full/10.1080/00396338.2016.1257201.

[40] Lino Miani, "Beyond Crimea: Hybrid War in Asia?" Affiliate Network, May 2, 2016, http://affiliatenetwork.navisioglobal.com/2016/05/beyond-crimea.

[41] Saalman, "Little Grey Men."

[42] James Stavridis, "Maritime Hybrid Warfare Is Coming," *Proceedings Magazine*, December 2016, https://www.usni.org/magazines/proceedings/2016-12-0/maritime-hybrid-warfare-coming.

[43] Daniel L. Kuester, "Naval War College Professors Testify on State of South China Sea," Navy News Service, September 30, 2016, https://www.navy.mil/submit/display.asp?story_id=96943.

[44] Paul A. Goble, "Moscow Acting in the Arctic the Way Beijing Is in the South China Sea, French Analyst Says," Euromaidan Press, February 16, 2017, http://euromaidanpress.com/2017/02/16/moscow-acting-in-the-arctic-the-way-beijing-is-in-the-south-china-sea-french-analyst-says-euromaidan-press.

## Scenarios

### Sino-Russian Alliance

The next few years will likely see a deepening of the comprehensive Sino-Russian defense and security partnership. The Chinese and Russian national security communities share common objectives that can be promoted through further cooperation, such as border security, military technology development, and counterterrorism. They also perceive threats from U.S. and allied positions and policies that they can cooperate to thwart, such as U.S. missile defense and Western military intervention in regional hotspots. They conversely see opportunities to expand their influence at the expense of the United States, including by undermining U.S. bilateral and multilateral alliances.

In theory, China and Russia could sign a more comprehensive mutual defense treaty, under which each country would render military aid to the other in cases of armed aggression against one partner by a third party. The Treaty of Good-Neighborliness and Friendly Cooperation, signed in 2001, promotes security ties but lacks a mutual defense clause such as that found in the mutual defense treaty that the PRC and Soviet Union signed in 1950. The 2001 treaty stresses mutual nonaggression, noninterference, peaceful coexistence, antiterrorism, international law, and respect for national sovereignty, equal security, and territorial integrity.[45] Although China has consistently denied any intent to seek foreign military alliances and bases, it has made major changes to its foreign security policies in recent years. In the South China Sea, Beijing has adopted a more assertive stance, pursuing massive construction projects and the militarization of artificial islands in disputed territories. China could likewise decide to revise its no-alliance policy, though this would be a major departure from recent policies. Perhaps the only factor that might force Beijing and Moscow to take such an overtly anti-American step would be if they both came to simultaneously fear a near-term U.S. military threat. Even U.S. military action against Iran or North Korea might not drive them to follow that course if, as with the use of U.S. military power in Syria, the limited scope of the action was clear.

More plausibly, China and Russia could deepen their defense collaboration by increasing the frequency, size, and ambitions of their military exercises and other engagements. In particular, they could prepare

---

[45] "Treaty of Good-Neighborliness and Friendly Cooperation between the People's Republic of China and the Russian Federation," July 24, 2001, available at http://www.fmprc.gov.cn/mfa_eng/wjdt_665385/2649_665393/t15771.shtml.

to conduct more extensive joint military campaigns, such as in Central or East Asia. Both countries seek capabilities meant to negate the United States' technological strengths and exploit asymmetrical weaknesses in U.S. defenses. For example, Chinese and Russian security experts have discussed ways to cooperate against U.S. missile defense systems, especially those in Northeast Asia, beyond their joint command post exercises.[46] More extensive Sino-Russian collaboration on ballistic missile defense (BMD) could range from simply exchanging more intelligence assessments to coordinating pressure against other countries in Europe or Asia to abstain from deploying U.S. BMD assets, selling each other BMD-penetrating weapons, and undertaking joint R&D programs for common anti-BMD technologies. Through the latter approach, China and Russia could pool their resources or expertise to overcome U.S. BMD systems stationed on their peripheries.[47] Yet despite closer security ties, envisioning a scenario where a combined Sino-Russian force engages in joint military action is difficult. Even in Central Asia, the SCO lacks standing military structures or traditional defense functions. As a result, Beijing and Moscow would have to cobble together a joint force in the midst of a crisis, such as if one of the governments were to come under threat from Islamist or pro-Western groups. There is also no evidence that China and Russia have been coordinating their political-military pressure against third parties like Japan on a regular basis.

## *Renewed Rivalry*

The shadow of past conflict and future competition hangs over a potential Sino-Russian military alliance. Despite being formal military allies at one time, China and Russia have a history of conflict, including a vicious border fight in 1969. Since then, Russian representatives have viewed the PRC's rapidly advancing military capabilities with some apprehension. Still, they mostly accept this trend as a preferable alternative to Western military power in Russia's neighborhood. They also tend to downplay, and possibly underestimate, China's growing military capabilities. Looking ahead, Russian leaders may increasingly fear a rising, aggressive China in their own backyard, especially if they see a declining West in the future. The over 2,600 mile border shared by China and Russia may also become

---

[46] "Russia, China to Hold Second Missile Defense Drill in 2017," Sputnik, October 11, 2016, https://sputniknews.com/military/201610111046212661-russia-china-missile-defense.

[47] For further discussion of Sino-Russian cooperation on BMD, see Richard Weitz, "A Way Forward on Ballistic Missile Defenses," China-US Focus, September 5, 2012, https://www.chinausfocus.com/peace-security/a-way-forward-on-ballistic-missile-defenses.

a renewed source of tension if Beijing revives its territorial claims. Yet it would probably take a direct, major, and simultaneous U.S. threat to both countries to drive them into another formal military alliance, given these obstacles and their general satisfaction with their currently strong but flexible alignment of limited liability.

Future trends may weaken the Sino-Russian security partnership even without overt U.S. countermeasures. Beijing's doubts about Moscow were earlier evident in Chinese concerns about Russia's capacity to ensure the security of Central Asia. This region has thus far not seen much overt rivalry between the two sides due to their harmonious near-term interests, but Central Asia's stability is becoming more crucial for the PRC's plans both for east-west integration and for securing its western borders against sub-state terrorist threats. Chinese anxiety about Russia's will and capacity to maintain Eurasian stability has been less evident following Russian military successes in Ukraine and Syria but could worsen again should Moscow show weakness in the face of mutual threats to Sino-Russian regional interests. If Chinese leaders believe it necessary to intervene militarily in Central Asia, Moscow could grow uneasy about the implications of China's rising power for Russian influence in Eurasia.[48]

Nonetheless, developments that could drive the two apart will likely have a limited impact, focused on a geographic region or functional area rather than comprehensively breaking up the Sino-Russian security alignment on a global scale. For example, should one of the Sino-Russian regional divergence scenarios discussed earlier come to pass, such as one pertaining to Central Asia and the Middle East, it would not necessarily follow that these differences would spill over into one area, let alone all others, where the two countries interact. They could probably contain the dispute in one sphere to prevent it from contaminating others.

## *Tightening Ties*

The favorable drivers of Sino-Russian defense cooperation will most likely deepen. Russia may sell China more advanced air, sea, and ground platforms. It may also begin buying military technologies from Chinese manufacturers, including major weapons systems like the Type 054A frigate, which joined the 2015 joint naval exercise with the Russian Navy in the Mediterranean Sea. As discussed earlier, China and Russia have

---

[48] U.S. Defense Intelligence Agency, *Russia Military Power: Building a Military to Support Great Power Aspirations* (Washington, D.C., 2017), 16, http://www.dia.mil/Portals/27/Documents/News/Military%20Power%20Publications/Russia%20Military%20Power%20Report%202017.pdf.

already agreed to co-develop new major weapons systems and sell them to third parties, which might include states hostile to U.S. interests. They could also plausibly deepen their defense collaboration by increasing the frequency, size, and ambitions of their military exercises and other bilateral engagements. In particular, they could prepare to conduct more extensive joint military campaigns in places like Central or East Asia.

Yet the obstacles to more substantial Russian arms sales to China are considerable. Russian weapons exporters seek to balance sales to China with new deals with other buyers. Some of these buyers, such as India and Vietnam, are potential Chinese military adversaries. China's need for Russian military imports is declining due to the improving capacity of the Chinese military-industrial complex, though the need persists in some niche areas such as high-performance engines. Russian arms dealers worry about having to compete with increasingly formidable Chinese weapons manufacturers, with PRC arms exports emerging as more serious competition to Russian weapons exporters in third markets. Thus far, Chinese defense exports have contested Russian military sales in only a few low-value markets. Yet Russian policymakers understand that Chinese technological prowess could allow the PRC to find a niche for its defense exports by selling lower-priced weapons that are only slightly less capable than their Russian equivalents. For instance, in 2016, Moscow expected the Royal Thai Army to order Russian T-90MS main battle tanks. Instead, Thailand negotiated to buy China's less expensive MBT-3000 tanks.

The traditional abandonment-entrapment dilemma further restrains collaboration; Russian and Chinese policymakers fear being dragged into a conflict by the other. For this reason, Beijing has distanced itself from Russian military activities in Ukraine, while Moscow has refrained from fully backing Chinese territorial claims in the East and South China Seas. While China has not joined Western states in condemning Russian actions in Georgia and Ukraine, it has not fully endorsed them either due to Chinese economic interests in both countries, a desire to shield itself from Russia's unpopularity in the West, and strong concerns about separatist movements. Russian policymakers, meanwhile, have strived not to antagonize traditional allies like India and Vietnam even as Russia builds ties with China. Even if they refuse to acknowledge such a position in public, some Russian policymakers may also see other Asian countries as potential balancers of a China whose military and other power has been rising rapidly relative to Russia.

A final consideration is that Chinese and Russian security concerns predominately focus on different geographic areas and functional issues.

This situation promotes but also constrains their defense relationship. Though both sides worry about Eurasian terrorism and stability, Russia prioritizes European security issues, while the PRC is preoccupied with the Asia-Pacific. Due to these different priorities, Russia and China do not presently have a major bilateral dispute where their vital national interests conflict. Equally important, neither country requires the other's help to achieve its most critical security goals, allowing them to accept with benign indifference cases when the other fails to render support.

## Policy Implications

Despite denials by China and Russia that their cooperation is directed against the United States or any other country, their wide-ranging ties present security challenges for Washington and its allies. These overlapping challenges include China's and Russia's growing nuclear and conventional power, hostile information policies such as state-sponsored discourse attributing malign motives to U.S. foreign policy, and hybrid tactics to neutralize the United States as a counterweight to Russian and Chinese regional power. The passive strategic reassurance that Moscow and Beijing provide to one another as they pursue their respective challenges to U.S. interests and leadership is sometimes amplified by more concrete and extensive cooperation on specific issues. For instance, Russian arms sales to China circumvent Western sanctions on both countries and give the PLA weapons that it cannot acquire from domestic suppliers.

The Trump administration's recently released national security, national defense, and nuclear strategies make clear that U.S. national security officials perceive China and Russia as a direct challenge to U.S. power, influence, and interests.[49] The Trump administration observes that both countries are "pursuing asymmetric ways and means to counter U.S. conventional capabilities."[50] For instance, they are developing A2/AD capabilities designed to keep the U.S. military away from their national territories. Of note, the PLA's A2/AD capabilities (e.g., cruise and ballistic missiles, cyber weapons, air defenses systems, and naval and land mines) have been enhanced by its purchase of Russian anti-aircraft and anti-ship missiles. Increased Chinese A2/AD could impede U.S. freedom of navigation

---

[49] White House, *National Security Strategy of the United States of America* (Washington, D.C., December 2017), https://www.whitehouse.gov/wp-content/uploads/2017/12/NSS-Final-12-18-2017-0905.pdf.

[50] U.S. Department of Defense, *U.S. Nuclear Posture Review* (Washington, D.C., February 2018), https://www.defense.gov/News/SpecialReports/2018NuclearPostureReview.aspx.

operations and the United States' ability to defend its allies and project power in the Asia-Pacific, while enabling China to continue to expand its presence in the western Pacific.[51]

Not only has the Sino-Russian arms trade provided the PLA with Russian military technologies, but the sales have also enhanced Russian military power indirectly through generating increased revenue for Russian defense firms. These companies reinvest these profits into R&D that benefits the Russian military. China's growing military power also forces the Pentagon to pay greater attention to Asian military contingencies rather than concentrating against Russian military power in Europe. In addition, Chinese and Russian arms sales proliferate A2/AD capabilities to other countries, potentially negating some U.S. conventional power-projection advantages and threatening U.S. primacy in the global commons. Russia, for example, is negotiating new arms deliveries to Iran worth billions of U.S. dollars. From a regional security perspective, such deals make U.S. deterrence less credible since U.S. adversaries like Iran and North Korea now see China and Russia as possible security counterweights against the United States. Such increased military cooperation also puts pressure on U.S. relationships with allies such as Japan, which look to Washington for protection against China and Russia. The Sino-Russian security partnership allows Moscow to focus its military efforts on Ukraine, Syria, and other areas outside Asia. Their overlapping security spheres, centered on their joint border region, give China and Russia a de facto secure "strategic rear"—a sphere where they do not perceive a threat from each other and that lies beyond the reach of the U.S. military.[52]

The two countries may cooperate more directly against U.S. interests in the future. Russia may sell more advanced weaponry to China as well as begin buying substantial military technologies from Chinese manufacturers. As discussed earlier, they have already agreed to co-develop new dual-use and dedicated weapons systems such as reconnaissance drones, transport helicopters, and large-body aircraft—some of which may be sold to third parties hostile to U.S. interests. Agreements between China and Russia to cooperate more on space exploration and satellites might include more

---

[51] Rakesh Krishnan Simha, "China Emulates Russian Military Strategy in the Pacific," Russia Beyond, August 20, 2015, http://rbth.com/blogs/2015/08/20/china_emulates_russian_miitary_strategy_in_the_pacific_48627.html.

[52] Artyom Lukin, "Why the Russian Far East Is So Important to China," Huffington Post, January 12, 2015, http://www.huffingtonpost.com/artyom-lukin/russian-far-east-china_b_6452618.html.

extensive collaboration on space security.⁵³ U.S. diplomats have been countering Sino-Russian initiatives to limit U.S. military use of outer space. China and Russia are also independently developing means to disrupt or destroy U.S. satellites. If they were to collaborate more directly, it could make U.S. space assets even more vulnerable. One reason that some U.S. analysts want to establish a new space force is to better counter Sino-Russian threats in this realm. Their growing foreign military activities may also increase the risk of accidents or inadvertent encounters with the U.S. and other militaries, given that confidence- and security-building measures are harder to negotiate on a trilateral, rather than bilateral, basis. China and Russia could also coordinate on security issues related to the Arctic region, which could challenge U.S. and European access to this region.⁵⁴

In the short term, arms control issues provide a means for the United States to amplify Sino-Russian differences. The Russian government has become increasingly insistent that future strategic arms control treaties encompass additional countries besides Russia and the United States, including China. The PRC's nuclear arsenal is growing in terms of numbers, diversity, and capabilities. Yet it remains opaque about the number and capabilities of its nuclear warheads and delivery systems, as well as about its targeting and nuclear weapons employment doctrines (beyond citing the country's no-first-use doctrine). According to independent estimates, Russia and the United States have thousands of nuclear warheads, while Britain, France, India, Israel, and Pakistan have only several hundred. Most Western analysts place the Chinese arsenal at several hundred deployed strategic nuclear warheads, which is roughly the same size as the arsenals of France and the United Kingdom.⁵⁵ However, there are a few Russian (and U.S.) analysts that estimate that China has more than one thousand warheads.⁵⁶ The U.S. government maintains that Moscow and Washington need to reduce their much larger arsenals before negotiating binding limits on other countries.

---

[53] "Russia, China to Hold Experiment to Increase Satellite Data Accuracy," TASS, July 5, 2018, http://tass.com/science/1012076; and "Russia, China Sign Memorandum on Cooperation in Space Exploration," TASS, June 8, 2018, http://tass.com/science/1008745.

[54] Sonja Jordan, "China, Russia Cooperating in Arctic as Region Gains Strategic Importance," *National Defense*, June 20, 2018, http://www.nationaldefensemagazine.org/articles/2018/6/20/china-russia-cooperating-in-arctic-as-region-gains-strategic-importance.

[55] "Nuclear Weapons: Who Has What at a Glance," Arms Control Association, June 2018, https://www.armscontrol.org/factsheets/Nuclearweaponswhohaswhat; and "World Nuclear Weapon Stockpile," Ploughshares, July 5, 2018, https://www.ploughshares.org/world-nuclear-stockpile-report.

[56] Alexei Arbatov, "Engaging China in Nuclear Arms Control," Carnegie Moscow Center, October 2014, http://carnegieendowment.org/files/Arbatov_China_nuclear_Eng2014.pdf. See also "GU Students Help Discover China's Hidden Nuclear Tunnels," Georgetown University, December 5, 2011, https://www.georgetown.edu/news/china-tunnels-discovery.html.

However, the Trump administration shares Russian anxieties about Beijing's growing nuclear capabilities. If Beijing and Moscow continue to diverge regarding these issues, the Trump administration may wish to explicitly call on Beijing to join the next round of forced cuts, adhere to the Intermediate-Range Nuclear Forces Treaty, and make other proposals to raise the prominence of these Sino-Russian differences on disarmament issues. The current U.S. policy of nonrecognition of Chinese and Russian subconventional assertiveness has not reversed either country's recent gains. The United States needs additional economic, diplomatic, legal, and other nonmilitary tools to complement military countermeasures to deter Chinese and Russian subconventional assertiveness without escalating conflicts into armed exchanges.

In the long term, Washington should devote more attention and resources to assessing Sino-Russian arms sales, military exchanges, and other security ties. This effort should encompass expanded dialogues with U.S. allies and friends, including building on recent U.S. efforts to limit major arms sales both to and from China and Russia.[57] Trade agreements and related measures could improve defense industrial ties with key U.S. partners and discourage them from buying Chinese or Russian weapons or selling defense technologies to either country. Just as Western energy sanctions on Russia have focused on denying transfers that China cannot substitute for, U.S. and other Western sanctions on China and Russia should target products and services that neither country can substitute for the other. The United States should continue to strive to maintain its military technological advantages over both states in critical areas such as air power, networked information technologies, and missile defense. Future U.S. administrations should also make a great effort to strengthen U.S. foreign defense and security alliances. While keeping such commitments can be costly in terms of defense spending and sometimes lives, they provide the United States with strategic advantages over Russia and China, including military allies, forward-operating and -staging bases, diplomatic and intelligence assistance, and international legitimacy for even primarily U.S. unilateral operations. The current administration's National Defense Strategy states the following about the importance of U.S. alliances and partnerships:

> Mutually beneficial alliances and partnerships are crucial to our strategy, providing a durable, asymmetric strategic advantage that no competitor or rival

---

[57] Though without providing details, Christopher Ford, assistant secretary of state and head of the State Department's Bureau of International Security and Nonproliferation, stated that the Trump administration had already deprived Russia of millions of dollars in potential arms sales. See Hudson Institute, Policy Podcast, April 2018, http://s3.amazonaws.com/media.hudson.org/PT6-ChrisFord.mp3.

can match....Every day, our allies and partners join us in defending freedom, deterring war, and maintaining the rules which underwrite a free and open international order. By working together with allies and partners we amass the greatest possible strength for the long-term advancement of our interests, maintaining favorable balances of power that deter aggression and support the stability that generates economic growth. When we pool resources and share responsibility for our common defense, our security burden becomes lighter.[58]

In addition to traditional regional allies like Japan and South Korea, the United States should deepen ties with developing partners like India and Vietnam. The latter could act as natural counterweights to Chinese military power in South and Southeast Asia, while targeted U.S. efforts could limit these countries' defense ties with Moscow. Although Turkey has insisted on buying Russian and Chinese weapons despite U.S. pressure, and the Trump administration has declined to apply sanctions against India and various Middle Eastern countries for buying Russian weapons, the threat of sanctions alone, such as limits to defense industrial cooperation with the United States, may help deter some sales.

## Conclusion

The depth of Sino-Russian defense cooperation should not be overstated. The mutual defense commitments between the two countries are modest, especially when compared with those between the United States and its allies in Europe and Asia. China and Russia lack joint standing defense structures and are not capable of conducting a large joint conventional military operation. Despite closer security ties between China and Russia, it is unlikely that there will be a scenario where a combined Sino-Russian fleet engages in joint military action. Even in Central Asia, the SCO lacks standing military structures or functions, and some of its other members, including new member India, would resist a Sino-Russian defense condominium at their expense. Even where their security concerns overlap, the two governments have not engaged in comprehensive joint countermeasures such as pooled R&D against U.S. ballistic missile defenses. Their tabletop exercises signal to the United States their joint concerns but do not advance their joint or individual capabilities. Russia and China both want to remain major but independent great powers, and there is little indication that they will soon enter a formal mutual defense alliance.

---

[58] U.S. Department of Defense, "Summary of the 2018 National Defense Strategy of the United States of America: Sharpening the American Military's Competitive Edge," January 2018, 8, https://dod.defense.gov/Portals/1/Documents/pubs/2018-National-Defense-Strategy-Summary.pdf.

The United States could more proactively try to counter Sino-Russian security ties through more assertive policies—though with the potential caveat of driving China and Russia closer together instead of apart. For example, by decisively challenging China in the 1950s, including making nuclear threats to deter Chinese aggression, the United States helped split Beijing from Moscow because Chinese leaders became frustrated when the Soviet Union would not offer to back China with its own nuclear threats due to the risk of nuclear war. Today, the United States has applied a range of sanctions and other measures against both China and Russia, but not any targeted directly at the Sino-Russian alignment and designed to discourage or punish one country from cooperating with the other. Under present conditions, such dual-aimed threats could succeed, but they also could drive them closer together.

Defense ties between China and Russia have increased dramatically and will probably continue to do so. Areas of focus will likely encompass regional security issues, weapons sales, bilateral and military exercises, and defense and security dialogues. Their security cooperation challenges U.S. interests in maintaining regional security balances and in preventing Sino-Russian ties from facilitating the circumvention of U.S. sanctions and constraining U.S. military access to key geographic and functional areas. These challenges would increase should China and Russia form a full-fledged defense alliance, such as that existing between Japan and the United States, though this scenario is unlikely to develop, given adequate and balanced U.S. countermeasures.

# EXECUTIVE SUMMARY

This chapter examines Russia's and China's political interference and influence operations and assesses how the context, goals, and tactics of the two states' operations differ in important ways.

MAIN ARGUMENT

Russia derives its interference and influence operations from a highly personalist leadership and a position of national decline. As such, it seeks to lower other states to its level by weakening them internally. By contrast, China develops and implements its operations via a Leninist party apparatus and a position of growing strength. It seeks continued security and modernization and increasing influence on the world stage. Tactically, the two states' operations diverge in their use of violence, the messaging of their propaganda, how they harness their respective diaspora communities, their use of cyberactivities, and the missions of their intelligence personnel and foreign agents. At present, there is insufficient evidence of Sino-Russian collaboration on influence or interference operations, though the two conduct similar operations in certain democratic countries—the cumulative effect of which is to weaken local institutions and governments irrespective of bilateral coordination.

POLICY IMPLICATIONS

- Investing time and institutional resources into building knowledge about the Kremlin and the Chinese Communist Party, developing requisite language capabilities, and understanding the tactics each regime uses to achieve success in its influence operations are all necessary aspects of dealing effectively with Russia and China for the foreseeable future.

- The scale, sophistication, and ideational motives of Russian and Chinese interference and influence operations can only be effectively countered by a community of common values that shares expertise and intelligence and works together to cultivate better strategies and countermeasures.

- Even though evidence of Sino-Russian coordinated or collaborative political influence is limited, the U.S. and its allies and partners should work to counter the cumulative effect of Russian and Chinese efforts to weaken their institutions.

Chapter 4

# Russian and Chinese Political Interference Activities and Influence Operations

*Peter Mattis*

In different countries, in different ways, the political influence operations of the People's Republic of China (PRC) and Russia burst onto the scene in 2017. The efforts of the Chinese Communist Party (CCP) to shape and subvert democratic polities received dramatic coverage, beginning with an Australian news program, *Four Corners*, that aired in June 2017. The program detailed the wheelings and dealings of two Australian-Chinese businessmen who were the nexus of Australian politics and the CCP's influence operators.[1] Later that summer in nearby New Zealand, a sitting member of parliament, Yang Jian, made headlines when it was learned that he probably was a former Chinese military intelligence officer.[2] In a report released just two weeks before President Donald Trump's inauguration, the U.S. intelligence community stated as fact that Russia interfered in the U.S. presidential election and that its efforts "demonstrated a significant escalation in directness, level of activity, and scope of effort compared to previous operations." Moreover, the analysts assessed that "Putin and the Russian Government developed a clear preference for President-elect

---

**PETER MATTIS** is a Research Fellow in China Studies at the Victims of Communism Memorial Foundation and a contributing editor at War on the Rocks. He can be reached at <contact@petermattis.com>.

The author would like to thank Lizzy Leary for her research assistance.

[1] Nick McKenzie and Sarah Ferguson, "Power and Influence," *Four Corners*, June 5, 2017, http://www.abc.net.au/4corners/power-and-influence-promo/8579844.

[2] Jamil Anderlini, "China-Born New Zealand MP Probed by Spy Agency," *Financial Times*, September 12, 2017, https://www.ft.com/content/64991ca6-9796-11e7-a652-cde3f882dd7b.

Donald Trump."³ Vladimir Putin later confirmed his preference for candidate Trump, and perhaps also efforts by his government to help the Trump campaign.⁴ While the U.S. intelligence community did not assess whether Russian activities directly affected the outcome of the election, the narrowness of Trump's victories in key states gives cause for wondering whether Moscow's influence tipped the scale.⁵

More examples accumulated throughout the year and suggested that democratic states were more vulnerable to manipulation than even had been feared. News investigations revealed that France's far-right National Front led by Marine Le Pen sought Kremlin-linked funding in 2014 and 2016.⁶ In the 2017 German elections, the nationalist party Alternative for Germany claimed 94 seats on the back of the country's migrant controversy and Russian-fueled agitprop about crimes committed by refugees.⁷ Of note, Russia's relationships also included the parties and candidates from the far left as much as the far right, suggesting that bringing about chaos was at least as important as "elite capture."⁸ In Australia, Senator Sam Dastyari from the Labor Party resigned after media revelations that he had warned CCP-linked fundraiser Huang Xiangmo about government surveillance and an audio tape put the lie to Dastyari's denials that he contradicted Labor Party policy on

---

³ Office of the Director of National Intelligence, *Assessing Russian Activities and Intentions in Recent U.S. Elections*, National Intelligence Council, Intelligence Community Assessment, ICA 2017-01D (Washington, D.C., January 6, 2017), https://www.dni.gov/files/documents/ICA_2017_01.pdf.

⁴ At a press conference in Helsinki following the Trump-Putin summit in July 2018, when asked, "[D]id you want President Trump to win the election and did you direct any of your officials to help him do that?" Putin replied, "Yes, I did. Yes, I did. Because he talked about bringing the U.S.-Russia relationship back to normal." "Remarks by President Trump and President Putin of the Russian Federation in Joint Press Conference," White House, July 16, 2018, https://www.whitehouse.gov/briefings-statements/remarks-president-trump-president-putin-russian-federation-joint-press-conference.

⁵ Fewer than 80,000 votes in three states swung the election in Trump's favor, despite Hillary Clinton winning the popular vote by more than 2.5 million. Philip Bump, "Donald Trump Will Be President Thanks to 80,000 People in Three States," *Washington Post*, December 1, 2016, https://www.washingtonpost.com/news/the-fix/wp/2016/12/01/donald-trump-will-be-president-thanks-to-80000-people-in-three-states/.

⁶ Gabriel Gatehouse, "Marine Le Pen: Who Is Funding France's Far Right?" BBC, April 3, 2017, https://www.bbc.co.uk/news/world-europe-39478066.

⁷ Amar Toor, "Germany Grapples with Fake News ahead of Elections," *Verge*, January 19, 2017, https://www.theverge.com/2017/1/19/14314680/germany-fake-news-facebook-russia-election-merkel; and Paul Kirby, "German Election: Why This Is a Turning Point," BBC, September 25, 2017, https://www.bbc.co.uk/news/world-europe-41094785.

⁸ "Turning Politics Up to 11: Russian Disinformation Distorts American and European Democracy," *Economist*, February 22, 2018, https://www.economist.com/briefing/2018/02/22/russian-disinformation-distorts-american-and-european-democracy; and Robert Windrem, "Senate Russia Investigators Are Interested in Jill Stein," NBC, December 19, 2017, https://www.nbcnews.com/news/us-news/why-are-senate-russia-investigators-interested-jill-stein-n831261.

the South China Sea for donations.[9] The Australian Security Intelligence Organization reportedly identified ten political candidates closely linked to China's intelligence services and, in mid-2018, outed a sitting member of parliament for links to Beijing.[10] In sum, the successful manipulation or penetration of democratic political systems by Beijing and Moscow could no longer be disputed by the end of 2017. This realization about authoritarian interference, however, could distort at least as much as illuminate the challenge posed by these revisionist states.

Political interference or political influence operations can be defined as deliberate efforts to disrupt the normal flow of political or social activity to generate desired outcomes for the influencer. Both the CCP's China and Putin's Russia see political influence operations as a critical and routine part of statecraft. Although this distinguishes both approaches from the special policy channels through which democratic states handle covert action, the two countries diverge from one another owing to several factors. First, China is trying to shape a functional but Sino-centric regional and global order as an emerging great power. Russia, however, can only be a powerful and influential country by bringing other countries down to its level. The country's demographic trends, economic structure, and poor performance present seemingly insurmountable barriers to regaining the kind of status once possessed by the Soviet Union.

The differences between the two approaches may not be as important as two basic features of the CCP's China and Putin's Russia. Political influence operations—what Americans would call covert actions—are a routine, day-to-day feature of these systems. The operators in both systems do not require special approvals or direct, specific orders to carry out their operations. This is not to suggest that operational approvals are not required in certain cases from the highest levels, but those approvals are not necessarily the norm as they would be in a Western democratic system. Both countries also define their security by the absence of threats, rather than the state's ability to manage them, and consider robust liberalism to

---

[9] "Sam Dastyari Resignation: How We Got Here," Australian Broadcasting Corporation, December 12, 2017, http://www.abc.net.au/news/2017-12-12/sam-dastyari-resignation-how-did-we-get-here/9249380; and Nick McKenzie, James Massola, and Richard Baker, "Labor Senator Sam Dastyari Warned Wealthy Chinese Donor Huang Xiangmo His Phone Was Bugged," *Sydney Morning Herald*, November 29, 2017, https://www.smh.com.au/politics/federal/labor-senator-sam-dastyari-warned-wealthy-chinese-donor-huang-xiangmo-his-phone-was-bugged-20171128-gzu14c.html.

[10] Paul Maley and Nicola Berkovic, "Security Agencies Flag Chinese Manchurian Candidates," *Australian*, December 9, 2017. One example revealed later in 2018 added concreteness to the intelligence leaks. See Nick McKenzie, Alexandra Smith, and Fergus Hunter, "This Sitting Labor MP Has Been Cultivated by Chinese Intelligence," *Sydney Morning Herald*, June 27, 2018, https://www.smh.com.au/politics/federal/this-sitting-labor-mp-has-been-cultivated-by-chinese-intelligence-20180627-p4znzp.html.

be a serious, if not existential, threat to their political systems. Indeed, the absence of threats in the world of ideas may well be the ultimate shared security objective of Zhongnanhai and the Kremlin. In a world with stronger democracies, preempting and shaping decisions in Western capitals is a necessity, not just a consideration.

This chapter is divided into the following four main sections. The first section discusses the overall objectives and top-level operational concepts underpinning CCP- and Kremlin-backed political interference. The second section outlines the organizational and personal ties that constitute both countries' influence-building systems. The third section compares the tactics of both sides through their use of propaganda, violence, influence in target countries, and cyberspace. The fourth section explores the challenges and opportunities for U.S. policymakers considering the divergent Chinese and Russian approaches to interference.

## Chaos and Construction: Active Measures vs. United Front Work

The problematic influence-building and interference in democratic societies of the CCP's China and Putin's Russia come from a shared vision of security defined by the absence of threats rather than the ability to manage them. Those threats are not limited to material or physical threats to both countries, their citizens, or their interests, but include the ideas that undermine the ways in which the two regimes rule.

In a broad sense, both countries share at least three substantial interests. First, they see a threat from Western liberalism that undermines their legitimacy at home. To the extent that democratic governance can be discredited, the CCP and Putin benefit from the lack of alternatives to their authoritarian rule at home. Second, they both benefit from a weakening of U.S. security partnerships and alliances. Without its allies and partners, the United States' ability to project force and restrain Chinese and Russian behavior in their near abroad would be limited. Third, the two regimes remain sensitive to China's and Russia's diaspora communities because of their ability to boost influence-building abroad and as a source of threat to the regimes at home.[11] Diaspora communities are best situated to serve as a bridge between each country's old and new societies because they

---

[11] Laura Rosenberger and John Garnaut, "The Interference Operations from Putin's Kremlin and Xi's Communist Party: Forging a Joint Response," *Asan Forum*, May 8, 2018, http://www.theasanforum.org/the-interference-operations-from-putins-kremlin-and-xis-communist-party-forging-a-joint-response.

possess the cultural fluency to translate foreign ideas back into their ethnic homeland in ways that resonate.

## National Objectives for New Situations

Russian leaders give every indication that their primary objective is a multipolar world in which Moscow can exercise influence.[12] Trends in the foundation of Russian power remain problematic for Putin's grand objectives, and there is little reason to envision Russia's re-emergence as a great power. Demographically, the country's population is aging as those born amid low birthrates in the 1990s have now entered into the workforce, which is shrinking by as much as 800,000 people per year. Even Putin has drawn attention to the issue.[13] Moscow relies heavily on raw materials and energy to keep the economy afloat, but U.S. actions and the international response to the Russian occupation of eastern Ukraine and Crimea have stressed the system. Both individual businesses and the overall economy have felt the bite, even if the Kremlin's behavior has not modified noticeably. The round of sanctions imposed in April 2018 badly damaged the stocks of key Putin allies, and Washington made it known that it has a list with the names of many more people who could be sanctioned. Russian GDP growth is down, and inflation is up; meanwhile, U.S. sanctions make it difficult to move dollars.[14] Moreover, many European countries were able to avoid damage themselves and compensate for the loss of Russian business by finding new markets.[15]

The weakness of Russia's position, particularly after sanctions were introduced in 2014, means that Putin's objectives cannot be achieved through growth—even if that already was evident beforehand. As the former head of U.S. counterintelligence Joel Brenner said, "The Russians know they have to play jiu jitsu with the [United States] instead of taking

---

[12] Julia Ioffe, "What Putin Really Wants," *Atlantic*, January/February 2018, https://www.theatlantic.com/magazine/archive/2018/01/putins-game/546548/1; and "Shift to Multipolar World: Lavrov Says Russia Working to Adjust Foreign Policy to New Reality," RT, April 10, 2016, https://www.rt.com/news/339082-russia-new-foreign-policy-multipolar.

[13] Tom Balmforth, "Another Worrying Sign for Russia's Dire Demographics," Radio Free Europe/Radio Liberty, September 27, 2017, https://www.rferl.org/a/russia-population-decline-labororeshkin/28760413.html.

[14] Tom Keatinge, "This Time, Sanctions on Russia Are Having the Desired Effect," *Financial Times*, April 13, 2018, https://www.ft.com/content/cad69cf4-3e40-11e8-bcc8-cebcb81f1f90; and John W. Schoen, "U.S. Sanctions Have Taken a Big Bite Out of Russian Economy," CNBC, July 25, 2017, https://www.cnbc.com/2017/07/25/us-sanctions-have-taken-a-big-bite-out-of-russias-economy.html.

[15] Edward Hunter Christie, "Sanctions after Crimea: Have They Worked?" *NATO Review*, July 13, 2015, https://www.nato.int/docu/review/2015/russia/sanctions-after-crimea-have-they-worked/EN/index.htm.

us on directly."[16] The Kremlin must bring other countries down to its level to expand its influence and strengthen its prestige. Study after study of Russian political influence operations in recent years has arrived at a similar conclusion. Operational objectives include subverting the local government, undermining its credibility, exploiting corruption, distorting and polluting democratic political discourse, trying to exacerbate polarizing political issues in the electorate, and disrupting viable alternatives to Russia's strongman rule.[17] This largely continues an old playbook developed by the KGB during the Cold War. A wide range of former Soviet Bloc intelligence officers have affirmed these objectives of Soviet and Russian political influence operations.[18] In part because the Kremlin cannot persuade, it seeks to capture foreign states through these other means.

In contrast, the CCP's objectives can be understood in terms of two interrelated and overarching goals: Chinese modernization and national security. The party's view of modernizing China has long taken the form of building the country into a great power. CCP general secretary Xi Jinping is simply the most recent example of a party leader describing this objective. At the 19th Party Congress in 2017, he stated: "The original aspiration and the mission of Chinese Communists is to seek happiness for the Chinese people and rejuvenation for the Chinese nation. This original aspiration, this mission, is what inspires Chinese Communists to advance." He also stated that "the Chinese nation, which since modern times began has endured so much for so long, has achieved a tremendous transformation: it has stood up, grown rich, and is becoming strong; it has come to embrace the brilliant

---

[16] David Lynch, "Russian Spies Adopt New Tactics to Battle an Old Enemy," *Financial Times*, December 14, 2016, https://www.ft.com/content/ae1cd0c2-c170-11e6-9bca-2b93a6856354.

[17] For example, Edward Lucas and Peter Pomerantsev, "Winning the Information War: Techniques and Counter-strategies to Russian Propaganda in Central and Eastern Europe," Center for European Policy Analysis, August 2016, https://docs.wixstatic.com/ugd/644196_fb18ae76bcf246148d0f1c8418497a2f.pdf; Heather A. Conley et al., *The Kremlin Playbook: Understanding Russian Influence in Central and Eastern Europe* (Washington, D.C.: Center for Strategic and International Studies, 2016), https://csis-prod.s3.amazonaws.com/s3fs-public/publication/1601017_Conley_KremlinPlaybook_Web.pdf; and U.S. House Permanent Select Committee on Intelligence, "Report on Russian Active Measures," March 22, 2018, https://intelligence.house.gov/uploadedfiles/final_russia_investigation_report.pdf.

[18] Evan Osnos, David Remnick, and Joshua Yaffa, "Trump, Putin, and the New Cold War," *New Yorker*, March 6, 2017, https://www.newyorker.com/magazine/2017/03/06/trump-putin-and-the-new-cold-war; Ladislav Bittman, *The KGB and Soviet Disinformation: An Insider's View* (Washington, D.C.: Pergamon-Brassey's, 1985); and Ronald J. Rychlak and Ion Mihai Pacepa, *Disinformation: Former Spy Chief Reveals Secret Strategies for Undermining Freedom, Attacking Religion, and Promoting Terrorism* (Washington, D.C.: WND Books, 2013).

prospects of rejuvenation."[19] Xi may have coined the term "China dream," but the objective has a longer history among Chinese reformers and within the CCP itself.[20]

Return to great-power status necessarily implies moving the international system from one characterized by U.S. unipolarity to one characterized by a multipolarity that includes China. Even though China must acquire a certain amount of material power and influence, CCP leaders consistently frame a component of this objective as ensuring the legitimacy of socialism on the international stage. Xi has been explicit about this requirement at least since he outlined his views of a "new type of great-power relations" to U.S. interlocutors in 2012.[21] His latest report at the 19th Party Congress affirmed that multipolarity is "surging forward," that "relative international forces are becoming more balanced," and that socialism with Chinese characteristics "offers a new option for other countries and nations who want to speed up their development while preserving their independence."[22] The subtext: socialism with Chinese characteristics is just as legitimate a national path as liberal democracy.

Greater engagement with an international system that is becoming increasingly multipolar, however, opens up China much more to external influences. This is why for each step forward toward openness, the CCP makes a corresponding move toward internal consolidation. Deng Xiaoping and the CCP accompanied "reform and opening" with the creation of the Ministry of State Security as well as the Anti-Spiritual Pollution Campaign. Xi merely reversed the order: the creation of the Central State Security Commission and the passage of national security legislation predated the Belt and Road Initiative and expanded alongside it. These developments illustrate a consistent fear about the union of domestic and overseas adversaries of the party.[23]

---

[19] Xi Jinping, "Secure a Decisive Victory in Building a Moderately Prosperous Society in All Respects and Strive for the Great Success of Socialism with Chinese Characteristics for a New Era," Report to the 19th National Congress of the Communist Party of China, October 18, 2017, available at http://www.xinhuanet.com/english/download/Xi_Jinping's_report_at_19th_CPC_National_Congress.pdf.

[20] For the shared objectives of Chinese reformers and political leaders since the late Qing Dynasty, see Orville Schell and John Delury, *Wealth and Power: China's Long March to the Twenty-First Century* (New York: Random House, 2013). For one CCP example invoking this history, see "Study, Disseminate, and Implement the Guiding Principles of the 18th CPC National Congress," in *The Governance of China* (Beijing: Foreign Languages Press, 2014), 12.

[21] Xi Jinping (speech at the National Committee on U.S.-China Relations and U.S.-China Business Council luncheon, Washington, D.C., February 15, 2012).

[22] Xi, "Secure a Decisive Victory."

[23] Samantha Hoffman and Peter Mattis, "Managing the Power Within: China's State Security Commission," War on the Rocks, July 18, 2016.

The CCP's view of security is marked by the absence of threat and the need to prevent social and cultural undermining of the party's legitimacy and ability to govern. This forces a preemptive approach to defeating threats to the party. An aggressive approach to identifying and neutralizing threats is not a product of the Xi era but has a long history within the CCP dating back at least to the 1950s.[24] The clearest official expression of this approach to security can be found in the National Security Law passed in 2015:

> National security refers to the relative absence of international or domestic threats to the state's power to govern, sovereignty, unity and territorial integrity, the welfare of the people, sustainable economic and social development, and other major national interests, and the ability to ensure a continued state of security. National security efforts shall adhere to a comprehensive understanding of national security, make the security of the people their goal, political security their basis and economic security their foundation; make military, cultural and social security their safeguard.[25]

Consequently, it seems fair to describe what the CCP is doing as working to eliminate threats by winning acceptance of its political and social system. Perhaps this goal can be achieved by undermining its potential adversaries, most notably the United States, but diminishing the power of states does not necessarily diminish the power of ideas.

## *Operational Concepts*

At the simplest level, the distinction between active measures and united front work is that the former aims at eliminating threats while the latter aims at building coalitions. Although the two concepts share a similar heritage in the Russian security state and international Communist movement, they lead to two very different views of the world and modes of operation.

The Russian concept of active measures (*aktivniye meropriyatiya*) describes a broad set of overt and covert actions intended to create political effects in target countries for the benefit of Moscow. The desired effects cover a range of outcomes, including sowing social contention and distrust, undermining confidence in political leaders or institutions, and pushing the target toward desirable actions. The tools include the full range of black, gray, and white propaganda; disinformation; provocation; intelligence and agents of influence; and "direct action" or "wet affairs," which describe

---

[24] Samantha Hoffman, "Programming China: The Communist Party's Autonomic Approach to Managing State Security" (Ph.D. diss., University of Nottingham, 2017), 31–46.

[25] "Zhonghua Renmin Gongheguo Guojia Anquan Fa" [National Security Law of the People's Republic of China], National People's Congress, July 1, 2015, http://www.npc.gov.cn/npc/xinwen/2015-07/07/content_1941161.htm.

assassination, kidnapping, or other violent intimidation.[26] The Soviet leaders incorporated many of these tools into their operational methods, because of their direct experience at the hands of the Tsarist secret police, the Okhrana, as well as their education from the Okhrana files they inherited from the fallen regime.[27]

One of the fundamental concepts of Russian information operations, "reflexive control," originated in the Soviet era as Moscow ramped up active measures worldwide. The concept was born from research into computer science, psychology, decision-making, and cybernetics in the 1950s, and it amounted to what Soviet civilian and military intelligence believed was a mathematically and scientifically supported process for influencing foreign government decisions. Reflexive control provided a four-part map—including the adversary's perception, goals, decision-making process, and the act of decisions—for influencing foreign governments, but also required a great deal of information that the intelligence services would need to collect.[28] Ultimately, active measures operating within the concept of reflexive control are intended to condition a target to accepting Kremlin-provided stimuli and acting in the desired way.

To paraphrase Mao Zedong, united front work is intended to mobilize one's friends to strike at one's enemies. In terms of Leninist theory, it mediates between the professional revolutionaries that form the party core and the social groups beyond the party that must be cultivated and directed.[29] This work divides the world beyond the CCP into three distinct groups: friends, neutrals, and adversaries. Neutrals need to be converted to the cause. Adversaries must be neutralized by converting them to the cause or to neutrality, or they must be isolated and defeated to prevent their influence. In practice, this means building relationships to insert the party or its priorities directly into the consideration of others.

Mao described united front tactics as one of three "magic weapons" that won the Chinese Revolution for the CCP, alongside armed struggle and party-building. He described the relationship between these magic weapons

---

[26] Richard Schultz and Roy Godson, *Dezinformatsia: Active Measures in Soviet Strategy* (Washington, D.C.: Pergamon-Brassey's, 1984), 1–3; and Kevin N. McCauley, *Russian Influence Operations against the West: From the Cold War to Putin* (Charleston: CreateSpace Independent Publishing, 2016), 4–7.

[27] Christopher Andrew and Oleg Gordievsky, *KGB: The Inside Story of Its Foreign Operations from Lenin to Gorbachev* (New York: Harper Perennial, 1991), chap. 1.

[28] McCauley, *Russian Influence Operations against the West*, 4, 10–21; and Clifford Reid, "Reflexive Control in Soviet Military Planning," in *Soviet Strategic Deception*, eds. Brian S. Dailey and Patrick J. Parker (Lexington, MA: Lexington Books, 1987), chap. 14.

[29] Vladimir Ilyich Lenin, "What Is To Be Done?" in *Lenin's Collected Works* (Moscow: Foreign Languages Publishing House, 1961), 347–530, https://www.marxists.org/archive/lenin/works/1901/witbd.

in the following way: "[T]he united front and armed struggle are the two basic weapons for defeating the enemy. The united front is a united front for carrying on armed struggle. And the Party is the heroic warrior wielding the two weapons, the united front and the armed struggle, to storm and shatter the enemy's positions."[30] The CCP uses united front work to draw people into the nation-building project that is socialism with Chinese characteristics. As Xi Jinping noted in his work report to the 19th Party Congress, "The united front is an important way to ensure the success of the Party's cause, and we must maintain commitment to it long term….We will encourage intellectuals who are not Party members and people belonging to new social groups to play the important roles they have in building socialism with Chinese characteristics."[31]

## Organizing for Influence

Both China and Russia possess formal bureaucratic units that conduct political influence operations abroad, but they are supplemented by elite networks that rally the ostensibly private resources of the nation to the cause. Three distinctions appear to mark how the two countries' operations differ from one another organizationally. First, the CCP governs China and retains the trappings of a Communist country, including a Leninist party structure with a clear hierarchy. Russia's authoritarianism revolves around the person of President Putin. Regardless of how well Russian methods work, the system is personalized rather than being embedded at every level like that of the CCP. Second, the role of the intelligence services is fundamentally different in each country. The Chinese intelligence services play a supporting role to the party's united front bureaucracy that contrasts with the essential role played by the Russian intelligence services. Third, the CCP integration of elite networks is more formalized from the central level down to the local level. Post–Cold War Russia simply lacks the ideological and institutional coherence of its Chinese counterpart.

### Russia's Organization for Political Influence

Russia's capacity for generating political influence abroad revolves around Putin and the circle around him that controls much of Russia's

---

[30] Mao Zedong, "Introducing The Communist," October 4, 1939, https://www.marxists.org/reference/archive/mao/selected-works/volume-2/mswv2_20.htm.

[31] Xi, "Secure a Decisive Victory."

wealth and industry. This is "an interlocking network of associations and clan-based politics centered on Putin," in the words of Karen Dawisha, "strengthening Putin's hold on power, silencing critics, and maximizing…economic benefits."[32] These arrangements comingle public and private interests, and each new participant benefits from "the power to award and reward—primarily through monetary means, but also through monopolistic power and influence."[33] One of the oligarchs close to the Kremlin, Oleg Deripaska, said, "I don't separate myself from the state. I have no other interests."[34] Even a Russian apologist prepared to explain away Moscow's actions writes: "Even the wealthiest business owner serves at the president's pleasure. It's not really a game but an abusive relationship with elements of codependency."[35]

These loyal oligarchs are the leading edge of Russian political influence operations because of their access and financial resources. Their efforts to invest outside Russia sometimes mask the political intentions of the Kremlin, and their resources help rope foreign political elites into business relationships that can be exploited.[36]

Russia's intelligence services, especially the Foreign Intelligence Service (Sluzhba Vneshney Razvedki, or SVR) and the Main Intelligence Directorate of the Russian General Staff (Glavnoye Razvedyvatel'noye Upravleniye, or GRU), are long-standing actors in the country's disinformation efforts. The SVR originated in the KGB's First Chief Directorate, which ran the agency's foreign intelligence operations and had a close connection with Service A, the KGB's disinformation organization.[37] This organization is first and foremost an intelligence service—and may be among the least influential of Russian intelligence organs—but it plays a critical operational role abroad in supporting active measures. First, it collects large amounts of the information necessary to support reflexive control. Second, it has both

---

[32] Conley et al., *The Kremlin Playbook*, xii.

[33] Ibid., xii–xiii.

[34] "Oleg Deripaska, Russian Oligarch under Siege for Putin Ties," *Financial Times*, May 4, 2018, https://www.ft.com/content/08f230b0-4dfb-11e8-8a8e-22951a2d8493.

[35] Leonid Bershidsky, "What 'Oligarchs Close to Putin' Really Means," Bloomberg, May 9, 2018, https://www.bloomberg.com/view/articles/2018-05-09/russian-oligarchs-close-to-putin-aren-t-what-they-seem.

[36] Veronika Víchová and Jakub Janda, eds., *The Prague Manual: How to Tailor National Strategy Using Lessons Learned from Countering Kremlin's Hostile Subversive Operations in Central and Eastern Europe* (Prague: European Values, 2018), http://www.europeanvalues.net/wp-content/uploads/2018/04/Prague-Manual.pdf; and Conley et al., *The Kremlin Playbook*.

[37] McCauley, *Russian Influence Campaigns against the West*.

officers based under traditional diplomatic and journalist covers as well as so-called illegals who operate without any official status.

After the Cold War ended and the KGB was carved apart, Moscow allowed much of its network of front organizations to wither from a lack of support.[38] Most of the KGB survived in the Federal Security Service (Federal'naya Sluzhba Bezopasnosti, or FSB). Technically responsible for internal security and counterintelligence, the agency saw Putin steadily expand its purview. In 2003, he folded the Russian signals and electronic intelligence service, the Federal Agency of Government Communications and Information (Federalnoye Agentsvo Pravitelstvennoi Svyazi i Informatsii, or FAPSI), into the FSB, giving it critically important capabilities abroad. FAPSI also had originally been a part of the KGB.[39] The FSB appears to be less involved in the softer side of active measures, but the service has been implicated in assassinations, such as that of Alexander Litvinenko in London in 2006, and kidnappings, such as that of Estonian intelligence officer Eston Kohver in 2014.[40]

The GRU traditionally was a human intelligence agency, using both overt and clandestine means to collect information and recruit sources. The most obvious of its officers posted overseas have long been Russian defense attachés. The agency, however, has become a significant player in cyberspace and is believed to have been behind a number of intrusions into political organizations such as the Democratic National Committee and the Bundestag. The GRU also may have taken the lead in interfering in the U.S. presidential election in 2016.[41] One cybersecurity researcher believes the GRU may employ several thousand officers to conduct operations in cyberspace.[42] The military agency, unlike its civilian counterparts, had not benefited from Putin's infusion of resources into intelligence operations until it stage-managed the takeover of Crimea in 2014 and provided a number

---

[38] McCauley, *Russian Influence Campaigns against the West.*

[39] Mark Galeotti, "The Spies Who Love Putin," *Atlantic*, January 17, 2017, https://www.theatlantic.com/international/archive/2017/01/fsb-kgb-putin/513272/.

[40] Shaun Walker, "Russia Jails Estonian Intelligence Officer Tallinn Says Was Abducted over Border," *Guardian*, August 19, 2015, https://www.theguardian.com/world/2015/aug/19/russia-jails-estonian-police-officer-allegedly-abducted-border-eston-kohver.

[41] Michael Weiss, "The GRU: Putin's No-Longer-So-Secret Weapon," Daily Beast, December 31, 2016, https://www.thedailybeast.com/the-gru-putins-no-longer-so-secret-weapon; Mark Galeotti, "Putin's Secret Weapon," *Foreign Policy*, July 7, 2014, https://foreignpolicy.com/2014/07/07/putins-secret-weapon; and Shaun Walker, "U.S. Expulsions Put Spotlight on Russia's GRU Intelligence Agency," *Guardian*, December 30, 2016, https://www.theguardian.com/world/2016/dec/30/us-expulsions-put-spotlight-on-russias-gru-intelligence-agency.

[42] Patrick Beuth et al., "Cyberattack on the Bundestag: Merkel and the Fancy Bear," *Die Zeit*, May 12, 2017, https://www.zeit.de/digital/2017-05/cyberattack-bundestag-angela-merkel-fancy-bear-hacker-russia.

of tactical intelligence successes that enabled the Russian military to defeat Ukrainian forces quite rapidly.

Created no later than 2013, the Internet Research Agency (IRA) in St. Petersburg is the newest player in Russian political influence operations. The IRA originally became known as a Russian "troll factory" and perpetuated a number of disinformation scams, such as reports about a chemical spill in Louisiana. In 2015 the *New York Times* profiled the IRA's tools—fake accounts and websites, the flooding of social media to create hype, manufactured media, and socially provocative fake news—previewing some of the tactics that would be seen in U.S. and European elections.[43] Russians working for the IRA, according to Clint Watts, "infiltrate audiences through false personas that look like and talk like the target audience, thus lowering normal cultural objections to foreign influence."[44] The IRA's owner, Yevgeny Prigozhin, is emblematic of the symbiotic relationship between Russian economic elites and the Kremlin. He began his career as a hot dog vendor and restaurant owner, and his first restaurant became a favorite of Putin's. This opened opportunities for government contracts, and Prigozhin made more than $8 billion in revenue from state catering contracts. He and the IRA technically operate outside the state apparatus, but they are still very much a part of the broad panoply of Russian active measures.[45]

## *Influence-Building Beyond United Front Work*

United front work is a useful concept for framing how the CCP interferes in foreign societies, but understanding how the party organizes and operates for influence requires going beyond united front work to include, among other operations, propaganda, liaison work, people-to-people diplomacy, and intelligence.[46] The CCP organization functions at three levels, including the party leadership, the core party bureaucracies, and the supporting ministries. This hierarchy shows that political influence operations are intertwined with the day-to-day activities of the party, and analysts would

---

[43] Adrian Chen, "The Agency," *New York Times*, June 7, 2015, https://www.nytimes.com/2015/06/07/magazine/the-agency.html.

[44] Clint Watts, "Russia's Active Measures Architecture: Task and Purpose," German Marshall Fund, Alliance for Securing Democracy, May 22, 2018, https://securingdemocracy.gmfus.org/russias-active-measures-architecture-task-and-purpose.

[45] "How to Be a Dadaist Troll: Inside the Internet Research Agency's Lie Machine," *Economist*, February 22, 2018, https://www.economist.com/briefing/2018/02/22/inside-the-internet-research-agencys-lie-machine.

[46] This section draws heavily from Peter Mattis, "An American Lens on China's Interference and Influence-Building Abroad," *Asan Forum*, April 30, 2017, http://www.theasanforum.org/an-american-lens-on-chinas-interference-and-influence-building-abroad.

be remiss to suggest that Beijing's interference is perpetuated by a rogue or overzealous cadre.

At the leadership level, four individuals in the Politburo control the essential party organs and play key roles in the party's policy implementation. The most senior official is the chairman of the Chinese People's Political Consultative Conference (CPPCC), who ranks fourth among the Politburo Standing Committee. This position has largely been dismissed by foreign analysts, but the past holders of the chairmanship underline the importance of this institution. Mao Zedong, Deng Xiaoping, Zhou Enlai, Li Ruihuan, Yu Zhengsheng, and now former Guangdong Party secretary Wang Yang all have held the position. While the early holders of the chairmanship need no introduction, the latter are known primarily for their competence as party bureaucrats as well as their connections with significant CCP elite groupings.

The directors of the party's United Front Work Department (UFWD) and Propaganda Department serve on both the Politburo and the Secretariat of the 19th Central Committee of the Communist Party of China. Because the Politburo does not meet regularly—its far-flung membership includes both central party bureaucrats and provincial party secretaries—the secretariat is empowered to make day-to-day decisions related to settled policy. This group is also responsible for moving paperwork among the central leaders and coordinating the party's actions. Secretariat membership is not related to relationships that the current UFWD and propaganda chiefs—respectively, You Quan and Huang Kunming—have but rather reflects the structure of post–Deng Xiaoping politics. These two positions simply have been represented on the Politburo and Secretariat for nearly four decades.

The fourth senior official with direct responsibility for united front and other influence-building work is a vice premier, seemingly without a portfolio. The last two holders of this position were both former UFWD directors, including current vice premier Sun Chunlan. This official presumably serves as the day-to-day operational chief, functioning as a bridge between the executive departments on the second level and the supporting agencies, which largely fall under the State Council, on the third level. This identification remains somewhat suppositional, but examinations of the protocol at united front events and the officials present strongly suggest that the vice premier is a principal player who outranks the UFWD director.[47]

On the second level, four CCP organizations at the central level oversee, coordinate, and execute the party's policies: the UFWD, Propaganda Department, CPPCC, and International Department. The UFWD mediates between the CCP and nonparty social groups. The UFWD operates at all levels of the party system from the center to the grassroots. The department plays a leading role in the following areas: Hong Kong, Macao, and Taiwan affairs; ethnic and religious affairs; domestic and external propaganda; entrepreneurs and nonparty personages; nonparty intellectuals; and people-to-people exchanges. The UFWD, alongside the All-China Federation of Industry and Commerce, takes the lead in establishing party committees in Chinese and now foreign businesses.[48] In addition to the political signs that Xi Jinping elevated the importance of united front work, the UWFD recently began a process of assimilating the Overseas Chinese Affairs Office (OCAO). The OCAO had served as a State Council adjunct for united front work, but it played a role somewhere between the supporting ministries below and the executive departments on this level.[49]

The Propaganda Department has been a core part of the CCP since 1924. The official description of its duties includes conducting the party's theoretical research; guiding public opinion; guiding and coordinating the work of the central news agencies, including Xinhua and the *People's Daily*; guiding the propaganda and cultural systems; and administering the Cyberspace Administration of China and the State Administration of Press, Publication, Radio, Film, and Television. The Propaganda Department cannot be regarded as an entirely internal organization that broadcasts outward to the extent that it is involved in influence-building abroad. For example, China Radio International developed in the 2000s a covert international network of

---

[47] For example, see the following articles and their accompanying pictures, "Yu Zhengsheng, Liu Yandong, Sun Chunlan, Du Qinglin, Xiangba Pingcuo deng zuo tong ji dida Lasa" [Yu Zhengsheng, Liu Yandong, Sun Chunlan, Du Qinglin, and Xiangba Pingcuo Arrived Together by Plane in Lhasa Yesterday], *Pengpai*, September 7, 2015, https://www.thepaper.cn/newsDetail_forward_1372371_1; and "Guanche luoshi Zhongyang guanyu zongjiao gongzuo zhongda juece bushu jingyan jiaoliuhui zai Jing zhaokai; Yu Zhengsheng chuxi bing jianghua" [Conference on the Implementation of the Central Committee's Exchange of Experience on Major Decision-making and Deployment of Religious Work Opens in Beijing; Yu Zhengsheng Attended and Spoke], *People's Daily*, September 12, 2017, http://cpc.people.com.cn/n1/2017/0912/c64094-29528941.html.

[48] "Zhongguo Gongchandang Tongyizhanxian gongzuo tiaoli (shixing)" [CCP United Front Work Trial Regulations], *People's Daily*, September 23, 2015, http://cpc.people.com.cn/n/2015/0923/c64107-27622040.html.

[49] Teddy Ng and Mimi Lau, "Fears about Chinese Influence Grow as More Powers Given to Shadowy Agency," *South China Morning Post*, March 21, 2018, https://www.scmp.com/news/china/diplomacy-defence/article/2138279/bigger-overseas-liaison-agency-fuels-fears-about.

radio stations to hide the CCP's direct role in broadcasting Chinese-language propaganda inside target countries. The Propaganda Department presumably also plays a role in the cooptation, intimidation, and purchase of Chinese-language print media outside China.[50]

The CPPCC ostensibly is a CCP advisory body, and it has largely been dismissed by external observers as an honorary or rubber-stamp advisory conference. Given the body's past and present leadership, this is not quite fair even if it is not an operational agency like the others on this second level. The CPPCC, according to its website, is "an organization in the patriotic united front of the Chinese people, an important organ for multiparty cooperation and political consultation." This description clearly identifies the CPPCC with the party's influence-building or united front system and highlights its purpose as a place where Chinese elites come together. Only 40% of the more than 2,200 members at the central level of the CPPCC belong to the CCP, and at lower levels of the consultative conference that percentage can be much smaller. Among the approximately 617,000 conference members at all levels are party elders, intelligence officers, diplomats, propagandists, military officers and political commissars, united front workers, intellectuals, and businesspeople.[51] The CPPCC offers a systematic approach for integrating Chinese elite at all levels into the political work of the party as recruitment is handled by the local standing committees.[52]

The International Department, founded in 1951, is the party's diplomatic arm, handling relationships with more than six hundred political parties and organizations as well as individual elites, who are primarily political.[53] The department previously handled the CCP's relationships between fraternal Communist parties and cultivated splinter factions of Moscow-dominated Communist parties after the Sino-Soviet split. The activist bent of the International Department disappeared as it began re-establishing itself in

---

[50] Koh Gui Qing and John Shiffman, "Beijing's Covert Radio Network Airs China-Friendly News across Washington, and the World," Reuters, November 2, 2015, https://www.reuters.com/investigates/special-report/china-radio; and Kelsey Munro and Philip Wen, "Chinese Language Newspapers in Australia: Beijing Controls Messaging, Propaganda in Press," *Sydney Morning Herald*, July 8, 2016, https://www.smh.com.au/national/chinese-language-newspapers-in-australia-beijing-controls-messaging-propaganda-in-press-20160610-gpg0s3.html.

[51] "Composition of the CPPCC," CPPCC, July 3, 2012, http://www.cppcc.gov.cn/zxww/2012/07/03/ARTI1341301498421103.shtml.

[52] This paragraph is drawn from Peter Mattis, "The Center of Chinese Influence: The Chinese People's Political Consultative Conference," in *The Corrosion of Democracy under China's Global Influence*, ed. J. Michael Cole and Hsu Szu-chien (forthcoming).

[53] "Wobu jianjie" [About Our Bureau], International Department, http://www.idcpc.org.cn/gywb/wbjj.

1970–71 following the tumultuous early years of the Cultural Revolution. Interestingly, the department itself may have been carved out of the UFWD.[54]

On the third level playing a supporting role are the State Council ministries and party-state bureaucracies. These organizations contribute to the CCP's political influence operations on a seemingly ad hoc basis. Although their focus is not on united front or propaganda work, they still have capabilities and responsibilities that can be used in support of operations normally outside their purview. Many of these agencies share cover or front organizations when they are involved in influence operations—a key indicator of organizations used for CCP influence-building is the presence of party and state officials from multiple organizations, especially from the preceding level, on an organization's board—and such platforms are sometimes lent to other agencies when appropriate. The organizations involved include, but are not limited to, the following:

- Ministry of State Security
- Ministry of Foreign Affairs
- Ministry of Culture
- Ministry of Education
- State Administration of Foreign Expert Affairs
- Ministry of Civil Affairs
- Xinhua News Agency

For instance, the Ministry of Education administers Hanban, which operates the Confucius Institute program active on more than five hundred university campuses worldwide.[55] Although many fear that the Confucius Institutes provide a conduit for propaganda or espionage—fueled in part by the words of China's own leaders—they are better understood as part of the united front system.[56] By bolstering the career of individual academics and administrators as well as testing the carefulness of university leadership,

---

[54] This latter responsibility faded in the 1960s and ended with the collapse of party bureaucracy in the Cultural Revolution. See Robert Suettinger, "The International Liaison Department of the Chinese Communist Party," Central Intelligence Agency, POLO Paper, no. 33, December 1971, https://www.cia.gov/library/readingroom/docs/polo-33.pdf.

[55] "Over 500 Confucius Institutes Founded in 142 Countries, Regions," Xinhua, October 7, 2017, http://www.chinadaily.com.cn/china/2017-10/07/content_32950016.htm.

[56] Alan H. Yang and Michael Hsiao, "Confucius Institutes and the Question of China's Soft Power Diplomacy," Jamestown Foundation, China Brief, July 6, 2012, https://jamestown.org/program/confucius-institutes-and-the-question-of-chinas-soft-power-diplomacy; and Peter Mattis, "Reexamining the Confucius Institutes," Diplomat, August 2, 2012, https://thediplomat.com/2012/08/reexamining-the-confucian-institutes.

Confucius Institutes serve as a gateway for other CCP efforts and help place sympathetic voices in university councils. The party also can exploit the university to promote cultural programs and propaganda by using the university's name to gain credibility in the local community.[57] None of these activities detract from Hanban and the role of Confucius Institutes in promoting Chinese-language education and standards for the Ministry of Education. However, they can and do open a pathway for the CCP's political influence operations to follow.

The People's Liberation Army (PLA) plays a special role that spans each of the three levels, mirroring the CCP's overall structure. This role is probably a legacy of the Chinese Revolution and the PLA's underground or guerrilla role far from CCP base areas. Every function of the party bureaucracy needed to be duplicated within the PLA because the party organs responsible for those functions would not be present. Mao expressed the need for the PLA to play a political role in his famous statement "On Correcting Mistaken Ideas within the Party" delivered at the Gutian Conference of 1929. Critiquing the view that the PLA existed primarily to fight on the battlefield, he wrote that "The Red Army fights not merely for the sake of fighting but in order to conduct propaganda among the masses, organize them, arm them, and help them to establish revolutionary political power."[58]

The PLA's first or leadership level includes the Central Military Commission, including the body's chairman Xi Jinping and the head of the Political Work Department (formerly the General Political Department). On the second level, the primary agency responsible for political warfare and influence-building is the Political Work Department's Liaison Bureau. On the third or supporting level, the PLA also sometimes draws on or coordinates with the State Council ministries or organizations associated with CPPCC members.[59]

---

[57] John Fitzgerald, "Unis Could Bide Their Time and Escape the Long Arm of Beijing," *Australian*, March 2, 2018, https://www.theaustralian.com.au/news/inquirer/unis-could-bide-their-time-and-escape-the-long-arm-of-beijing/news-story/202b5b9462af59a9f38f57aaee13b7b8.

[58] Mao Zedong, "On Correcting Mistaken Ideas within the Party," December 1929, https://www.marxists.org/reference/archive/mao/selected-works/volume-1/mswv1_5.htm.

[59] Bethany Allen-Ebrahimian, "This Beijing-Linked Billionaire Is Funding Policy Research at Washington's Most Influential Institutions," *Foreign Policy*, November 28, 2017, https://foreignpolicy.com/2017/11/28/this-beijing-linked-billionaire-is-funding-policy-research-at-washingtons-most-influential-institutions-china-dc.

## Comparing and Contrasting Tactics

This section offers some thumbnail sketches of distinctions that can be drawn at the tactical level of CCP- and Kremlin-run political influence operations. In many cases, the distinctions can be understood primarily as those between direct and indirect uses of violence. Another distinguishing feature is how comparable state institutions in the two countries utilize propaganda, and to what end. Third, Beijing and Moscow differ in how they harness their respective diaspora communities to generate influence in target countries. Finally, the two regimes diverge in the nature of their cyberactivities.

### *Use of Violence: Direct vs. Indirect*

The Russian state under Putin employs violence directly in ways that are difficult to hide from international scrutiny. From the murder of former FSB officer Alexander Litvinenko with Polonium 210 in 2006 to the attempted murder of former military officer Sergei Skripal with a nerve agent in 2018, Putin's Kremlin barely has camouflaged the violence it has used against regime opponents and defectors.[60] Chinese coercion and violence to shape the political environment mostly remain in the category of suspicious but unproven. Although violence is used against regime opponents and seemingly political figures opposing central leaders, the CCP does not hold press conferences like the Kremlin to taunt and dismiss those who blame it for attacks.

Russian political violence at home and abroad appears to have had two purposes. The first is to silence regime critics and forestall investigations into corruption that might implicate Putin's circle "by demonstrating the long and extralegal reach of the Kremlin."[61] Perhaps the most notable murders have been those of the individuals who linked Putin and the Russian security services to the Moscow apartment bombings in 1999 that helped fuel Putin's succession of President Boris Yeltsin. This may include, among others, Litvinenko, journalist Yuri Shchekochikhin, and opposition politician Sergei Yushenkov.[62] Around the fringes of the investigation into Russian meddling in the U.S. presidential campaign in 2016, there is some reason to doubt

---

[60] "Alexander Litvinenko: Profile of Murdered Russian Spy," BBC, January 21, 2016, https://www.bbc.co.uk/news/uk-19647226; and Joel Gunter, "Sergei Skripal and the 14 Deaths under Scrutiny," BBC, March 7, 2018, https://www.bbc.co.uk/news/world-europe-43299598.

[61] McCauley, *Russian Influence Campaigns against the West*, 9.

[62] David Filipov, "Here Are 10 Critics of Vladimir Putin Who Died Violently or in Suspicious Ways," *Washington Post*, March 3, 2017, https://www.washingtonpost.com/news/worldviews/wp/2017/03/23/here-are-ten-critics-of-vladimir-putin-who-died-violently-or-in-suspicious-ways.

the mysterious deaths by suicide, accident, or health problems of Russian officials or possibly even their intermediaries associated with the efforts to influence U.S. elections.[63]

The second is to help consolidate Kremlin control over key resources or media platforms. For example, Olga Kotovskaya, a television journalist in Kaliningrad, fell to her death—initially reported as a suicide and barely covered in Russian media—after winning control back of her station. She had lost control because Kaliningrad officials seized her station, which had been criticizing local officials, and presented a document with Kotovskaya's forged signature to make the seizure legal.[64]

The CCP's record of violence to shape behavior outside China is much more opaque. Beijing thus far has escaped diplomatic consequences for its actions in part because the linkage between the murders, violence, or coercion can be more difficult to trace. One of the signature cases probably is the suicide of convicted CIA spy Larry Wu-Tai Chin in an Alexandria jail before his sentencing in federal court. Family members and reporters who spoke with Chin following his conviction believed the suicide seemed out of character.[65] However, Chin's last visitor was a Ministry of State Security officer under journalist cover.[66] His death unfroze his bank accounts so that his wife would be supported, and the ministry avoided a former agent telling U.S. counterintelligence about their handling of him. The only assassination for which the CCP has claimed credit was that of the Chinese spy for the CIA, Yu Qiangsheng, who reportedly betrayed Chin to U.S. authorities.

---

[63] Amy Knight, "Was This Russian General Murdered over the Steele Dossier?" *Daily Beast*, January 23, 2018, https://www.thedailybeast.com/was-this-russian-general-murdered-over-the-steele-dossier; and Jonathan Chait, "Will Trump Be Meeting with His Counterpart—Or His Handler?" *New York Magazine*, July 8, 2018, http://nymag.com/daily/intelligencer/2018/07/trump-putin-russia-collusion.html.

[64] Scott Simon, "Why Do Russian Journalists Keep Falling?" NPR, April 21, 2018, https://www.npr.org/2018/04/21/604497554/why-do-russian-journalists-keep-falling; and Luke Harding, "Colleagues Urge Investigation into Russian Journalist's Death," *Guardian*, December 1, 2009, https://www.theguardian.com/world/2009/dec/01/olga-kotovskaya-journalist-death-kaliningrad.

[65] Caryle Murphy, "Chinese Spy Chin Apparently Kills Self," *Washington Post*, February 22, 1986, https://www.washingtonpost.com/archive/politics/1986/02/22/chinese-spy-chin-apparently-kills-self/23603e62-148f-44d7-bf25-db2daae62233; and Caryle Murphy, "To Family, Chin's Conviction 'a Horrible Error,'" *Washington Post*, February 27, 1986, https://www.washingtonpost.com/archive/local/1986/02/27/to-family-chins-conviction-a-horrible-error/67da5984-280a-4c30-9c99-30608dfd3061.

[66] Wang Taotang, "Former FBI Head Refutes Claim That Chinese Spy Was Assassinated," *Epoch Times*, March 3, 2016, https://www.theepochtimes.com/former-fbi-head-refutes-claim-that-chinese-spy-was-assassinated_1982209.html.

This widely repeated claim, however, was bogus—despite its repetition as late as 2016—and Yu died peacefully of old age.[67]

Applying coercion to encourage suicide or to return to China to face politically motivated charges seems to mark a number of the country's attempts to deal with opponents, irrespective of the truth of any specific case. This indirect approach helps fire conspiratorial imaginations, even when a case seems reasonably accidental like that of HNA Group chairman Wang Jian's fatal fall in July 2018. Nor are such developments clarified when dozens of deaths inside China of purged officials or political opponents are attributed to suicide or health ailments where none previously existed in the middle of factional infighting.[68]

Beijing also has kidnapped or coerced some Chinese living abroad to return home from Australia, the United States, and possibly other countries.[69] Conversely, family members inside China have been used to control or threaten those outside, most notably in the case of Uighurs and human rights activists.[70] The CCP does organize physical violence against regime opponents abroad, but this tool appears to be used sporadically. Examples of violence used or organized by CCP security officials include that during the Olympic torch relay in 2008, Falun Gong community events in New York State, and protests at Mar-a-Lago during the Trump-Xi summit in April 2017.[71] Threats and intimidation are not confined to Chinese or

---

[67] Jamil Anderlini and Tom Mitchell, "Top Chinese Defectors Passes Secrets to U.S.," *Financial Times*, February 4, 2016, https://www.ft.com/content/4e900936-cb20-11e5-a8ef-ea66e967dd44; Taotang, "Former FBI Head Refutes Claim That Chinese Spy Was Assassinated"; and Kerry Brown, *The New Emperors: Power and Princelings in China* (London: I.B. Tauris, 2014), 161.

[68] Charlotte Gao, "HNA Group Chairman's Sudden Death Stokes Conspiracy Theories," *Diplomat*, July 5, 2018, https://thediplomat.com/2018/07/hna-group-chairmans-sudden-death-stokes-conspiracy-theories; Didi Kirsten Tatlow, "Spate of Suicides by Chinese Officials Tied to Drive Against Graft," *New York Times*, September 11, 2014, https://www.nytimes.com/2014/09/12/world/asia/suicide-cases-across-china-tied-to-drive-against-graft.html; "Chinese General Commits Suicide as Xi's Corruption Crackdown Grinds On," Bloomberg, November 28, 2017, https://www.bloomberg.com/news/articles/2017-11-28/senior-chinese-military-officer-commits-suicide-xinhua-reports; and Jun Mai "Princelings Put Their Political Views Aside to Remember Chen Xiaolu," *South China Morning Post*, March 31, 2018, https://www.scmp.com/news/china/policies-politics/article/2139770/princelings-put-their-political-views-aside-remember.

[69] Zach Dorfman, "The Disappeared," *Foreign Policy*, March 29, 2018, https://foreignpolicy.com/2018/03/29/the-disappeared-china-renditions-kidnapping.

[70] For example, Austin Ramzy, "After U.S.-Based Reporters Exposed Abuses, China Seized Their Relatives," *New York Times*, March 1, 2018, https://www.nytimes.com/2018/03/01/world/asia/china-xinjiang-rfa.html; Bethany Allen-Ebrahimian, "Chinese Police Are Demanding Personal Information From Uighurs in France," *Foreign Policy*, March 2, 2018, https://foreignpolicy.com/2018/03/02/chinese-police-are-secretly-demanding-personal-information-from-french-citizens-uighurs-xinjiang; and Josh Elliot, "'I'm Really Scared': Miss World Canada Says Father Threatened in China," CTV News, May 25, 2015, https://www.ctvnews.ca/canada/i-m-really-scared-miss-world-canada-says-father-threatened-in-china-1.2389775.

[71] Author's interviews in Washington, D.C., January 2018.

official minorities. New Zealand scholar Anne-Marie Brady's home and office were broken into, and she received at least one threatening letter.[72]

## Messaging: Creating Doubt vs. Creating a Positive Narrative

The Russian and Chinese approaches to propaganda have diverged substantially from their days when shared Marxist-Leninist ideology led to similar conclusions and forms of analysis. Moscow's propaganda narratives have taken on a conspiratorial feel, sometimes with only a tenuous relationship to the truth. Former Anglo-Russian producer and consultant Peter Pomerantsev observed that Russian media plays to the notion that if "nothing is true, then anything is possible." He went on to explain "insisting on the lie, the Kremlin intimidates others by showing that it is in control of defining 'reality'…We're rendered stunned, spun, and flummoxed by the Kremlin's weaponization of absurdity and unreality."[73] The attempted murder of Sergei and Yulia Skripal in 2018 provides a telling example of the Russian approach to propaganda. RT, Sputnik, Russia 1, and other media channels put out more than twenty different narratives about what might have happened to the Skripals in the United Kingdom. Here are just a few of the narrative streams:

- Novichok, the nerve agent used in the attack, does not exist, or at least is not military grade or necessarily manufactured in Russia.[74]

- Moscow has no reason to kill Sergei Skripal because he no longer has any relevant knowledge and could not pose a threat.[75]

- Anyone could have manufactured Novichok by following the description and guidance published in a book by a Russian defector in 2008. Russia is not the only possibility.[76]

---

[72] "SIS Needs to Tell Us Who Was behind Brady Break-Ins," *New Zealand Herald*, February 21, 2018, https://www.nzherald.co.nz/nz/news/article.cfm?c_id=1&objectid=11998319.

[73] Peter Pomerantsev, "Russia and the Menace of Unreality," *Atlantic*, September 9, 2014, https://www.theatlantic.com/international/archive/2014/09/russia-putin-revolutionizing-information-warfare/379880.

[74] John Laughland, "Blaming Russia for Skripal Attack Is Similar to 'Jews Poisoning Our Wells' in Middle Ages," RT, March 15, 2018, https://www.rt.com/op-ed/421434-skripal-poisoning-russia-uk/.

[75] "Russian Intelligence Veteran Explains What's Wrong with Skripal Case in UK," Sputnik, March 15, 2018, https://sputniknews.com/analysis/201803151062569505-skripal-uk-veteran.

[76] "UK Gov't Skripal Story Is 'Speculative, Ideological'—Investigative Journalist," Sputnik, March 15, 2018, https://sputniknews.com/analysis/201803151062574161-uk-skripal-story-investigation-journalist.

- The Porton Down facility, whose staff identified the presence of Novichok, either experimented on the Skripals intentionally or leaked the nerve agent accidentally.[77]
- The United States, UK, Israel, Ukraine, Sweden, Czech Republic, and Slovakia all are possible sources of the Novichok used in the attack.[78]

The Chinese approach to propaganda and censorship, by contrast, floods traditional and social media channels with messages emphasizing positive aspects of CCP rule. Although such information may not be entirely believable, China's media environment is defined by the relative absence of information that discredits the party. The party also makes it difficult to find alternative information, creating friction that enervates the user. The Great Firewall is the most well-known tool because it draws a clear line between what is inside and outside China. The censoring of specific names and topics, especially when news blows up, is not perfect. Chinese netizens create homophonic codewords and related catchphrases to communicate about such issues. Following these stories, however, requires a great deal of time and attention to keep abreast of current usage and ahead of the official censors.[79]

There are few alternatives for PRC residents who do not look beyond the Great Firewall, and even if residents find their news outside China, then they also must use another language. The CCP continues to squeeze independent Chinese-language media out of the market by purchasing newspapers and outlets directly or by proxy as well as by providing content to external media outfits. Falun Gong– and foreign government–supported media now are the largest Chinese-language media outlets internationally that remain autonomous of the CCP. In Australia, the edition of one Chinese-language newspaper told reporters that he estimated that 95% of the Chinese media in Australia was controlled by the party.[80]

---

[77] "UK Gov't Skripal Story Is 'Speculative, Ideological'"; Megan Martin, "Porton Down: Lab behind Skripal Poison Probe Has Dark History of Human Testing," RT, April 4, 2018, https://www.rt.com/uk/423190-porton-down-human-testing; and "Russia Spy Row: UK Lab Could Be Poison Source, Says Ambassador," BBC, March 18, 2018, https://www.bbc.co.uk/news/uk-43446312.

[78] Tony Wesolowsky, "A Timeline of Russia's Changing Story on Skripal Poisoning," Radio Free Europe/Radio Liberty, March 21, 2018, https://www.rferl.org/a/timeline-deny-distort-novichok-russia-changing-stories-poisoning/29113561.html.

[79] Margaret E. Roberts, *Censored: Distraction and Diversion Inside China's Great Firewall* (Princeton: Princeton University Press, 2018).

[80] Kelsey Munro and Philip Wen, "Chinese Language Newspapers in Australia: Beijing Controls Messaging, Propaganda in Press," *Sydney Morning Herald*, July 8, 2016, https://www.smh.com.au/national/chinese-language-newspapers-in-australia-beijing-controls-messaging-propaganda-in-press-20160610-gpg0s3.html.

## Use of the Diaspora: A Shared Springboard for Influence

Both Beijing and Moscow use their respective diaspora communities as a springboard for generating influence in target countries. They are a source of intelligence on local culture and politics as well as on how to deliver important propaganda themes. They can be rallied, albeit imperfectly, as a voting bloc to support desirable political candidates in democracies, or even provide pro-Beijing or pro-Moscow candidates. Although exploiting these communities for their parochial benefit would seem to endanger Chinese and Russians abroad, it is not clear that either country's leaders care. Suspicion of their diaspora communities reinforces the very kind of social distrust that Russian and, to a lesser extent, Chinese leaders want. More importantly, suspicion of Chinese and Russians in host nations isolates them from the government and society, making them less likely to pose a security risk to Beijing and Moscow.

Just because the CCP's and the Kremlin's policies seek to exploit their respective diaspora communities does not mean they always will be or even can be successful. The brutal legacies of Maoist China and Soviet Russia led to large ethnic communities that wish nothing to do with the governments in Beijing and Moscow. FBI director Christopher Wray said that the party mobilizes a whole-of-society effort, but just because the policy targets the whole society does not mean it succeeds.[81]

The Kremlin uses the Russian diaspora community, which it largely defines as anyone who speaks Russian as a first language or who self-identifies as Russian, to sow dissent in democratic states and as a political prop. For the former, according to a study by Edward Lucas and Peter Pomerantsev, Russian propaganda "falsely claims that these segments of the population face discrimination or outright persecution because of their ethnic, civic or linguistic affiliations."[82] Concerns over the safety of Russian-speaking citizens in eastern Ukraine, for instance, could provide a justification to intervene on their behalf, argued President Putin, as early as May 2014.[83] Researchers have found numerous calls from the Kremlin or its

---

[81] Michael Kranz, "The Director of the FBI Says the Whole of Chinese Society Is a Threat to the U.S.," *Business Insider*, February 13, 2018, https://www.businessinsider.com/china-threat-to-america-fbi-director-warns-2018-2?r=UK&IR=T.

[82] Lucas and Pomerantsev, "Winning the Information War," 5.

[83] Kathy Lally and Will Englund, "Putin Says He Reserves Right to Protect Russians in Ukraine," *Washington Post*, March 4, 2014, https://www.washingtonpost.com/world/putin-reserves-the-right-to-use-force-in-ukraine/2014/03/04/92d4ca70-a389-11e3-a5fa-55f0c77bf39c_story.html.

proxies to protect the Russian diaspora in Latvia, Moldova, and Azerbaijan among others.[84]

The CCP views the Chinese diaspora worldwide as a potential conduit for influence as well as a force to be harnessed for national modernization. The party's two goals, modernization and security, dovetail quite precisely with the language used. He Yafei, the former diplomat and deputy director of the Overseas Chinese Affairs Office, explained the importance of the overseas Chinese community as a conduit for Beijing's soft power and public diplomacy: "They are good at selecting from the broad and profound Chinese culture the contents that are easily accepted by the citizens living in the country, choosing the ways and means by which they will be well-received, and carrying out public diplomacy in the role of 'party'. This makes their message more persuasive and contagious."[85]

Beijing also has been prepared to step into elections by mobilizing its diaspora to vote or participate directly. Retired senior Singaporean diplomat Bilahari Kausikan highlighted one example of Chinese interference in a recent speech. He pointed out that the Chinese ambassador to Malaysia had campaigned openly for the Malaysian Chinese Association president in his parliamentary constituency in violation of diplomatic protocols.[86] The most provocative cases, however, have occurred in Australia. Press leaks in 2017 from the Australian Security Intelligence Organisation indicated that the CCP was directing at least ten political candidates.[87] That report received some corroboration in spring 2018. Australian intelligence agencies gathered information linking Ernest Wong, a member of the Upper House from the Labor Party, to Chinese intelligence officers. Wong had risen in the ranks of the Labor Party due to his ability to raise millions of dollars from the Chinese diaspora, and his political engagement led him into contact with Chinese intelligence and the UFWD.[88] In late 2017, a Chinese-language letter

---

[84] Lucas and Pomerantsev, "Winning the Information War," 25; and Víchová and Janda, *The Prague Manual*, 7, 42.

[85] Zhang Hong et al., "Zoujin guoqiao ban: Siwei fuzhuren tan qiaowu" [Inside the Overseas Chinese Affairs Office: Four Deputies Discuss Overseas Chinese Affairs Work], *People's Daily*, April 12, 2014, http://paper.people.com.cn/rmrbhwb/html/2014-04/12/content_1414072.htm.

[86] "Amid Rise of Identity Politics, S'poreans Need to Beware Foreign Manipulation: Bilahari Kausikan," *Today*, July 12, 2018, https://www.todayonline.com/singapore/amid-rise-identity-politics-sporeans-need-beware-foreign-manipulation-bilahari-kausikan.

[87] Paul Maley and Nicola Berkovic, "Security Agencies Flag Chinese Manchurian Candidates," *Australian*, December 9, 2017, https://www.theaustralian.com.au/national-affairs/national-security/security-agencies-flag-chinese-manchurian-candidates/news-story/81e6dad4b472180141f543d2f08e3e25.

[88] Nick McKenzie, Alexandra Smith, and Fergus Hunter, "This Sitting Labor MP Has Been Cultivated by Chinese Intelligence," *Sydney Morning Herald*, June 27, 2018, https://www.smh.com.au/politics/federal/this-sitting-labor-mp-has-been-cultivated-by-chinese-intelligence-20180627-p4znzp.html.

circulated on WeChat urging the substantial Chinese minority in Bennelong to vote against the government because of its China-phobia. The letter began circulating through UFWD-connected Chinese-Australians, suggesting a direct party hand.[89]

## Cyberspace: Boosting Active Measures vs. Preserving the Propaganda Edge

Russia has taken its active measures toolkit into cyberspace, exploiting newfound avenues to reach a broader audience in target countries. What Russia is doing here does not represent a departure from past practices of using intelligence to inform the reflexive control process or disseminating disinformation to poison public discourse. The difference is the amplification of these methods. Rather than manufacturing documents embarrassing to the Democratic Party to which it might have to respond, the GRU could break into the servers and find original documents that would exacerbate internal divisions in the American left. Rather than trying to build an original dataset on U.S. voters and figure out in general terms what messaging might work, Russian actors could steal such data and target their efforts to geographic constituencies crucial to the U.S. election.[90] Rather than try to evaluate whether the messages were working or reaching their intended audience, Facebook, YouTube, and other social media provided feedback on whether the message resonated.

The CCP's primary tactics in cyberspace are various forms of censorship inside China and within Chinese-language communities overseas. Major foreign social media outlets are banned in the PRC, but the party has kept a tight grip over Weibo, WeChat, and the other significant social media and messaging services. These allow it to reach abroad because many Chinese-language speakers overseas use the apps to communicate with friends and relatives in China and to keep apprised of information there.

A much smaller amount of the party's activity appears to follow the more malicious Russian model. Attacks on computer networks have been used to disrupt gatherings of Chinese dissidents by bringing down a venue's sound system, which is necessary for microphones and simultaneous translation. In one incident, the collateral damage to other exposed parts of the building

---

[89] Henry Belot, "Mysterious Letter Shows Influence of Chinese Community in Crucial Bennelong By-Election," Australian Broadcasting Corporation, December 14, 2017, http://www.abc.net.au/news/2017-12-14/bennelong-by-election-mysterious-letter-chinese-community/9258696.

[90] Manu Raju, Dylan Byers, and Dana Bash, "Russian-Linked Facebook Ads Targeted Michigan and Wisconsin," CNN, October 4, 2017, https://edition.cnn.com/2017/10/03/politics/russian-facebook-ads-michigan-wisconsin/index.html.

led the venue owners to ban the organizers and Chinese dissidents from their facilities.[91] This may be a single incident, but the silence that surrounds CCP intimidation suggests that other stories probably exist. Against Taiwan, PRC actors have started to feed disinformation into the LINE app—Taiwan's rough equivalent of WeChat—to exacerbate social tensions and fuel distrust. Some of this work has been automated through content farms that have been traced back to the PRC.[92]

## Agents of Influence vs. Influenced Agents[93]

In keeping with the differences in the roles of intelligence services, Russia relies heavily on intelligence officers, their ability to pound the pavement and socialize, and their recruited agents. The Russian services appear perfectly willing to recruit agents simply for active measures, and they also cultivate collaborators who may not understand with whom they are dealing or why. For example, according to the Robert Mueller investigation's indictments in July 2018, Russian hackers communicated with "a person who was in regular contact with senior members of the presidential campaign"—later revealed to be Roger Stone—though the indictment did not specify that Stone knew that his interlocutors were Russian.[94]

Russian tactics for spreading disinformation have a long history, as the Soviet era makes clear. A first tactic has been simply to hire or recruit individuals to produce manipulative cultural products to discredit political figures and hostile institutions. A second tactic is developing ever more sophisticated ways of producing doctored or forged documents that could then be passed discreetly to newspapers or researchers. One public example is the case of Pierre-Charles Pathé, a French journalist sentenced to five years in prison in 1980 for his distribution of Soviet disinformation through his newsletter. Pathé's subscribers included roughly 400 French parliamentarians, 50 foreign embassies, and another 50 journalists and publications. On at least one occasion, the Soviets handed Pathé an entire draft that he went on to publish in his own name. Pathé also provided

---

[91] Author's interviews in Washington, D.C., December 2016.

[92] Russell Hsiao, "CCP Propaganda against Taiwan Enters the Social Age," Jamestown Foundation, China Brief, April 24, 2018, https://jamestown.org/program/ccp-propaganda-against-taiwan-enters-the-social-age.

[93] This section draws from Peter Mattis, "Contrasting China's and Russia's Influence Operations," War on the Rocks, January 16, 2018, https://warontherocks.com/2018/01/contrasting-chinas-russias-influence-operations.

[94] Mark Mazzetti and Katie Benner, "12 Russian Agents Indicted in Mueller Investigation," *New York Times*, July 13, 2018, https://www.nytimes.com/2018/07/13/us/politics/mueller-indictment-russian-intelligence-hacking.html.

the KGB dossiers on influential French politicians, businesspeople, and journalists of his acquaintance.[95] The recruitment of journalists and writers is echoed from other sources, such as KGB defector Stanislav Levchenko. He claimed to have four journalists among the ten agents he handled during his tour in Tokyo in the late 1970s. Sergei Tretyakov also described handling a Canadian environmental lawyer to agitate U.S.-Canadian relations in the 1990s as well as the continuing Russian efforts to sow mischief through other agents and propaganda materials unattributed to Russian intelligence.

Russian tactics seem to have changed from planting fake stories in Western media outlets to promoting fake content across online platforms in recent times. This occurred during the 2016 U.S. presidential election campaign. Russian operatives, working for the St. Petersburg–based IRA (one of the more sizable Russian troll farms), purchased numerous advertisements featuring fake content that were viewed by as many as 150 million Facebook users.[96] Here the work seems to have been directed by Putin's closest associates and not directly tied to Russia's traditional intelligence services.

The CCP approach generally appears much softer, perhaps because the formal intelligence organizations play a less prominent role. Gatekeepers who facilitate inroads and make connections to open the door for Chinese agents in foreign countries are more common than intelligence officers. People like Sheri Yan (convicted on bribery charges) and Chau Chak Wing of Australia or Chinese-American Katrina Leung fulfilled this kind of role. Leung also reportedly served as a conduit for the Chinese leadership to feed information through the FBI to the White House. The kind of elite relationship-building that these individuals demonstrate and that seem to be the hallmarks of Chinese influence are what make flirtations with ethics violations difficult to dismiss out of hand. From then ambassador to China Gary Locke's rushed sale of his Maryland home to Chinese businesspeople to the trademark grants by Ivanka Trump or Jared Kushner's backchannel communications with Beijing, the activity may be completely innocent or routine. Or it may be something more devious. The surface-level indicators are the same.

---

[95] Daniel Souherland, "France the Height of International Intrigue; Paris Copes with a New Kind of Spy," *Christian Science Monitor*, September 24, 1980, https://www.csmonitor.com/1980/0924/092450.html.

[96] Thomas G. Mahnken, Ross Babbage, and Toshi Yoshihara, "Countering Comprehensive Coercion: Competitive Strategies against Authoritarian Political Warfare," Center for Strategic and Budgetary Assessments, May 2018, https://csbaonline.org/uploads/documents/Countering_Comprehensive_Coercion%2C_May_2018.pdf; and Hannah Kuchler, "Russian Meddling in U.S. Election Reached 150m Facebook Users," *Financial Times*, November 2, 2017.

Mao and the CCP exploited foreign contacts from the very beginning to shape the story of China's revolution, gain support, and discredit their adversaries. Journalists Edgar Snow and Theodore White presented the CCP of the 1930s and 1940s to Americans as made up of charismatic, peasant-focused revolutionaries who brought self-government and genuine resistance against Japan. They were not the only ones duped by the Communists' selective openness. As Yu Maochun chronicled, U.S. officials in China erred in exaggerating the Kuomintang's faults and corruption—Chiang Kai-shek and the Kuomintang sacrificed the cream of their army in 1937 in an attempt to unify China and rally the warlords—as surely as they misjudged the CCP's noble resistance.[97] The reality was far different. The transcripts of Snow's interviews with Mao were edited by the CCP. Rather than fighting an all-out war against Japan, CCP leaders often collaborated, providing intelligence to the Japanese army on the Kuomintang while husbanding their own strength.[98] To the best of our knowledge, none of those who misjudged the CCP based on their managed contact with Communist leaders, including controversial or sympathetic figures like John Service, was a spy or did so under CCP direction.

## China's Taiwan Caveat

The CCP's evolving tactics against Taiwan deserve special mention because the party appears to be evolving toward a more aggressive, Russian-like approach.[99] Beginning in 2016 after the election of President Tsai Ing-wen of the Democratic Progressive Party, Beijing placed more pressure internally and externally on Taiwan. The political trends—the solidification of Taiwanese identity, the absence of Taiwanese interest in unification under the CCP, and the collapse of the Kuomintang's internal cohesion—suggested to the CCP that it needed to change public opinion in Taiwan itself rather than rely on a pro-mainland partner to move the needle gradually.

---

[97] Maochun Yu, *OSS in China: Prelude to Cold War*, reprint ed. (Annapolis: Naval Institute Press, 2011).

[98] Anne-Marie Brady, *Making the Foreign Serve China: Managing Foreigners in the People's Republic* (Lanham: Rowman and Littlefield, 2003), 46–47; and Homare Endo, "Mao Zedong, Founding Father of the People's Republic of China, Conspired with the Japanese Army," Japan Policy Forum, Discuss Japan, no. 33, May/June 2016, https://www.japanpolicyforum.jp/archives/diplomacy/pt20160517095311.html.

[99] For a more thorough description of these changes, see Peter Mattis, "Responding to the PRC's Increased Pressure on Taiwan," in "U.S.-Taiwan Defense Relations," National Bureau of Asian Research, May 2018, http://nbr.org/downloads/pdfs/psa/us-taiwan_defense_relations_roundtable_may2018.pdf.

The new tactics resembled Russia's efforts to undermine the trust in the political system and discredit Taiwan's leaders.[100] The CCP's proxies, such as former organized crime leader Chang An-lo and his China Unification Promotion Party, have fueled pension protests and violent counter-demonstrations against youth activists and even begun preparing for armed unrest. Beijing's intelligence services also have taken a more active role, recruiting journalists, scholars, and pundits as agents of influence and guiding the pro-PRC New Party, whose leadership was arrested. These operations against Taiwan provide a warning of what the CCP is prepared to do and what it is capable of doing when political trends appear unfavorable from Beijing's perspective.

## Challenges and Opportunities

One example of a shared target is the Czech Republic, where China and Russia have very close ties to the political leadership.[101] While there are no indications of collusion between Beijing and Moscow, Czech researchers suggest that some degree of coordination may be taking place to lower the defenses of the Czech Republic and other Eastern European countries.[102] In part, this is reflected in operations that are similar in nature. For instance, much as it does in Taiwan, the PRC uses tactics in the Czech Republic that mimic Russian influence operations.[103] In particular, Martin Hala describes China's use of corrupt capitalism to influence Czech politics and society to fit the interests of the CCP.[104] In the annual public report released by the Czech Republic's Security Information Service, Russia and China are the largest actors conducting covert operations to influence the Czech Republic.[105] The report also mentions a similarity between Russian and Chinese campaigns,

---

[100] J. Michael Cole, "China Acting on 'Lebanonization' Threat against Taiwan," *Taiwan Sentinel*, May 8, 2018, https://sentinel.tw/china-acting-on-lebanization-threat-against-taiwan.

[101] Bethany Allen-Ebrahimian and Emily Tamkin, "Prague Opened the Door to Chinese Influence. Now It May Need to Change Course," *Foreign Policy*, March 16, 2018, https://foreignpolicy.com/2018/03/16/prague-to-czech-chinese-influence-cefc-energy-communist-party.

[102] Author's interviews in Prague, March 2017.

[103] Laura Rosenberger and John Garnaut, "The Interference Operations from Putin's Kremlin and Xi's Communist Party: Forging a Joint Response," *Asan Forum*, May 8, 2018, http://www.theasanforum.org/the-interference-operations-from-putins-kremlin-and-xis-communist-party-forging-a-joint-response.

[104] Martin Hala, "China's Gift to Europe Is a New Version of Crony Capitalism," *Guardian*, April 18, 2018, https://www.theguardian.com/commentisfree/2018/apr/18/chinese-europe-czech-republic-crony-capitalism.

[105] Security Information Service (Czech Republic), "Annual Report of the Security Information Service for 2016," 10, https://www.bis.cz/public/site/bis.cz/content/vyrocni-zpravy/en/ar2016en.pdf.

in that China has adopted "hybrid campaigns" that were previously considered a type of Russian influence operation.[106] The CCP's campaign involved attempting to influence public opinion regarding the South China Sea by targeting the Chinese diaspora community. Articles that were in favor of China's interests were published, with the involvement of the Chinese embassy in Prague, and those articles were then translated into Mandarin to give the Chinese public the impression that support for China was strong in the Czech Republic.

Of course, China and Russia do share interests in weakening Western political institutions. Even if there is no evidence of collaborated or coordinated political influence efforts, the cumulative effect can make great strides in weakening the institutions, irrespective of whether the efforts themselves are coordinated.

Collaboration has its own downsides as well. One could easily imagine the horror of Chinese officials at Russian active measures to influence U.S. political elections should they be invited to join such efforts, because the approaches are so radically different from how China prefers to operate. Moreover, collaboration in some countries might easily be turned into competition in regions where the two have competing visions and goals, such as in Central Asia.

While the record is murky with regard to influence operations, China and Russia have been known to share intelligence that could be used against foreign governments.[107] The nature and breadth of intelligence-sharing efforts is not known, however, largely due to the sensitivity of such efforts. The question is whether the pathways for sharing intelligence, especially related to the United States, also provide a means for running joint intelligence operations and coordinating efforts to weaken U.S. influence.

Addressing the challenges posed by CCP and Russian political influence operations cannot be done by avoiding the issue. The only natural tension point in what each country is doing is whether Chinese leaders begin to believe that Russian operations are tearing apart countries that Beijing would prefer to stay intact or to build up itself. To the extent that CCP political or

---

[106] Security Information Service (Czech Republic), "Annual Report of the Security Information Service for 2016," 12.

[107] For instance, China and Russia reportedly shared knowledge and training related to countering and targeting U.S. government officials and operations. See Tom Winter, Ken Dilanian, and Jonathan Dienst, "Alleged CIA China Turncoat Lee May Have Compromised U.S. Spies in Russia Too," NBC News, January 19, 2018, https://www.nbcnews.com/news/china/cia-china-turncoat-lee-may-have-compromised-u-s-spies-n839316; and Brian Bennet and W.J. Hennigan, "China and Russia Are Using Hacked Data to Target U.S. Spies, Officials Say," *Los Angeles Times*, August 31, 2015, http://www.latimes.com/nation/la-na-cyber-spy-20150831-story.html.

economic penetration corrupts countries on Russia's periphery, the Kremlin has little reason for concern. Belt and Road projects would increase demands for Russian energy resources and raw materials, while corruption created by CCP investments and infiltration only would make it easier for the Kremlin to do the same.

The distinctions between the PRC and Russian approaches to political influence operations highlight a central tension in how democratic states respond to authoritarian interference. To avoid demonizing their ethnic Chinese and Russian citizens and residents, democracies need to craft laws and measures that provide effective protections, regardless of which state's influence activities cross the line. Yet countering the CCP or the Kremlin requires a great deal of specific knowledge about the adversary, language capability, and vectors through which they approach the political core of their targets. Investing the time and resources necessary to build that knowledge and capability will force tradeoffs, and the long timeline necessary to devise capable countermeasures makes the process vulnerable to being crowded out due to more immediately pressing matters, such as counterterrorism, that might involve the life and death of citizens.

Investing in such resources is a necessary part of living and dealing with Russia and China as they are presently governed. Few countries, however, have a robust counterintelligence service capable of addressing the scope and scale of the challenge. The need to preempt in a world of ideas, as implied by both countries' security concepts, will keep Russia and China pushing up against democracies, undermining their political values, and seeking to discredit democracy in practice. For these political influence operations to stop, Western democracies would likely need to either give up their democracy or give up their power.

Countering these operations offers a means to repair the transatlantic alliance and strengthen cooperation badly damaged by decades of conflict in the Middle East and the inappropriate management of alliance issues. Pockets of expertise are too few and too isolated for any one country to work effectively alone. Although there is a great of deal of public knowledge of and experience with what Russia does, knowledge of CCP operations is much slimmer. Even knowing what an adversary does is no guarantee that a country possesses the practical expertise to prevent damage to its political system. Only in a practitioner community of shared values will ideas and countermeasures be tested and resilience demonstrated.

Moving forward, democratic states have no choice but to address the Chinese and Russian efforts to undermine them from within. The cautious and the critics are right to be concerned about the potential backlash.

The last time Western societies dealt with infiltration and subversion, the United States entered a dark period of McCarthyism and others saw government coalitions collapse almost overnight. The cost of not addressing these concerns, however, will be the integrity of democratic politics and policymaking. Democratic states have many different tools with which to respond. The national security toolkit is a blunt instrument, and where possible, other measures should be used.

The first steps should include transparency measures to cast sunlight into the shadowy areas where united front work and active measures reside. Many Westerners barely believe such conspiratorial activities exist, much less are conducted on a daily basis by agents of Beijing and Moscow. A free press, then, is indispensable, as are researchers operating out in the open to expose such operations. Legislation, such as the Foreign Agent Registration Act, or administrative measures, such as changing visa and entry questionnaires, also can assist by penalizing the failure to report one's connections. Governments would be remiss not to consider the benefits of civic education in schools and what kind of curriculum or activities might be appropriate for nurturing engaged citizenship.

Legal and law-enforcement institutions also need to be stress-tested against Beijing's and Moscow's political interference. The same elements responsible for conducting counterintelligence and tracking foreign spies will be the units responsible for rooting out foreign interference. If they have had trouble making relatively straightforward espionage cases, then Western counterintelligence will struggle to address the more opaque interference-related problems. Criminal and civil liberties statutes can supplement the more focused national security–related measures to protect against intimidation, surveillance, and violence. Such measures benefit from asking democratic governments to live up to their promises and their values rather than raising the specter of another McCarthyite scare.[108]

The long-term ability of the United States and other democratic states to execute a recalibrated and strategic approach to Russia and China depends in large part on an effective response to their political influence operations. Supporting public discussion and sunshine measures is at least as important as the national security response because these raise awareness and activate the antibodies that protect democratic governance. Ultimately, democracy is something that citizens must practice, not a ring that they possess.

---

[108] Samantha Hoffman and Peter Mattis, "China's Incursion on American Campuses Is Nothing to Take Lightly," *Hill*, May 3, 2018, https://thehill.com/opinion/education/386078-chinas-incursion-on-american-campuses-is-nothing-to-take-lightly.

## Conclusion

Both China and Russia view political influence operations as critical elements of statecraft, though they diverge in some of the core objectives behind these operations, how they organize them, and the defining tactics they employ. As an emerging great power, China aspires to shape a Sino-centric regional and eventually global order. By contrast, dire economic, demographic, and other trends prevent Russia from regaining the great-power status of the Soviet Union and instead require it to bring other countries down to its level.

However, both regimes view ultimate security as the absence of all threats to their legitimacy and ability to govern. In particular, both Xi and Putin view the threats from Western liberalism and democratic norms as undermining their domestic legitimacy and see benefits from weakening U.S. security partnerships and alliances. Both countries aim to move the international system toward a multipolar order in which each country dominates its own spheres of influence. Even if there is little publicly available evidence that China and Russia collaborate in political influence operations, there are clear indications that they share intelligence that could be used against foreign governments like the United States. Moreover, their complementary actions compound the individual challenges they pose to the United States and its partners and allies around the globe, a challenge that is only growing more formidable with time.

## EXECUTIVE SUMMARY

This chapter provides a comprehensive view of Sino-Russian cooperation across the security, economic, and political realms and considers policy options for the United States.

### MAIN ARGUMENT
Cooperation between China and Russia has advanced considerably in the past decade. Their cooperation is driven both by shared interests, including the preservation of their authoritarian regimes and statist economic policies, and by opposition to the perceived U.S. efforts to impose a liberal international political and economic order. Their coordination in the political realm focuses on opposing U.S. efforts in existing international organizations to institutionalize liberal norms and on creating alternative political and economic organizations that are more conducive to their interests. The principal challenges to the U.S. stem from the individual policies of China and Russia rather than their combined efforts, but their increased willingness to coordinate policies complicates the U.S. ability to respond effectively to those dangers.

### POLICY IMPLICATIONS
- Explicit U.S. policies designed to try to slow down or reverse this coordination are not likely to be effective without a substantial reorientation of U.S. policy in ways that would harm fundamental U.S. economic, political, and security interests.

- The U.S. can best meet the challenge posed by Sino-Russian cooperation by strengthening international engagement and support for U.S. allies and partners who share its interests and values.

- While the U.S. should not accommodate China's or Russia's demands solely for the sake of disrupting their cooperation, it should be prepared to take steps (consistent with core U.S. interests) to reduce the danger of an unintended security spiral with both China and Russia.

Chapter 5

# China-Russia Cooperation: How Should the United States Respond?

*James B. Steinberg*

On June 8, 2018, in a ceremony held in advance of the 18th annual Shanghai Cooperation Organisation (SCO) summit, President Xi Jinping presented President Vladimir Putin with the Medal of Friendship, hailing the Sino-Russian relationship as the "most significant relationship between major countries in the world."[1] As the 70th anniversary of the founding of the People's Republic of China (PRC) approaches, ties between China and Russia appear to have come full circle: from the PRC's early days when Mao Zedong announced the policy of "leaning to one side," to the brink of war in 1969, back to what Chinese foreign minister Wang Yi has termed "the best period of history."[2]

The Sino-Russian rapprochement has triggered alarm bells in Washington. In his forward to the recent NBR Report "Russia-China Relations: Assessing Common Ground and Strategic Fault Lines," Robert Sutter observed: "Russian-Chinese relations [have] advance[d] in ways that seriously affect the interests of the United States and its allies and partners."[3]

---

**JAMES B. STEINBERG** is University Professor of Social Science, International Affairs, and Law in the Maxwell School of Citizenship and Public Affairs at Syracuse University. He can be reached at <jimsteinberg@syr.edu>.

The author would like to thank Elise Roberts for her invaluable research assistance.

[1] "China This Week: China Awards Putin First Medal of Friendship," *China-US Focus*, June 8, 2018, https://www.chinausfocus.com/focus/china-this-week/2018-06-08.html.

[2] Mao Zedong, "On the People's Democratic Dictatorship: In Commemoration of the Twenty-Eighth Anniversary of the Communist Party of China," June 30, 1949, History and Public Policy Program Digital Archive, trans. from *Selected Works of Mao Tse-tung*, vol. 4 (Peking: Foreign Languages Press, 1961), 411–23; and Shannon Tiezzi, "China, Russia 'Show Americans' Their Close Relationship," *Diplomat*, April 10, 2018, https://thediplomat.com/2018/04/china-russia-show-americans-their-close-relationship.

[3] Robert Sutter, "Foreword," in "Russia-China Relations: Assessing Common Ground and Strategic Fault Lines," National Bureau of Asian Research (NBR), Special Report, no. 66, July 2017, v.

This threat perception has led policymakers and analysts, with increasing urgency, to criticize past failures to address this problem and to propose a variety of policy measures to respond to the perceived threat.

Advocates for this approach in effect advance a complex syllogism: (1) cooperation between China and Russia is increasing dramatically, (2) this cooperation seriously harms U.S. interests, (3) their cooperation stems in important part from U.S. policies that are driving them together, (4) the U.S. interests served by these policies are small in comparison to the costs to the United States of their deepening cooperation, and (5) if the United States stops doing those things, China and Russia will stop cooperating with each other and the United States will be better off.

Each of these premises is debatable. A strong case can be made that the extent of Sino-Russian cooperation faces real constraints; that its impact (beyond the individual challenges posed separately by Russia and China) is limited; that what is driving them together is only partly due to U.S. policies; that to the extent that U.S. policies are driving Russia and China together, the United States is motivated by very important interests that would be costly to sacrifice; and that even if the United States were to reverse these policies, this would be unlikely to have a significant impact on their cooperation. This chapter explores the underlying arguments in support of each of these perspectives and concludes by drawing implications for U.S. policy going forward.

There is little doubt that in recent years ties between China and Russia have grown closer. Their leaders increasingly tout the importance of the bilateral relationship as a central focus of their national strategies. The rhetoric is matched by an impressive array of activities across the security, economic, and political domains. By almost any metric—looking at the frequency, breadth, and intensity of their interactions—cooperation between China and Russia is on the rise. The question for U.S. policymakers thus is twofold. First, how worried should the United States be about these developments? Second, to the extent that there is cause for concern, what can and should the United States do?

To answer these questions, the chapter will begin by examining the historical evolution and contemporary developments in Sino-Russian relations before offering an assessment of the implications of that cooperation for U.S. security, economic, and political interests. The analysis will then review a range of proposed U.S. strategies suggested by other practitioners and analysts to respond to the perceived risks to the United States and provide a "net assessment" of the costs and benefits of the proposed courses of action. The chapter concludes by considering an alternative approach, drawing on historical U.S. policy strengths that would allow the United States to respond to the real challenges while reinforcing its core interests and values.

## The Shadow of the Past

Any assessment of the importance of contemporary Sino-Russian cooperation must contend with the shadow of the past, which looms large over the current policy debate. Fear of a Sino-Soviet condominium was an important factor in the debates over U.S. policy during China's civil war: advocates of the United States providing support to China's nationalists focused on the danger that a Communist China would join hands with the Soviet Union to pose a global threat to the West.[4] Events following the triumph of the Chinese Communist Party in 1949, from the Korean War to Soviet support for China's nuclear program, seemed to confirm those fears.[5] By contrast, President Richard Nixon's bold move to open U.S. relations with the PRC at the same time that he pursued nuclear arms negotiations with the Soviet Union was seen as a way to advance U.S. interests by exploiting the growing split in the Communist world to lessen the danger to the United States and to provide the United States with leverage in its negotiations with each country. The apparent success of the idea of "trilateral diplomacy"—positioning the United States so that its ties with both China and Russia were "better" than their ties

---

[4] See, for example, U.S. Department of State, *The China White Paper* (Stanford: Stanford University Press, 1949), https://archive.org/stream/VanSlykeLymanTheChinaWhitePaper1949/Van+Slyke%2C+Lyman+-+The+China+White+Paper+1949_djvu.txt. There is considerable debate among historians on the degree to which such a "monolithic" threat existed. See for example Odd Arne Westad, *Cold War and Revolution: Soviet-American Rivalry and the Origins of the Chinese Civil War* (New York: Columbia University Press, 1993); and Douglas J. Macdonald, "Communist Bloc Expansion in the Early Cold War: Challenging Realism, Refuting Revisionism," *International Security* 20, no. 3 (1995–96): 152–88.

[5] For a comprehensive review of Sino-Soviet cooperation during the first decade after the establishment of the People's Republic of China (PRC), see Zhihua Shen and Yafeng Xia, *Mao and the Sino-Soviet Partnership, 1945–1959: A New History* (New York: Lexington Books, 2015). The authors argue that shared interests, more than shared ideology, drove the partnership in its early years. For an evaluation of this argument, see the contributions in "H-Diplo Roundtable XVIII, 17 on Mao and the Sino-Soviet Partnership, 1945–1959: A New History," February 27, 2017, https://networks.h-net.org/node/28443/discussions/168915/h-diplo-roundtable-xviii-17-mao-and-sino-soviet-partnership-1945.

with each other—became a hallmark of U.S. strategy.[6] The approach was deepened during the Carter administration when the United States not only formalized diplomatic ties with the PRC and supported its entry into the United Nations but also launched a range of efforts to build bilateral security, economic, and political cooperation with Beijing while at the same time conducting arms control negotiations with Moscow.[7]

Events of the early 1990s seemed to offer a further opportunity to pursue this approach. The end of the Cold War and the ascension of the democratic and pro-Western leadership of Boris Yeltsin offered the prospect of better political ties between Russia and the United States. At the same time, Deng Xiaoping's "reform and opening up" revealed new and potentially vast vistas of Sino-U.S. economic collaboration, even as political tensions fueled by the Tiananmen Square events plagued political and security ties. Sino-Russian relations, which had warmed slightly following the death of Mao and improved further following the rise of Mikhail Gorbachev,[8] remained difficult, in part because China's Communist leaders feared the implications of democratic reform in Russia for their own hold on power. In the early post–Cold War years of the Clinton presidency, it was thus not difficult to imagine that the United States would have better relations with both China and Russia than they had with each other.

But in the early 2000s the landscape began to change, bringing China and Russia closer together and the United States farther apart from both. The rise of Vladimir Putin and an increasingly authoritarian leadership in Russia widened the political gap between the United States and Russia, while narrowing Moscow's differences with Beijing. A series of developments, from Russia's actions in Chechnya to its military intervention in Georgia, further strained ties. U.S. sanctions in response to the invasion of Ukraine in 2014 accelerated both trends, further distancing Russia from the West, while enhancing the value of China as an economic partner to lessen the impact of Western sanctions. Russian meddling in the U.S. presidential election

---

[6] Whether U.S. engagement in fact provided the United States with leverage in dealing with the Soviet Union is a matter of considerable debate. "Despite the claims of its practitioners, U.S. triangular diplomacy did not yield Washington tangible leverage in U.S.-Soviet negotiations....[T]hroughout the 1970s and 1980s developments in U.S.-China relations failed to significantly moderate Soviet policy toward the United States." Robert S. Ross, "Conclusion: Tripolarity and Policy Making," in *China, the United States, and the Soviet Union: Tripolarity and Policy Making in the Cold War*, ed. Robert S. Ross (Armonk: M.E. Sharp, 1993), 179–80. The chapters collected in this book offer a comprehensive look at the evolution of tripolarity from the perspectives of each of the three countries during the critical period beginning with Nixon's initiative to the end of the Cold War.

[7] Michael B. Yahuda, "The Significance of Tripolarity in China's Policy toward the United States since 1972," in Ross, *China, the United States, and the Soviet Union*, 21–24.

[8] See Chi Su, "The Strategic Triangle and China's Soviet Policy," in Ross, *China, the United States, and the Soviet Union*, 48–57.

in 2016 sent U.S.-Russian relations to a level of conflict not seen since the height of the Cold War.

At the same time, a comparable process was unfolding in Sino-U.S. relations. Trade frictions mounted between China and the United States following China's accession to the World Trade Organization (WTO) in 2001. Job losses in the United States due to Chinese competition and protectionism, compounded by allegations of China's theft of American intellectual property, clouded the landscape, especially following the 2008–9 financial crisis. China's military modernization, fueled by the country's economic growth, became an increasing cause for concern in Washington. More "assertive" Chinese policies in the South and East China Seas seemed to foreshadow a more confrontational approach to China's relations with the United States and its East Asian allies. The failure of China's economic modernization to translate into domestic political reform, including the festering human rights concerns about Chinese policies in Tibet, Xinjiang, and Hong Kong, also served to cloud U.S.-China ties, as did escalating tensions across the Taiwan Strait following the election of Chen Shui-bian, the independence-minded Democratic Progressive Party (DPP) candidate, in Taipei. Cross-strait tensions moderated following the election of the Kuomintang candidate Ma Ying-jeou in 2008 and then re-emerged with the DPP's victory in 2016. Although there have been bright spots, and China-U.S. relations have been more mixed than the tense relations between Washington and Moscow, both Washington and Beijing increasingly view each other with mistrust and a growing emphasis on elements of competition, rivalry, and even conflict rather than cooperation.

This reversion to early Cold War patterns among the three powers has led some to call for a revival of the Nixon/Kissinger playbook. Andrew Kuchins, for example, recently gave voice to that sentiment in counseling the newly elected Donald Trump: "The incoming administration would be well advised to review some of the principles of triangular diplomacy as practiced by Henry Kissinger in the Nixon administration."[9]

While history can provide valuable analogies, it is vital to examine them closely.[10] To the extent that Nixon's strategy was successful, it hinged

---

[9] Andrew C. Kuchins, "Releveraging U.S. Power amid Sino-Russian Rapprochement," in *Chinese Soft Power and Its Implications for the United States: Competition and Cooperation in the Developing World*, ed. Carola McGiffert (Washington, D.C.: Center for Strategic and International Studies, 2009), https://csis-prod.s3.amazonaws.com/s3fs-public/legacy_files/files/media/csis/pubs/090403_mcgiffert_chinesesoftpower_web.pdf.

[10] For a discussion of the use and misuse of historical analogies in informing policy, see Richard E. Neustadt and Ernest R. May, *Thinking in Time: The Uses of History for Decision-makers* (New York: Free Press, 1986).

on some very specific features of the time. Hindsight has shown that the Sino-Soviet bond was never as close or durable as many had thought during the early years following the Communist victory in China; common interests were matched with areas of deep tension, and the shared ideological rivalry with the United States was not enough to ensure common action by the two Communist giants. Moreover, the United States had something important to offer both sides that they could not provide each other—in the case of the Soviet Union, détente and the easing of the Cold War arms race; in the case of China, an economic outlet to fuel its growth, as well as security cooperation against Soviet dominance. Moreover, historians and analysts continue to debate whether U.S. engagement with China really provided the United States an advantage in dealing with the Soviet Union.[11]

Although there are important similarities between circumstances today and that earlier era, the differences are pronounced.[12] Only through carefully examining the nature of contemporary Sino-Russian cooperation and its implications for the United States can we evaluate what if any lessons can be learned from the prior era to inform contemporary policy.

## The Reality of the Present

A growing literature, both scholarly and journalistic, has documented the deepening engagement between China and Russia. Before assessing the extent to which this trend poses a threat to U.S. interests, it is useful to review the evolution of the relationship over the past decade or so.

### Security

From the earliest days of the PRC, cooperation between China and the Soviet Union included a security dimension.[13] Indeed, military support from Russia to the Chinese Communist Party contributed to its victory in China's civil war and its engagement in the Korean War. But from the beginning, the Soviet Union was cautious in the amount and type of military support provided to the PRC, particularly in high-end capabilities, including nuclear weapons. This caution stemmed in part from a desire to retain the upper hand in the relationship and also because of persistent tensions between the

---

[11] See the discussion in fn. 6 above.
[12] See Yahuda, "The Significance of Tripolarity," 15. Yahuda argues that "the strategic triangle, far from being a permanent fixture on the international landscape, was of transitory significance."
[13] See ibid.

two countries, especially over their shared border. Indeed, these restrictions were an important source of friction. As the overall relationship began to improve in the Gorbachev era, security cooperation too began to improve but restrictions on transferring systems like state-of-the art fighters and air defense systems remained.

Security cooperation experienced a step-wise improvement in the last decade, driven by a range of factors, including Russia's need for export income from arms sales, a recognition that China would soon be able to develop its own indigenous capabilities (so that any Russian restraint was self-defeating), and overall improvement in bilateral relations. This cooperation now extends beyond highly capable military systems to include exchanges, joint exercise, and training.

Since the 1990s, China has been one of Russia's largest arms importers, providing much-needed revenue to support state finances and the overhead costs of the Russian arms industry.[14] These arms sales have played an important role in China's quest to modernize its military quickly by supplying it with the high-tech weapons and equipment that the West has refused to sell. Between 2006 and 2010, Russia supplied over 80% of China's imports. However, as China's capacity to develop and produce its own weapons systems grows—due in part to reverse engineering of Russian technology—arms sales have declined.[15] In response to this trend, Russia has been increasingly willing to open up sales of advanced technologies like surface-to-air missiles, jet fighters, and submarines to gain more Chinese sales.

Exercises and exchanges between China and Russia have likewise increased. The first large-scale joint military exercises involving China and Russia occurred in 2005 with the SCO's Peace Mission drills. Although the scale of the exercises declined significantly in the early years, they have grown in size since 2014. Russia and China have also conducted a number of bilateral maritime exercises with an emphasis on search and rescue, antisubmarine warfare, and amphibious assaults.[16] In addition to their land and sea cooperation, Chinese and Russian defense agencies have worked together to counter U.S. military advances in the region, staging two computerized missile defense simulations in May 2016 and December 2017 in response to the installation of the Terminal High Altitude Area

---

[14] Richard Weitz, "Sino-Russian Security Ties," in "Russia-China Relations: 31.

[15] Paul J. Bolt, "Sino-Russian Relations in a Changing World Order," *Strategic Studies Quarterly* 8, no. 4 (2014): 47–69.

[16] Joshua Kucera, "Russia and the SCO Military Exercises," *Diplomat*, August 28, 2014, https://thediplomat.com/2014/08/russia-and-the-sco-military-exercises.

Defense (THAAD) missile defense system in South Korea.[17] In addition, representatives from both countries have held private meetings to discuss missile defense issues during international summits.[18]

## Economic

Economic ties, too, date to the early days of the PRC, when the Soviet Union provided not only a model for China's own development strategy but also critical technology, expertise, and capital. With "reform and opening up," however, China's economic focus in all three dimensions turned to the West, which provided not only crucial inputs for China's development but also markets for its burgeoning manufacturing sector. That pattern continues today. As Charles Ziegler discusses in his chapter for this volume on energy and trade cooperation, with the important exception of the energy sector and military technology, Russia has relatively little to offer China, while China's economic ties to the United States and U.S. allies (including the European Union, Japan, and South Korea) are central to the country's economic growth.[19] Even in energy, where Russia has been China's primary supplier of crude oil since 2016,[20] China has taken advantage of Russia's need for alternative markets in the wake of Western sanctions to strike favorable deals, while at the same time diversifying its own sources of energy and commodities among Central Asia, Myanmar, the Middle East, and even Western partners like Australia and Chile. On investment, despite repeated high-level pledges to enhance engagement, Chinese investment in Russia has slowed in recent years. Chinese investors remain extremely distrustful of the business environment in Russia, including its opaque regulatory system,

---

[17] See Franz-Stefan Gady, "China Claims 'New Breakthroughs in Anti-Missile Cooperation' with Russia," *Diplomat*, December 19, 2017, https://thediplomat.com/2017/12/china-claims-new-breakthroughs-in-anti-missile-cooperation-with-russia.

[18] Yu Bin, "Between Past and Future: Implications of Sino-Russian Relations for the United States," *Asia Policy* 13, no. 1 (2018): 12–18.

[19] After a decline in trade and investment between the two countries beginning in 2012, bilateral trade has increased significantly since 2015, with year-on-year growth increasing by 20% in 2017 to a total of $84 billion. These trends are likely to continue, with recent pledges by Moscow and Beijing to boost trade volumes to $200 billion by 2020. Nonetheless, these volumes pale in comparison to U.S.-China trade flows, which amounted to $636 billion in goods (import and export) in 2017. "Russia-China Trade Volume Exceeds Expectations, Hitting $84 Bn," RT, January 12, 2018, https://www.rt.com/business/415692-russia-china-trade-turnover.

[20] Russia surpassed Saudi Arabia in energy trade and is likely to maintain its position. The volume of its exports increased in 2017 and is likely to continue to increase in 2018, following the completion of a second East Siberia–Pacific Ocean pipeline in January and increased imports across the board. "Russia Remains China's Top Oil Supplier as Pipeline Expands," Reuters, February 24, 2018, https://www.reuters.com/article/us-china-economy-trade-crude/russia-remains-chinas-top-oil-supplier-as-pipeline-expands-idUSKCN1G808M.

high levels of corruption, and potential for greater economic instability.[21] The majority of investment that does occur comes from Chinese sovereign wealth funds like the Russia Direct Investment Fund and the Russia-China Investment Fund. With the exception of some notable infrastructure projects (like a high-speed rail connecting Moscow and Beijing), these investments have focused primarily on developing the energy and raw materials sectors and the Russian Far East.

By contrast China looms larger in Russia's economic calculus. Following the end of the Cold War (and with it the end of the Cold War–based constraints on trade, technology, and investment in Russia), Russia, like China, initially focused on the West as both a model and economic partner. However, the disruptive effects of the Yeltsin years soured many Russians on Western economic liberalism,[22] and new restrictions on Russia's trade with the United States, stemming from concerns about human rights (the Magnitsky Act), corruption, and most dramatically events in Crimea, led Russia to seek alternative economic partners. China is Russia's most important export market and is the fourth most important source of FDI.[23] Thus, the relationship is highly asymmetrical: China is Russia's largest bilateral trading partner, but Russia rarely makes it into China's top ten.[24]

In addition to efforts to strengthen bilateral economic cooperation and therefore reduce dependence on the United States and its allies, Russia and China have also worked to lessen the influence of the dollar in international economic governance, in part to reduce U.S. leverage over each of them. This includes promoting the reform of the International Monetary Fund (IMF) and World Bank, establishing alternative economic forums such as the BRICS (Brazil, Russia, India, China, and South Africa) summit and the associated New Development Bank, and proposing the Asian Infrastructure Investment Bank (AIIB). An additional aspect of this campaign is to promote the use of the renminbi as an international currency and reduce the primacy of the dollar.[25] Russia and China conduct a large proportion of their trade in rubles and renminbi following a currency swap agreement

---

[21] "China and Russia in 2017: An Intricate Path of Growth," EY and Partnership with Russia-China Investment Fund, April 2017, https://www.ey.com/ru/en/issues/ey-china-and-russia-in-2017.

[22] During the period of Dmitri Medvedev's presidency, Russia again began to look to strengthen economic ties with the United States and the West (including by joining the WTO and active participation in the G-8), but these efforts lapsed with the return of Putin in 2012.

[23] "China and Russia in 2017," 13.

[24] "China Monthly Trade Data," World Bank, World Integrated Trade Solutions, https://wits.worldbank.org/CountrySnapshot/en.

[25] Evan S. Medeiros and Michael S. Chase, "Chinese Perspectives on the Sino-Russian Relationship," in "Russia-China Relations," 1–25.

in 2014. The Bank of Russia nearly tripled its holdings of renminbi in the fourth quarter of 2017 from just 1.0% percent of its foreign exchange to 2.8%.[26] China and Russia have also been developing an alternative payment system that would lessen the impact of Western sanctions.[27]

## Political

Political cooperation between Russia and China has also increased in recent years. During the Cold War, despite the U.S. tendency to see the two Communist powers as a monolithic force in global affairs, their agendas frequently diverged. From China's own role in trying to forge a third force of neutral and developing countries in the Bandung Conference and the Non-Aligned Movement to Mao's support for radical revolutionary movements in the third world, which diverged from Moscow's more cautious approach, and the Sino-Russian competition for preeminence in the developing world, the two were frequently at odds in the international arena. This tendency was reinforced following the rapprochement between China and the United States in the 1970s and Deng Xiaoping's decision to focus China's external policy on improving the climate for economic growth—which meant easing tensions with the United States and the West at a time when Washington and Moscow were engaged in a range of proxy confrontations around the world, from Afghanistan to the Horn of Africa.

The end of the Cold War and the emergence of the United States as a self-proclaimed "sole superpower" gradually began to change the calculations of the two. A shared interest in countering perceived U.S. hegemony caused each to consider supporting the other as a counterweight to the assertion of U.S. power. The impulse began as early as 1997 with the signing of the Joint Declaration on a Multipolar World and the Establishment of a New International Order and was codified in the (largely rhetorical) Treaty of Good-Neighborliness and Friendly Cooperation (signed in 2001).

Sino-Russian cooperation in the international political arena is perhaps most evident in the countries' shared effort to counter U.S. efforts to extend the "liberal international order," particularly on issues such as the promotion of human rights and democracy, which both countries see

---

[26] Olga Tanas, "Bank of Russia Got Ahead of the World with Quest for Yuan Assets," Bloomberg, July 2, 2018, https://www.bloomberg.com/news/articles/2018-07-02/yuan-chases-loonie-s-share-as-bank-of-russia-adds-chinese-assets.

[27] Vladimir Soldatkin, "Russia Eyes Unified Payment Systems with China: PM," Reuters, November 4, 2016, https://www.reuters.com/article/us-russia-china-payments-sanctions/russia-eyes-unified-payment-systems-with-china-pm-idUSKBN12Z1RU.

as a direct threat to their regimes.[28] Both place considerable emphasis on the inviolability of sovereignty as embodied in Article 2(4) and 2(7) of the UN Charter (though clearly selectively applied by Russia in the cases of Georgia and Ukraine) and opposition to international intervention as embodied in doctrines such as the Responsibility to Protect.[29] Similarly, they have worked together to influence the international rules governing cyberspace, with an eye to maximizing sovereign control over the internet and limiting protections for free speech and international commerce.[30]

More broadly, China and Russia have a shared interest in reducing the role and influence of the United States in international institutions, working together either to reduce the United States' clout within those organizations (e.g., IMF and the World Bank) or to build alternative institutions in which the U.S. voice is either excluded or has limited weight, such as the SCO, the Conference on Interaction and Confidence Building Measures in Asia (CICA), and the AIIB.[31]

To date, each of these organizations has had limited impact. The SCO has at times aspired to play a broad role in managing regional security and has expanded its membership and geographic scope to include South Asia

---

[28] The recent push by Russia and China to use the budget process to take down a key office for human rights promotion at the United Nations is but one example of the way that China and Russia have used their position in the Security Council to try and reshape the current international order. See Colum Lynch, "At the UN, China and Russia Score Win in War on Human Rights," *Foreign Policy*, March 26, 2018, https://foreignpolicy.com/2018/03/26/at-the-u-n-china-and-russia-score-win-in-war-on-human-rights. For a discussion of Russia's and China's historical voting patterns at the United Nations, see Carla Monteleone, "Coalition Building in the UN Security Council," *International Relations* 29, no. 1 (2015): 58–59. Anthony Cordesman discusses the Russian and Chinese perceptions that the United States tried to undermine Russian leadership by helping create the 2004 Orange Revolution in Ukraine, the 2005 Tulip Revolution in Kyrgyzstan, and the 2012 Rose Revolution in Georgia. See Anthony H. Cordesman, "Russia and the 'Color Revolution': A Russian Military View of a World Destabilized by the United States and the West," CSIS, May 28, 2014, https://www.csis.org/analysis/russia-and-%E2%80%9Ccolor-revolution%E2%80%9D. Leaders from both countries have issued public statements vowing to combat these color revolutions and resist attempts at foreign interference in states' domestic politics.

[29] This view was formalized in the Declaration of the Russian Federation and the People's Republic of China on the Promotion of International Law, June 30, 2016, available at http://www.mid.ru/en/foreign_policy/position_word_order/-/asset_publisher/6S4RuXfeYlKr/content/id/2331698.

[30] The cooperation included proposals to the UN General Assembly for a Code of Conduct for Information Security and a joint statement. See Lincoln Davidson, "Despite Cyber Agreements, Russia and China Are Not as Close as You Think," Council on Foreign Relations, June 30, 2016 https://www.cfr.org/blog/despite-cyber-agreements-russia-and-china-are-not-close-you-think. See also the "Joint Statement between the People's Republic of China and the Russia Federation on Cooperation in Information Space Development," June 26, 2016, available at http://www.chinadaily.com.cn/china/2016-06/26/content_25856778.htm.

[31] See Bolt, "Sino-Russian Relations in a Changing World Order," 50–51.

and parts of the Middle East,[32] but its concrete achievements have been limited. The addition of India (as well as Pakistan) in 2017 to the membership further reduces the chances that the SCO will become an anti-U.S. security and political organization (although India does share some of Russia's and China's concerns about U.S. trade policy).[33] The CICA is largely a Chinese creation designed to provide an "Asia only" counterpart to trans-Pacific organizations like the East Asia Summit, which includes the United States and its allies (Japan and Australia) as well as Russia and China. By contrast, the United States is only an observer in CICA. Development-oriented organizations like the BRICS New Development Bank and AIIB (as well as China's own Belt and Road Initiative) fill a niche by potentially meeting infrastructure investment needs without the transparency safeguards required by U.S.-dominated development agencies. Taken together, these organizations represent a theoretical challenge to U.S. interests, but their achievements to date have been modest. Even within these organizations, China's and Russia's views are not always aligned.

On global issues, the degree of mutual political support remains rather limited, even in areas of key importance to each of the "partners."[34] Given its deep reservations about international intervention, China has been cautious about Russia's actions in Georgia and Ukraine. While it sees benefits in tensions between Russia and the West, it has refused to recognize the independence of Abkhazia, South Ossetia, or Crimea.[35]

The Middle East illustrates the complex mix of shared and divergent interests between the two countries with areas of cooperation as well as rivalry.[36] Both are concerned with the threat posed by Islamist terrorist organizations to their respective countries and have opposed Western efforts

---

[32] President Xi has described the union as promoting both security and development in the region, stressing the organization's support for free trade and the WTO. "China's Xi Welcomes India, Pakistan to SCO, Hails 'Unity,'" Radio Free Europe/Radio Liberty, June 10, 2018, https://www.rferl.org/a/china-russia-putin-xi-welcomes-india-pakistan-sco/29281818.html.

[33] See Jaloliddin Usmanov, "The Shanghai Cooperation Organization: Harmony or Discord?" *Diplomat*, June 26, 2018, https://thediplomat.com/2018/06/the-shanghai-cooperation-organization-harmony-or-discord.

[34] Analysts disagree about the significance of China's and Russia's mutual political support. Robert Sutter, for example, argues that "the independent goals of both China and Russia have been accepted by the other state, as can be seen by China's support for Russian involvement in Syria and Russian support for China's action in the South China Sea." See Robert Sutter, "America's Bleak View of Russia-China Relations," *Asia Policy* 13, no. 1 (2018): 42. Others focus on the lukewarm nature of the support. See, for example, Bolt, "Sino-Russian Relations in a Changing World Order," 53.

[35] See Bolt, "Sino-Russian Relations in a Changing World Order," 53.

[36] For a comprehensive look at the Russian and Chinese roles in the Middle East, see Galia Lavi and Sarah Fainberg, "Russia and China in the Middle East: Rapprochement and Rivalry," Institute for National Security Studies, Strategic Assessments, January 2018, http://www.inss.org.il/publication/russia-china-middle-east-rapprochement-rivalry.

to support democracy movements like the Arab Spring, which threaten the region's autocracies. China has given limited support to Russia's role in Syria, and the two jointly vetoed six of seven UN Security Council resolutions relating to Syria's use of chemical weapons.[37] But China's actual involvement in the country has largely been limited to the provision of humanitarian aid and support for a political settlement.[38] More broadly, analysts have suggested that Beijing has offered only tepid support for Russia in the Middle East, in part due to China's growing economic interests, especially access to energy and increasingly arms sales, which have led to close ties with Saudi Arabia (Russia's adversary in the region).[39]

Similarly, Russia has given only limited support to China's position in the South China Sea—for example, by refusing to back the United Nations Convention on the Law of the Sea (UNCLOS) arbitral panel decision in the case brought by the Philippines and by supporting China's position that the disputes should be resolved by the claimants without "outside" (i.e., U.S.) interference—while not explicitly endorsing China's sovereignty claims. On North Korea, there has been a fair degree of cooperation between Russia and China. Both countries have stressed the need for a political solution, opposed the U.S. deployment of THAAD, and jointly offered the "freeze for freeze proposal." Russia has recognized China's vital interests in the future of North Korea and has been generally respectful of China's lead role.[40] China and Russia jointly vetoed the UN Security Council action on North Korean human rights in 2014 and issued a joint statement on the North Korean nuclear situation in 2017.[41] Here, too, their positions are not identical. At least until recently, Russia has taken a somewhat stronger anti-proliferation line, driven in part by concerns about horizontal proliferation in the region and the erosion of its role as one of the five "authorized" nuclear powers under the Nuclear Non-Proliferation Treaty. At least until 2014, when North

---

[37] It is noteworthy that on the seventh resolution, where China abstained while Russia vetoed, the vote took place shortly after a meeting between Presidents Trump and Xi. See Lavi and Fainberg, "Russia and China in the Middle East," 52.

[38] In May, China held an international symposium on the prospect of a political settlement of the Syrian issue in Shanghai, which involved a number of international actors, including the special envoys to Syria from the United Nations, UK, and France. There are reports that China has also provided some military training and advice to the Syrian army. See ibid., 63.

[39] See Gilbert Rozman, *The Sino-Russian Challenge to the World Order: National Identities, Bilateral Relations, and East versus West in the 2010s* (Stanford: Stanford University Press, 2014).

[40] For a comprehensive review of Russia's position on North Korea, see Artyom Lukin et al., "Nuclear Weapons and Russia–North Korea Relations," Foreign Policy Research Institute, December 2017, https://www.fpri.org/wp-content/uploads/2017/11/NuclearWeaponsRussiaDPRKDec2017.pdf.

[41] See "Joint Statement by the Russian and Chinese Foreign Ministries on the Korean Peninsula's Problems," July 4, 2017, available at http://www.mid.ru/en/foreign_policy/news/-/asset_publisher/cKNonkJE02Bw/content/id/2807662.

Korean–Russian ties intensified, Russia appeared more willing to support Korean unification under the leadership of Seoul.[42] Ironically, as China began to crack down on North Korea, Russia evolved slightly in the opposite direction as it sought to take advantage of deteriorating Sino–North Korean relations to improve its economic position in the North.

## Net Assessment

### Outlook for Sino-Russian Cooperation

There continues to be a wide range of views about the nature and significance of cooperation between China and Russia. While many see a dramatic change in the scale and importance of their collaboration, especially in the security sphere,[43] others offer a more cautious assessment. Gilbert Rozman, for example, concludes that "Sino-Russian relations may be warm on the outside, tepid on the inside, and chilly underneath."[44] As Richard Weitz argues, "The leaders of both countries view their changed security relationship as a major success that they strive to sustain. Nonetheless, their mutual defense commitments are tenuous and their engagements remain below that found in a traditional military alliance."[45]

It is difficult to know whether the trend to greater Sino-Russian cooperation has natural limits and the current level represents an apex or whether deeper engagement may be possible in the future. Many analysts have identified key remaining barriers, and mutual suspicions continue

---

[42] See Ilya Dyachkov et al., "From Joseph Stalin and Kim Il-sung to Vladimir Putin and Kim Jong-un," in Lukin et al., "Nuclear Weapons and Russia–North Korea Relations."

[43] In his foreword to the 2017 NBR report on Russia-China relations, Robert Sutter notes: "One hundred leading U.S. specialists on Russia and China participating in the NBR project 'Strategic Implications of Russia-China Relations' are in broad agreement on the causes of the challenges that Russia and China pose to the United States. They agree that Sino-Russian relations increasingly undermine U.S. interests and that past views of the relationship as an 'axis of convenience' with little significance for the United States no longer hold." Sutter, "America's Bleak View of Russia-China Relations," 39.

[44] Rozman, *The Sino-Russian Challenge to the World Order*, 266–67. Along the same vein, see Lyle J. Goldstein, "A China-Russia Alliance?" *National Interest*, April 25, 2017, http://nationalinterest.org/feature/china-russia-alliance-20333; and Bobo Lo, *A Wary Embrace: What the China-Russia Relationship Means for the World* (Sydney: Penguin, 2017).

[45] Weitz, "Sino-Russian Security Ties," 28.

to constrain ties.⁴⁶ The two countries compete for political influence and economic leverage in Central Asia, a competition intensified by China's expanding activities under the Belt and Road Initiative. They also have different interests in the Middle East: Russia is motivated by arms sales and access to Mediterranean geopolitical influence, which has led to a de facto alignment with Iran, while China seeks to maintain good ties with all of the region's energy producers.⁴⁷ In addition, there are profound differences in their approach to globalization (which is vital to China's economic development, while Russia remains highly autarchic economically) and transnational challenges such as climate change. Moreover, Russia continues to maintain important political and security ties to potential Chinese adversaries, including Vietnam and India.

Nonetheless, it seems clear that some U.S. policies are driving China and Russia closer together. U.S. support for democracy and human rights in third countries is seen as a direct threat to the leadership of both Russia and China and gives them an incentive to work together. Both see U.S. alliances in Europe and East Asia as an element of a containment strategy. Each challenges U.S. support for neoliberal economic policies on trade and investment in international organizations like the IMF, World Bank, and WTO, and they have worked together to build alternative institutions that do not embrace U.S. values. Both are concerned about Washington's use of extraterritorial legislation, especially third-country sanctions.

But in the end, the key question for U.S. policymakers is not the extent of cooperation per se, but rather how problematic is the current and potentially even greater future Sino-Russian partnership for U.S. interests? More specifically, is the United States worse off if China and Russia are working together or in parallel? To answer this question, it is important to go beyond the simple enumeration of where they are acting in concert to assess whether and how their common efforts could adversely impact U.S. interests.

---

⁴⁶ Bolt asserts that "while the Chinese-Russian strategic partnership is substantive and productive, it is based on both dissatisfaction with a U.S.-led world order and very practical considerations. The relationship is not grounded in a shared long-term positive vision of world order, and the conditions that have given rise to the partnership will also limit it and perhaps even erode it in the long term, as seen in disagreements over energy, weapons sales, and Russia's annexation of Crimea." In addition, he states that "the foundations of the Sino-Russian partnership may not be stable for the long term. As China rises in power, its conception of the ideal world order is likely to diverge from Russia's viewpoint." One of the potential sources of friction in the partnership may arise over a competition for influence in Central Asia. Bolt, "Sino-Russian Relations in a Changing World Order," 49, 52.

⁴⁷ Sutter, "America's Bleak View of Russia-China Relations," 42.

## The Impact of Sino-Russian Cooperation on U.S. Interests

There are a number of ways that Sino-Russian cooperation might harm U.S. interests: by enhancing their mutual capabilities, emboldening them to act knowing they will have each other's support, enhancing the perceived legitimacy of their "alternative" world order in the eyes of third countries, and reducing the United States' ability to influence their policies (through sanctions, for example).

*Capabilities.* One way in which Sino-Russian cooperation might affect the United States would be by increasing their mutual capabilities to harm U.S. interests. After all, one of the key arguments for alliances is that combining forces makes the alliance stronger than the sum of individual parts. On an operational level, it is challenging to imagine circumstances in which the two countries would fight together against the United States—for example, China participating in a Russian invasion of the Baltics, or Russia engaging in naval operations in the South or East China Sea.[48] It is also true that China's military capability has been enhanced by arms and technology transfers from Russia.[49] However, as China improves its own technological capabilities (both military and civilian), the value of this is likely to wane significantly in the relatively near future. Intelligence sharing is another area where cooperation could enhance mutual capabilities against the United States, especially to the extent (which seems plausible) that Chinese and Russian intelligence assets are complementary rather than duplicative.[50]

*Emboldenment.* Another reason the United States might fear a deeper partnership is the idea that each country might be emboldened to act more forcefully against the United States because it can count on the backing of the other. China might not send volunteers to Eastern Ukraine or Syria, but it can still back Russia politically in international forums like the United Nations. Similarly, China might be more willing to aid Iran or North Korea knowing that its actions might be supported by Russia. Each side clearly takes comfort in numbers (for example, in their mutual efforts in the

---

[48] Weitz contends that "despite closer security ties, it is unlikely that there will be a scenario where a combined Sino-Russian fleet engages in joint military action." See Weitz, "Sino-Russian Security Ties," 34. Some, however, have suggested that Sino-Russian rapprochement provides a "secure rear area," which allows each to concentrate its full capabilities against the United States. For further discussion, see Weitz, "Sino-Russian Security Ties," 33.

[49] See ibid., 28.

[50] To date, there is no publicly available evidence that the two countries are sharing military or political intelligence directed against the United States, though the two participate in antiterrorism intelligence sharing with others under the aegis of the SCO and other organizations. See Shubhajit Roy, "Intel Chiefs of Russia, China, Iran and Pakistan Discuss IS Threat," *Indian Express*, July 12, 2018, https://indianexpress.com/article/india/intel-chiefs-of-russia-china-iran-and-pakistan-discuss-is-threat-5255825.

UN Human Rights Council), but it is difficult to assess how much this might affect decision-making. We have seen in recent U.S. history, both under President George W. Bush and President Trump, that the fear of political isolation has not necessarily been a brake on U.S. action, especially where the U.S. interests at stake are high and there is domestic support. Russia's actions in Georgia and Ukraine demonstrate a similar willingness to act despite a lack of international support, including from China.

To the extent that the two countries see their partnership as "strategic," they may be prepared to support each other even when their interests diverge, as well as when, in the absence of the partnership, one or the other might abstain or even support the U.S. view (what some might call "backscratching"). China's responses to Russian actions in both Georgia and Crimea are possible examples of this phenomenon: given its strong attachment to sovereignty, China might have been expected to oppose these cross-border interventions. Its reticence to join others in criticizing Russia can be seen as an effort not to antagonize its partner.

*Legitimation.* A number of analysts have suggested that Sino-Russian cooperation in the political realm could enhance the spread of anti-liberal norms, just as Communism provided an alternative model during the Cold War. By working together, China and Russia can block liberal initiatives in existing institutions, create alternative institutions that embody their shared approach, and provide political, economic, and even military support to nondemocratic regimes that resist liberal reforms. As a result of these combined efforts, the credibility and legitimacy of this nonliberal alternative is arguably more convincing than if it were promulgated by either country alone.

*Reduced U.S. leverage.* A related concern is that Sino-Russian cooperation will reduce the United States' leverage to influence Russian and Chinese policies. The most obvious example is in the case of sanctions, where the availability of alternative partners can make a big difference in the efficacy of economic measures. This can be seen in Russia's turn to China to reduce the impact of Western energy sanctions, or China's reliance on Russia to mitigate the post-Tiananmen limits on U.S. arms and technology sales to China. Under what circumstances the availability of an "alternative" might reduce the efficacy of sanctions depends on a number of factors, including the issues at stake and how much of an alternative the other offers. For example, the partnership with Russia does not offer China much relief in cases where sanctions restrict China's access to the U.S. consumer market or international banking system. In a number of important cases such as human rights and democracy, experience shows that even in the face of strong U.S. economic pressure, China and Russia are extremely unlikely to change their approach, whether or not they have each other as an alternative.

## *Most Likely Future Scenarios and the Bottom Line*

Sino-Russian cooperation is primarily driven by both countries' interest in promoting an international order that is conducive to the survival of their authoritarian, economically mercantilist regimes and thus is deeply rooted in their national strategies. Putin and Xi command strong domestic support, and to the extent that this support continues, their cooperation is likely to continue. At the same time, the growing asymmetry of power (both military and economic), differences in their level of engagement in the global economy, and persistent tensions in their interests in Central Asia, the Middle East, and the Russian Far East suggest limits to the further development of Sino-Russian cooperation. In particular a formal military or political alliance is unlikely. China and Russia will continue to coordinate their positions in existing international institutions, but the alternatives they have promoted are unlikely to gain much more traction, given the many other countries (the European Union, India, Japan, and Australia, for example) that will be reluctant to abandon current organizations in favor of those dominated by China and Russia.

There are three kinds of developments that might alter this scenario. First, despite the strengths of the current regimes, both face serious domestic problems. A significant change to the current system is conceivable in both countries, which would have a profound effect on their cooperation. Second, if U.S. policy were to become more willing to accommodate Russia's or China's security and political interests (such as by abandoning support for democracy or conceding regional spheres of influence), this would weaken the rationale for their cooperation, which would have achieved the goals it was designed to achieve. Although there appears to be some support for this approach from President Trump, bipartisan congressional opposition makes this scenario less likely. Finally, the United States could adopt a more determined "regime change" strategy toward both countries, which would drive them even closer together, to include the possibility of a defensive military alliance.

The most likely scenario suggests that the Sino-Russian partnership will make it somewhat harder for the United States to achieve its goals. In most cases, however, the problems would arise whether or not the two countries were cooperating (or working in parallel), and thus the effect of their cooperation is on the margin. Put another way, in deciding to pursue policies that are inconsistent with U.S. interests, neither China nor Russia is influenced significantly by the support (or the absence of support) from the other. Nonetheless, in a number of areas both countries are pursuing similar policies opposed to the United States (either in cooperation or in parallel), which makes the achievement of U.S. goals somewhat more difficult. For this reason, it is important to explore what, if anything, the United States can do.

## Policy Options

Analysts have suggested a number of strategies to put a brake on or even reverse the trend toward increasing cooperation between China and Russia. Ian Bond has suggested four possibilities: (1) oppose both Russia and China, (2) oppose China and seek a partnership with Russia, (3) oppose Russia and seek a partnership with China, and (4) seek partnerships with both Russia and China.[51] The first option is similar to the approach presented in the Trump administration's National Security Strategy.[52] Edward Luttwak and (and to some extent) former U.S. ambassador to China Stapleton Roy propose the second, while Bond himself advocates for the third choice. Bobo Lo's prescription tracks the fourth option.

The Trump National Security Strategy sees China and Russia as presenting a common challenge: "China and Russia want to shape a world antithetical to U.S. values and interests."[53] While not fully ruling out the possibility of cooperation, the strategy focuses on measures that the United States should take to counter each country across the full range of security, economic, and political realms.

Luttwak makes a classic balance-of-power argument: "In the 1970s, the United States embraced China to offset the Soviet power upsurge.

---

[51] Ian Bond, "Russia and China: Partners of Choice and Necessity?" Centre for European Reform, December 2016, https://www.cer.eu/publications/archive/report/2016/russia-and-china-partners-choice-and-necessity.

[52] White House, *National Security Strategy of the United States of America* (Washington, D.C., 2017), https://www.whitehouse.gov/wp-content/uploads/2017/12/NSS-Final-12-18-2017-0905.pdf. Whether this reflects the "authentic Trump" is open to debate. See Lawrence Freedman, "Authentic Trump versus the Trump Administration: Donald Trump as Foreign Policy Disrupter," H-Diplo, ISSF, July 3, 2018, https://issforum.org/roundtables/policy/1-5bh-authentic.

[53] White House, *National Security Strategy of the United States of America*, 25. The report argues that "China and Russia challenge American power, influence, and interests, attempting to erode American security and prosperity....These competitions require the United States to rethink the policies of the past two decades—policies based on the assumption that engagement with rivals and their inclusion in international institutions and global commerce would turn them into benign actors and trustworthy partners. For the most part, this premise turned out to be false." Ibid., 2–3.

Now, Trump should do the opposite: Focus U.S. strength against an increasingly militaristic China, and enlist Russia in that effort. It is Geopolitics 101 not to confront both countries at the same time, and Russia is clearly less of a threat to the United States."[54] Roy argues that U.S. policy in Eastern Europe has played a central role in fostering Sino-Russian cooperation ("an avoidable confrontation whose consequences drove Russia into the arms of China") and that China now occupies the privileged position of having better relations with both Russia and the United States than they have with each other.[55] He further argues that the United States can and should redress this balance: "To the extent that Western actions in Europe partly explain the current unnaturally close alignment between Moscow and Beijing, then easing tensions between the West and Russia in Europe could help restore a more normal and limited pattern of cooperation between Russia and China."[56]

In contrast, Bond's argument for "tilting" toward China is based on an assessment that Russia poses the greater threat to the United States and its allies: "China may be revisionist in the sense of wanting a stronger position on the global chess board, but it has shown less inclination than Russia to tip over the board entirely."[57] Bobo Lo offers a different strategy, suggesting that the United States show more deference to both countries: "it is vitally important to treat China and Russia as individual great powers."[58]

Rather than favor China or Russia, some have proposed as a fifth alternative that the United States might seek to drive a wedge between the two countries by siding with one where their interests diverge or by casting doubt on the reliability of the other as a partner, perhaps building on the inherent

---

[54] See Edward N. Luttwak, "5. Play Russia Against China," in "6 Out-of-the-Box Ideas for Trump," *Politico Magazine*, January/February 2017, https://www.politico.com/magazine/story/2017/01/outside-the-box-ideas-policies-president-trump-administration-214661.

[55] J. Stapleton Roy, "Sino-Russian Relations in a Global Context: Implications for the United States," in "Russia-China Relations," 40.

[56] Roy also argues that tensions between the United States and Russia are "diverting scarce U.S. resources away from the western Pacific, where China has assumed the role of the United States' major strategic competitor." Roy, "Sino-Russian Relations in a Global Context," 48. In addition to advocating a new approach to Russia on Ukraine/Eastern Europe, Roy also recommends restoring confidence in U.S. engagement and leadership in fostering strategic stability. Ibid., 49.

[57] The idea of a strategic "tilt" implies a decision to favor one side irrespective of the merits of the particular issue in question. The concept gained fame through Kissinger's advocacy of a tilt toward Pakistan in managing U.S. relations in South Asia. For contrasting views of the Nixon/Kissinger strategy toward South Asia in the early 1970s, compare Gary J. Bass, *The Blood Telegram: Nixon, Kissinger and a Forgotten Genocide* (New York: Alfred A. Knopf, 2013) with Robert Blackwill, "In Defense of Kissinger," *National Interest*, January 2, 2014. https://nationalinterest.org/article/defense-kissinger-9642?page=0%2C1.

[58] Lo, *A Wary Embrace*, 76.

tensions and suspicions in their bilateral relationship.[59] Weitz has sketched out how this option might be implemented in his chapter for this volume.

## Can Any of These Options Work?

Do any of these strategies have a reasonable chance of success? After all, the split between China and Russia during the Cold War was not a product of U.S. policy; rather, the United States was able to take advantage of underlying differences between the two Communist powers. Today, the opposite is true. Most analysts argue that shared interests, at least as much as if not more than U.S. policy, are the critical factor in the rapid improvement in Sino-Russian relations.[60] Even to the extent that U.S. policy does contribute to Sino-Russian cooperation, there are reasons to question whether the United States could succeed at a self-conscious strategy designed to slow down or reverse this trend. As several regional experts have argued, "an attempt…to drive a wedge between Russia and China would be so transparent as to be understood by Moscow and Beijing for what it is—a clumsy geopolitical ploy."[61]

Success in improving bilateral ties with either China or Russia—for example, by accommodating them on important issues such as Ukraine or the South China Sea—might produce benefits, but this would not necessarily lead to reduced cooperation. These accommodative moves might simply be pocketed by one or both countries, or even used as leverage to achieve objectives in their bilateral relationship with each other. For example, a more accommodative stance by the United States on Russian energy exports to Europe might simply allow Russia to extract a higher price for gas from China. As Eugene Rumer notes, "the unintended consequences of outreach to Russia.…could enable Russia to engage in its own geopolitical maneuvering in the European theater while doing little to weaken China."[62] He goes on to argue that "a renewed partnership is unlikely to result in Russia being willing to forgo its close relations with China and side with the

---

[59] For example, during the Cold War, the Nixon and Ford administrations' pursuit of détente and arms control with Moscow created uncertainties among China's leaders about the reliability of U.S. opposition to the Soviet Union.

[60] Offering a Russian perspective, for example, Alexander Lukin writes that "the Sino-Russian rapprochement is a natural result of broader changes taking place in world politics, while the U.S. policy hostile to both countries has had the effect of accelerating that process." Alexander Lukin, "A Russian Perspective on the Sino-Russian Rapprochement," *Asia Policy* 13, no. 1 (2018): 19. For a more comprehensive statement of the argument, see Alexander Lukin, *China and Russia: The New Rapprochement* (Cambridge: Polity Press, 2018).

[61] Eugene B. Rumer, "Russia's China Policy: This Bear Hug Is Real," in "Russia-China Relations," 15, 22.

[62] Ibid., 13.

United States, should the Trump administration challenge Beijing's position on Taiwan, trade, the disputes in the South China Sea, or North Korea—the major issues identified by the new team as its priorities with China."[63]

To address this risk, the United States could try to condition improvement in Russian-U.S. or Sino-U.S. relations on distancing from the other partner. For example, Weitz suggests that the United States might condition sanctions relief for Russia on restraining arms sales to China.[64] But such conditionality would be hard to specify (what would the United States ask either China or Russia to stop doing with each other?) and even harder to enforce. Moreover, the effort might simply accelerate China's already strong determination to improve its indigenous capabilities. To have any chance of success, the conditional inducement that the United States would need to offer would have to outweigh the benefit of cooperation. This leads to the core question: what price would the United States need to pay and is the benefit worth it?

## *Is It Worth It?*

Given the many positive factors that are driving Russia and China together, a strategy designed to thwart their cooperation against the United States faces a dilemma. Small accommodations are unlikely to affect either country's calculus, while the larger ones that might—such as concessions on support for democracy, human rights and the rule of law, alliances in Europe and East Asia, and the liberal economic order—would require a fundamental rethinking of U.S. national strategy.[65]

Would the United States be better off if it were to modify these policies—or to put it more sharply, to accede to Russia's and China's preferred views on these questions? Throughout U.S. history there have been those who have argued that the United States would be better served by an approach to international relations based solely on considerations of balance of power, a Palmerstonian view that "we have no eternal allies, and

---

[63] Rumer, "Russia's China Policy," 22.

[64] See Weitz, "Sino-Russian Security Ties," 36. This would probably require at least the acquiescence, if not approval, of Congress, which thus far has set strict conditions for sanctions relief.

[65] Others have noted the potentially high price that the United States would need to be pay to lessen Sino-Russian cooperation: "A change in Russian arms sales policy toward China would require major shifts in the U.S. defense posture—such as abandoning missile defense programs in Europe and Asia—that would be highly improbable under any U.S. administration, no matter how favorably inclined toward Russia." Rumer, "Russia's China Policy," 25.

we have no perpetual enemies. Our interests are eternal and perpetual."[66] Up until now those arguments have failed to carry the day, not only because that is not "who we are"[67] but because we have learned that the United States' greatest strengths derive precisely from the principled grounding of our leadership.

Nonetheless, there are elements of the Trump administration's approach that would suggest that President Trump thinks the answer is yes. This perspective was on full display in the president's address to the UN General Assembly, where he argued that respect for national sovereignty is at the core of international stability, implicitly accepting that the United States was prepared to mute its call for domestic political reform in return for better state-to-state relations.[68] But this view is at odds with the administration's own National Security Strategy, which sees relations between the United States and the other two powers not simply in great-power terms but as a contest over the nature of the international order.

Although Sino-Russian cooperation certainly complicates the U.S. calculus, there is little reason to believe that a strategy whose *raison d'être* is designed to reduce their cooperation would really benefit the United States. Such an approach risks the worst of both worlds—a strategy that fails to derail cooperation between China and Russia while sacrificing core U.S. values and interests. Indeed, to adopt such a strategy would be a vindication of their strategy, as the threat of cooperation would be seen as a successful ploy to force the United States to modify its course.

## What Then Is to Be Done?

Rather than seeking a way to discourage Sino-Russian cooperation, U.S. strategy should focus on how the United States can deal with Russia and China from a position of strength. Policies that might please them—conceding one or both a regional sphere of influence, abandoning U.S. convictions about the universality of fundamental human rights, or acquiescing in a mercantilist international economic order—are precisely those that jeopardize the United States' most precious assets—its allies and

---

[66] This realpolitik view is often attributed to John Quincy Adams, as well to Kissinger, although in both cases it represents an oversimplification of their approach. See John Bew, *Realpolitik: A History* (Oxford: Oxford University Press 2016), especially chap. 15.

[67] See President Barack Obama's farewell speech, January 10, 2017, available at https://www.npr.org/2017/01/10/509137106/watch-live-obama-addresses-the-nation-in-farewell-speech.

[68] "In America, we do not seek to impose our way of life on anyone, but rather to let it shine as an example for everyone to watch." Donald J. Trump (remarks to the 72nd Meeting of the UN General Assembly, New York, September 19, 2017), https://www.whitehouse.gov/briefings-statements/remarks-president-trump-72nd-session-united-nations-general-assembly.

its principles. Rather than prioritizing ways to placate Moscow or Beijing, the United States needs to strengthen its partnerships with those who share its values and interests. If it is looking for others to "accommodate," Washington should focus first on those who will likely reciprocate rather than alienating its natural allies by shortsighted policies of "America first" or "raison d'état." Rejoining the Trans-Pacific Partnership, strengthening the North American Free Trade Agreement, and recommitting to a strong, cohesive NATO and a constructive partnership with the European Union are far more important for meeting the challenge posed by China and Russia, singularly or together. In addition, as so many have observed, the United States should cultivate its domestic strengths—a vibrant open economy that affords opportunity for all, political tolerance, and innovation. By strengthening the appeal at home and abroad of the economic and political order it has helped create since World War II, the United States will be better positioned to counter the alternative narrative offered by China and Russia.

At the same time, there may be areas where seeking to find common ground with Russia or China could reap meaningful benefits, and U.S. policymakers can and should factor that possibility into their decision-making.[69] Just because the United States should not capitulate on core matters of national interest, the country is ill served by a view that sees any understanding between the United States and either Russia or China as a sign of weakness. The National Security Strategy's Manichean view of Russia and China as strategic adversaries not only risks driving the two closer together but also alienates U.S. allies and friends that do not wish to be forced into a binary choice of "with us or against us." Similarly, a strategy that emphasizes U.S. dominance or primacy forecloses any possibility of meaningful cooperation between the United States and either Russia and China and simply reinforces their own felt need to work to counter it.[70] Such an approach is both counterproductive and ultimately unsustainable, likely triggering an arms race and security competition that will make all three countries worse off.

How might the United States better approach relations with China and Russia in a way that lessens their need to work together to counter the United States without sacrificing core U.S. interests? Effectively managing

---

[69] Hans Morgenthau long ago argued that what he called "accommodation" is essential to the stable management of international relations. Hans J. Morgenthau and Kenneth W. Thompson, *Politics Among Nations: The Struggle for Power and Peace*, 6th ed. (New York: Alfred Knopf, 1985), 587.

[70] Ashley J. Tellis and Robert D. Blackwill, *Revising U.S. Grand Strategy toward China* (New York: Council on Foreign Relations Press, 2015), https://www.cfr.org/report/revising-us-grand-strategy-toward-china.

the long-term competition between the United States and both China and Russia requires a selective exercise of power that recognizes that neither China nor Russia will willingly acquiesce to all U.S. preferences, and that the United States' power is not great enough, even with its allies, to insist on its way in all cases. The management of Taiwan over the past four decades reflects the kind of nuanced calculation that is needed. The United States has not acquiesced to China's effort to impose "reunification," but at the same time it has carefully managed sensitive issues such as arms sales and official visits. The Obama administration's effort to address Russian concerns over European theater missile defense is another example. A similar effort could be made vis-à-vis both China and Russia with respect to theater missile defense in Northeast Asia. Economic policy is another area where nuance could be helpful: rather than simply opposing initiatives like the AIIB, on the grounds that they undermine the United States' preferred institutions (the World Bank and Asian Development Bank), Washington could have chosen to work within the new entity to encourage policies consistent with the U.S. worldview. Such an approach, which blends reassurance and resolve in dealing with these two important powers, requires an element of judgement more complex than a simplistic balance-of-power prescription but is likely to prove more successful and sustainable over the long run.

# EXECUTIVE SUMMARY

This chapter provides an overview of the scope and implications of China-Russia relations, explains why Sino-Russian cooperation against U.S. interests has increased during the past decade, assesses key determinants, and examines U.S. policy options.

MAIN ARGUMENT

The preceding chapters in this volume show how the China-Russia relationship continues to deepen and broaden, with ever more negative implications for the U.S. The drivers of Sino-Russian cooperation overshadow the brakes on forward movement at the U.S. expense. This momentum is based on (1) common objectives and values, (2) perceived Russian and Chinese vulnerabilities in the face of U.S. and Western pressures, and (3) perceived opportunities for the two powers to expand their influence at the expense of the U.S. and its allies that are seen as in decline. The current outlook is bleak, offering no easy fixes for the U.S. Nonetheless, there remain limits on Sino-Russian cooperation. The two governments continue to avoid entering a formal alliance or taking substantial risks in support of one another in areas where their interests do not overlap. Longer-term vulnerabilities include Russia's dissatisfaction with its increasing junior status relative to China, China's much stronger interest than Russia in preserving the existing world order, and opposition to Russian and Chinese regional expansion on the part of important lesser powers in Europe and Asia seeking U.S. support.

POLICY IMPLICATIONS
- The chapters of this volume support multiyear and wide-ranging domestic and international strengthening of the U.S. military, economic, and diplomatic position to better situate the U.S. to deal with the challenges from China and Russia.

- The chapters differ on the appropriate amount of strengthening, but all favor various mixes of strengthening and accommodation requiring compromise of U.S. interests.

- Specialists from Russia and China in the NBR China-Russia project, but few others, favor major change in existing U.S. policy to accommodate both Moscow and Beijing.

Chapter 6

# U.S. Policy Opportunities and Options

*Robert Sutter*

The judgments and analysis of this volume are the culmination of a two-year research and policy engagement project conducted by the National Bureau of Asian Research (NBR) on the strategic implications of China's and Russia's advancing relations. The purpose of this concluding chapter is to assess what we have learned regarding policy options and opportunities for the United States that flow from the recent and prospective trajectory of Sino-Russian relations. Such an assessment is complicated and challenging for three reasons.

First, as shown in the chapters written by Richard Weitz and Charles Ziegler in particular, reflecting developments in their respective areas of concern—military relations and economic relations—the partnership between China and Russia has become stronger and multifaceted as it has matured and broadened after the Cold War, with serious negative consequences for U.S. interests. The drivers of cooperation overshadow the brakes on forward movement at the United States' expense. The momentum is based on (1) common objectives and values, (2) perceived Russian and Chinese vulnerabilities in the face of U.S. and Western pressures, and (3) perceived opportunities for the two powers to expand their influence at the expense of U.S. and allied powers that are seen as in decline. The dispositions of Presidents Vladimir Putin and Xi Jinping support forecasts of closer relations over the next five years and probably beyond. The relationship has gone well beyond the common view a decade ago that

---

**ROBERT SUTTER** is Professor of Practice of International Affairs at George Washington University and the principal investigator of the project "Strategic Implications of China-Russia Relations" at the National Bureau of Asian Research (NBR). He can be reached at <sutterr@gwu.edu>.

This chapter is adapted from Robert Sutter, "China-Russia Relations: Strategic Implications and U.S. Policy Options," NBR, NBR Special Report, no. 73, September 2018.

Sino-Russian ties represented an "axis of convenience" with limited impact on U.S. interests.[1]

Russia and China pose increasingly serious challenges to the U.S.-supported order in their respective priority spheres of concern—Russia in Europe and the Middle East, and China in Asia along the country's continental and maritime peripheries. Russia's challenges involve military and paramilitary actions in Europe and the Middle East, along with cyber and political warfare undermining elections in the United States and Europe, European unity, and NATO solidarity. China undermines U.S. and allied resolve through covert and overt manipulation and influence peddling that employs economic incentives and propaganda. Chinese cyberattacks have focused more on massive theft of information and intellectual property to increase China's economic competitiveness and accelerate its efforts to dominate world markets in key advanced technologies at the expense of leading U.S. and other international companies. At the same time, China's coercion and intimidation of its neighbors, backed by an impressive buildup of military and civilian security forces, has expanded its regional control and influence.

Russia and China work both separately and together to complicate and curb U.S. power and influence in the international political, economic, and security realms. They coordinate their moves and support one another in their respective challenges to the United States and its allies and partners in Europe, the Middle East, and Asia. These joint efforts include diplomatic, security, and economic measures in multilateral forums and bilateral relations involving U.S. opponents in Iran, Syria, and North Korea. The two powers further support one another in the face of U.S. and allied complaints about their coercive expansion and other activities to challenge the regional order and global norms and institutions backed by the United States. Their cooperation today is more than an axis of convenience; today they form an axis of significant strategic cooperation.

American specialists involved with the NBR project differ on the importance of Sino-Russian cooperation opposing and undermining U.S. interests. Some focus on the respective problems posed for the United States by Russian and Chinese policies and practices, deeming their cooperation of significantly less concern. In contrast, Richard Ellings's chapter for this volume highlights potential major challenges to the United States posed by the complementarity of Chinese and Russian interests in Asia and Europe,

---

[1] See Bobo Lo, *Axis of Convenience: Moscow, Beijing, and the New Geopolitics* (Washington, D.C.: Brookings Institution Press, 2008).

which in a worst-case scenario could lead to a two-front war. Even short of such a war, there remain major challenges for the United States as it is compelled to divide resources and attention between two theaters, as seen in the concurrent coercive use of military and other state power by Russia in Ukraine and China in the South China Sea.

Overall, the United States' ability to deal with these rising challenges is commonly seen as being in decline. The U.S. position in the triangular relationship among the United States, Russia, and China has deteriorated, to the satisfaction of leaders in Moscow and Beijing opportunistically seeking to advance their power and influence. Russia's tension with the West and ever-deepening dependence on China, in conjunction with Washington's ongoing constructive interaction with Beijing, have given China the advantageous "hinge" position in the triangular relationship that the United States used to occupy.

Second, there are significant disagreements among specialists regarding the nature of the problem and what should be done. Russian and Chinese specialists generally argue in favor of U.S. actions to accommodate Russia and China and thereby create a more positive U.S. relationship with these powers. In contrast, the main recommended U.S. policy option for most of the experts from the United States and allied countries involves multiyear and wide-ranging plans to strengthen the United States—militarily, economically, and diplomatically—to better position it domestically and internationally to deal with the China-Russia challenges.

Nonetheless, U.S. specialists differ regarding the importance and negative impact of Sino-Russian cooperation for U.S. interests. In this volume, James Steinberg sees the respective challenges of China and Russia to U.S. interests as very important, but he judges that "in deciding to pursue policies that are inconsistent with U.S. interests, neither China nor Russia is influenced significantly by the support (or the absence of support) from the other." In contrast, Ellings asks whether a "full Sino-Russian alliance" can be prevented and argues that "the details of China-Russia strategic cooperation matter enormously."

For this and other reasons, while supporting U.S. strengthening, participants in the NBR project differ on the appropriate amount of strengthening, with some urging the United States to pursue sustained primacy and most others favoring various mixes of strengthening and accommodation requiring the compromise of U.S. interests. In determining the appropriate amount of strengthening and accommodation to apply, project participants exhibit the following spectrum of views:

- Some project participants view Russia as the leading danger, warranting U.S. accommodation of China to counter Russia.
- Others seek to work cooperatively with Russia against China, seen as a more powerful longer-term threat.
- Others view the above maneuvers as futile in the face of strongly converging Sino-Russian interests and identities.
- As noted above, Russian and Chinese specialists, but few others, favor major changes in existing U.S. policy in order to accommodate both Moscow and Beijing.

In the main, the authors in this volume favor U.S. strengthening but avoid taking sides between China and Russia, apart from Ellings, who urges U.S. policymakers to interact quite firmly but pragmatically with Russia in seeking closer ties in the face of a rising China.

Third, significantly adding to the complexity of the situation in contemporary U.S.-China-Russia relations is the uncertainty as to whether the avowedly unpredictable President Donald Trump will follow his administration's declared national security strategy that opposes adverse and predatory behavior by China and Russia or adopt more accommodating approaches in line with his repeated expressions of respect and support for both countries' leaders.[2] Thus, as is discussed below, in laying out specific options for U.S. policy toward Russia and China, the NBR project findings and the analysis of this volume differ from other authoritative studies. The reason is that, unlike these other studies, they see the United States not as a constant among variables—notably, an actor assumed as able and willing to employ the recommendations offered by the project. Rather, U.S. policy and behavior are viewed as a major uncertain variable affecting international dynamics, notably including the China-Russia relationship.

## Context for Current U.S. Policy: Consensus on Five Policy Judgments

To provide a proper frame of reference for the discussion on U.S. policy options and opportunities below, this section explains five general points of agreement among the NBR project experts from countries other than Russia and China concerning U.S. policy opportunities and choices for dealing with

---

[2] White House, *National Security Strategy of the United States of America* (Washington, D.C., 2017), https://www.whitehouse.gov/wp-content/uploads/2017/12/NSS-Final-12-18-2017-0905.pdf.

the adverse strategic implications of China-Russia relations for U.S. interests. Those five general points are supported by the assessments in the chapters of this volume.[3]

*Pursue strengthening and consider alternative policy choices amid international and domestic uncertainty.* The broad recommendations in the NBR project for dealing with the negative strategic implications of China-Russia relations for the United States are in line with the recommendations of other authoritative studies in calling for wide-ranging efforts by the United States to strengthen its economic, military, and diplomatic power and influence.[4] The goal is to create a more favorable balance of power supporting the U.S.-backed international order now challenged by Chinese and Russian actions. Building national power at home and abroad requires greater domestic cohesion and less partisan discord and government gridlock. Strategies employed need to be realistic and effectively implemented. However, in laying out specific options for U.S. policy toward China and Russia, the NBR project differs from other authoritative studies, as noted above, in treating U.S. policy and behavior as an uncertain rather than a constant variable.

*Recognize that there are no easy fixes.* None of the chapters in this volume offers easy fixes for U.S. difficulties resulting from China-Russia cooperation. There is general agreement among the experts participating in the NBR project that the problems posed by Sino-Russian relations are big and that there are no quick solutions. To fix them will require prolonged whole-of-government approaches that are difficult for U.S. policymakers to carry out amid many high-profile distractions at home and abroad. Such large-scale U.S. government foreign policy approaches often involve extensive publicity used to rally domestic and international support for the new effort against the perceived foreign danger or threat. Unless carefully managed by the U.S. administration, such publicity is seen negatively by some participants in the

---

[3] The very different Chinese and Russian experts' perspectives will be treated in a separate forthcoming NBR publication.

[4] Major studies include Julianne Smith, "A Transatlantic Strategy for Russia," Carnegie Endowment for International Peace and Chicago Council on Global Affairs, 2016; Angela Stent, "Russia, China and the West after Crimea," Transatlantic Academy, 2016; Lisa Sawyer Samp et al., *Recalibrating U.S. Strategy toward Russia: A New Time for Choosing* (Washington, D.C.: Center for Strategic and International Studies, 2017); Eugene Rumer, Richard Sokolsky, and Andrew Weiss, "Guiding Principles of a Sustainable U.S. Policy toward Russia, Ukraine, and Eurasia: Key Judgments from a Joint Task Force," Carnegie Endowment for International Peace and Chicago Council on Global Affairs, Policy Outlook, February 2017; Julianne Smith and Adam Twardowski, "The Future of U.S.-Russia Relations," Center for a New American Security, January 2017; Ashley J. Tellis and Robert D. Blackwill, *Revising U.S. Grand Strategy toward China* (New York: Council on Foreign Relations Press, 2015); Orville Schell and Susan Shirk, "U.S. Policy toward China: Recommendations for a New Administration," *Asia Society*, February 2017; and Bobo Lo, *A Wary Embrace* (Sydney: Penguin, 2017).

NBR project as more likely than not to feed Chinese and Russian perceptions of the United States as a weak opponent—an angst-ridden, declining power seeking in vain to reassert its previous dominance. In sum, it is difficult for the U.S. government to carry out strengthening strategies effectively over time in a low-key and resolved manner reflecting confidence and assurance.

*Avoid counterproductive tactical moves.* U.S. policymakers choosing between confrontational and accommodating policy choices in relations with China and Russia need to do so with awareness of how such moves affect the longer-term objective of strengthening the United States nationally and internationally and possibly other goals sought by U.S. policymakers. For example, as argued by Steinberg in this volume, accommodation of China or Russia to expand the United States' room for maneuver or other tactical benefits could be counterproductive by weakening domestic resolve and the resolve of U.S. allies and partners. Similarly, specialists from Russia and China are correct in arguing that applying greater U.S. pressure and tougher measures toward either power also could be troublesome. The results might not be in line with domestic interests and those of U.S. international supporters. Meanwhile, Weitz and Ziegler show limited advantage for the United States in maneuvering tactically between China and Russia in those authors' respective areas of concern—military relations and economic relations.

*Play the long game by targeting vulnerabilities in the China-Russia relationship.* Those authors in the volume proposing options see a low likelihood of quick success through specific moves toward Russia and China. The NBR project participants generally recommend that U.S. policymakers play a long game in seeking to exploit vulnerabilities in Sino-Russian collaboration. As discussed in the chapters in this volume by Weitz, Ziegler, and Steinberg, areas of China-Russia cooperation that show little susceptibility to being influenced by U.S. policy include arms sales, some aspects of Russian energy exports to China, and some aspects of the U.S.-led international order that Beijing and Moscow seek to change. More promising issues warranting U.S. attention and possible exploitation involve the very different standing that China and Russia have with the United States and the asymmetry in their respective worldviews and international ambitions.

For example, as illustrated in the chapters in this volume, as well as in the interim reports from the NBR project, because Russia is an avowed opponent of the United States on various key issues bilaterally and in regard to the U.S.-led international order, U.S.-Russian relations have declined to the lowest point since the Cold War. Whatever positive cooperative elements in the relationship remain are fully overshadowed by differences and disputes. In contrast, China benefits much more from stable relations with the United States and the existing U.S.-led international order. As Steinberg and others make clear, although China's disputes with the United States have been growing in recent years, they have not yet reached a stage of overshadowing Chinese interests in sustaining a good working relationship. Such calculations persuaded some participants in the NBR project to favor the United States working cooperatively with China to seek an advantage against Russia.

However, Ellings in this volume and some other participants in the NBR project see China as the greater threat—not only to the United States but also eventually to Russia. Asymmetries in the Sino-Russian relationship make Russia more dependent on China and more distant from re-establishing its great-power status. Against this background, some argue that the United States should seek cooperation with Russia in order to offset the common danger posed by China's rise.

Another promising vulnerability in China-Russia relations involves their respective coercive strategies in pursuit of regional leadership at the expense of neighboring powers. The countries' goals are at odds with the core interests of most of their neighbors. Taken together, Beijing and Moscow favor the fragmentation of NATO, the European Union, the U.S. alliance structure in Asia, and regional groupings led by ASEAN and other organizations that impinge on Chinese or Russian ambitions. The United States opposes coercive changes to the status quo and supports existing boundaries, stronger regional collective security, and the sovereignty and aspirations of all states in accordance with international norms. As seen in project deliberations and an interim report featuring experts from Europe, Japan, and South Korea, a strong United States provides a welcome counterweight for Asian and European nations affected by Chinese and Russian ambitions.[5] Meanwhile, U.S. contributions to the capabilities and resolve of neighboring states can be justified on their own merits without direct reference to China or Russia. As Weitz recommends, such steps provide a significant outlet for U.S.-backed strengthening against adverse Chinese and Russian practices that nonetheless is less directly confrontational than the application of U.S. power against China or Russia.

*Consider China and Russia together as well as separately.* Most recommendations from other authoritative studies of U.S. policy dealing with China and Russia focus on one or the other country but not the two

---

[5] Shoichi Itoh et al., "Japan and the Sino-Russian Entente: The Future of Major-Power Relations in Northeast Asia," NBR, NBR Special Report, no. 64, April 2017.

together. And, as noted above, there is disagreement among NBR project experts on the actual importance of Sino-Russian cooperation against U.S. interests. Nevertheless, overall the NBR project finds the recommendations of other authoritative studies to be useful but contends that they need to be incorporated with recommendations looking at China and Russia together in order to fully address the implications of their relationship for U.S. interests.

- One cannot discern appropriate U.S. policy toward China and Russia without careful consideration of the main differences between the two that can be used by U.S. policy.
- U.S. policy that does not deal with China-Russia cooperation risks ineffectiveness in the face of the two countries' actions together reinforcing their respective challenges to the United States. It also risks reinforcing the perception that the United States is passive and declining in the face of Sino-Russian advances.
- The different standing that Russia and China have in their relations with the United States means that U.S. policy needs to be tailored to both at the same time in ways that avoid worsening the United States' overall position. For instance, if Trump were to make significant compromises with Putin as the United States pursues a trade war to put major economic pressure on China, Putin might see these compromises as tactical ploys to increase pressure on China with little lasting benefit for Russian interests. Steinberg warns against what he sees as ill-advised efforts by some in the Trump administration to accommodate Russia in seeking an advantage for the United States against China.
- Assessing U.S. policy toward both powers facilitates the difficult task of determining with greater accuracy what the trade-offs are for the United States as it seeks an advantage in moving forward with changes in U.S. policy toward one power or the other. Ellings acknowledges that his interest in pursuing a firm but more pragmatic U.S. approach toward Russia that seeks possible common ground against China is tempered by the possibility of Moscow or Beijing exploiting unwarranted U.S. flexibility and accommodation of Russia.

## U.S. Policy Opportunities and Options

The policy options and their opportunities for U.S. interests explained below start with a choice about whether the United States should seek accommodation of China and Russia. This option is not highlighted in this volume and generally is not favored by the participants in the NBR project, with the exception of specialists from those countries. The discussion then moves to examine three policy choices involving varying degrees of U.S. strengthening in opposition to Chinese and Russian challenges and U.S. accommodation of China and Russia. Those three options are:

- U.S. strengthening to oppose both China and Russia, an approach favored by most authors in this volume
- Applying U.S. strengthening and accommodation in seeking better relations with China for an advantage against Russia
- Applying U.S. strengthening and accommodation in seeking better relations with Russia for an advantage against China, an approach favored by Ellings and in varying degrees others in the project, including this author, who sees China as a much more dangerous challenger to the United States than Russia

Favoring the first of the above three options are the majority of NBR project experts. This includes those few favoring sustained U.S. global primacy; many more, including the authors in this volume, who support pursuing rivalry with Russia and China through a mix of strengthening and accommodation; and those who see U.S. attempts to divide Russia and China and gain an advantage by accommodating one and pressuring the other as futile. Most volume authors avoid explicit views on this judgment of futility, though Steinberg leans in this direction when he considers U.S. efforts to seek an advantage by accommodating Russia or China on core interests.

## *Accommodation to Meet Russia and China Halfway*

Russian and Chinese leaders voice support for this policy choice. This choice also is supported by some U.S. specialists but enjoyed little support during the project deliberations apart from Chinese and Russian participants.[6] The choice involves U.S. actions reducing both existing sanctions on Russia and military, economic, and political pressures on Russia and China (such as military deployments and surveillance in Asia and Europe, trade and investment restrictions, and criticism of human rights conditions) as means to improve relations and ease tensions.

---

[6] Examples of U.S. scholars supporting this option include Lyle J. Goldstein, "Is It Time to Meet China Halfway?" *National Interest*, May 12, 2015; Michael Swaine, "Creating a Stable Asia: An Agenda for a U.S.-China Balance of Power," Carnegie Endowment for International Peace, 2016; and Artyom Lukin and Rensselaer Lee, "U.S. and Russia: A Pacific Reconciliation?" Australian Institute of International Affairs, October 28, 2016.

The benefit of accommodation is that it avoids costly military and other strengthening, eases tensions with Russia and China, is seen as reducing the chance of conflict, allows the United States to conform peacefully to a new international order featuring a rising China and resurgent Russia, and permits the United States to focus more on various domestic problems. Russia and China would be outwardly supportive and presumably find that this policy choice meets their current goals.

One drawback of accommodation is that it would likely be seen in the United States and elsewhere as poorly timed, coming amid growing Sino-Russian challenges to U.S. interests in Europe, the Middle East, and Asia, as well as in international economics, politics, and security, and would add to the perception of U.S. weakness and decline that prompts these challenges. Accommodation also risks being viewed domestically as "appeasement," which is not favored by most Americans and certainly not by Republican leaders in Congress. Finally, it could undermine U.S. alliances and emerging partnerships with key nonaligned powers (e.g., India, Egypt, and Vietnam).

### *Strengthening to Sustain U.S. Primacy*

The majority of experts participating in the NBR project recommend that the United States give top priority to sustaining its position as the world's leading power, especially military power, which supports a vibrant U.S.-led international order favorable to U.S. interests. As seen in an interim project publication, this policy choice involves facing directly the many challenges posed by China and Russia and mobilizing international partners and domestic resources in a coherent strategy to deter further challenges, deal with existing ones, and exploit Sino-Russian differences—all from a position of greater strategic strength.[7] A military buildup and international economic activism would accompany improved U.S. domestic governance, economic growth, social cohesion, diplomatic activism, and international attraction—i.e., soft power.

One advantage of this policy choice is its broad domestic political support. It echoes the "preserve peace through strength" theme highlighted in the Trump administration's National Security Strategy and National

---

[7] Michael S. Chase et al., "Russia-China Relations: Assessing Common Ground and Strategic," NBR, NBR Special Report, no. 66, July 2017.

Defense Strategy[8] and is widely supported by congressional Republican leaders, the Republican Party platform, and many defense-minded Democrats. The reported parochialism of the rank-and-file Republican Party members known as the "base," who strongly support President Trump, does not seem to apply to important national security threats. This influential contingent in the party seems to support more rather than fewer resources for defense at home and abroad, according to President Trump and his close associates.[9] Allies and partners would be reassured by the United States' demonstrated willingness to bear the costs and risks of this version of U.S. leadership. China and Russia would be put on guard and perhaps would need to recalibrate their challenges to U.S. interests and their perception of U.S. decline, leading to greater moderation on the part of Moscow and Beijing.

However, the costs of this effort are very high, thus tempering wholehearted support for this option. One does not easily move from a 280-ship navy to President Trump's endorsed 350-ship navy without spending enormous resources. This option will face major budget hurdles involving the Budget Control Act and deficit financing not supported by some leading Republicans. The costs may require political compromises opposed by some in the Republican majority in Congress in order to accommodate Democrats and thereby reach a budget arrangement allowing for substantial and sustained increased outlays for military and other involvement for years to come. Administration and congressional leaders seeking greater burden-sharing by allies and partners may find those states continuing to free ride under the umbrella of resurgent U.S. protection. Meanwhile, the objective of primacy appears unrealistic to those Americans who judge that the United States cannot stop China's rise, Russian resurgence, or the numerous international challenges caused by Iran, Syria, ISIS, and North Korea. This policy choice also risks driving Russia and China closer together against the United States.

## *Mixing Strengthening and Accommodation*

Most experts in the NBR project, including to varying degrees the authors in this volume, favor the United States adopting a variety of

---

[8] White House, *National Security Strategy of the United States of America*, 4; and U.S. Department of Defense, "Summary of the 2018 National Defense Strategy of the United States of America: Sharpening the American Military's Competitive Edge," January 2018, 1, https://dod.defense.gov/Portals/1/Documents/pubs/2018-National-Defense-Strategy-Summary.pdf?mod=article_inline.

[9] Jake Novak, "President Trump's Military Parade Plan Is a Brilliant Political Move," CNBC, February 8, 2018, https://www.cnbc.com/2018/02/08/trumps-military-parade-plan-is-a-brilliant-move.html.

initiatives that meet the interests of Russia and China while at the same time endeavoring to engage in domestic and international efforts to strengthen the U.S. position in the world balance of power amid rivalry and competition with these two states. The positive initiatives could involve gestures to advance common ground and ease sanctions and other economic, military, and diplomatic pressures as means to manage tensions and possibly improve relations. For example, the United States could seek greater cooperation with Russia over the conflicts in Syria, issues in the Arctic, and nuclear arms control. Much more extensive is the potential for the United States to expand common ground with China through various political, economic, and security initiatives. Examples include cooperating on North Korea, reducing U.S. surveillance flights near China, and easing U.S. restrictions on Chinese investment in the United States. Meanwhile, both Russia and China have more important interests in Central Asia than does the United States. By supporting each power's peaceful efforts to expand its interests in Central Asia, the United States could show goodwill and ease tension with both powers. The above positive U.S. steps would be carried out as the United States concurrently implements domestic and international strengthening measures to counter challenges posed by the two countries.

The advantage of an approach that includes accommodation is that it could help avoid conflict as the United States strengthens against Russia and China. On the one hand, it would reduce the large costs in emphasis on strengthening without concurrent positive moves toward Russia and China. On the other hand, it would diminish the chance that allies and partners would be upset as accommodation is accompanied by a reassuring strengthening of U.S. commitments to its allies and partners. Moscow and Beijing would likely remain wary of U.S. intentions but receptive to positive initiatives. Moreover, this policy choice could keep Russia and China on the defensive and off balance, perhaps encouraging both countries to exercise caution as they discern U.S. strength, weakness, and resolve. It also could result in more fluidity in Russia's and China's relations with the United States and one another, possibly providing more opportunities for the United States to exploit differences between them.

One drawback of accommodation is that Russia and China could focus on the U.S. strengthening against them and dismiss the positive initiatives, risking greater tension and costs by driving the two countries closer together in working against U.S. interests. Another risk is that Russia and China could become stronger as a result of the United States easing sanctions and investment restrictions. Possibly viewing the accommodations as signs of weakness, they could use their added strength to double down on negative pressures and challenges to U.S. interests.

*An example mixing strengthening and accommodation: Amid strengthening, the Trump administration plays down the promotion of human rights, democracy, and U.S. values.* This illustrative policy choice is consistent with the Trump administration's more pragmatic approach to defending American values in international affairs. In particular, the current government has demonstrated to Russia, China, other authoritarian governments, and other states seen as carrying out policies offensive to American views of human rights and democracy promotion that it is much less likely than previous administrations to seek to intervene in the internal affairs of other countries regarding human rights and democracy.

The benefits of such an approach are that it reduces a major incentive for Russia and China to work together or separately against heretofore perceived U.S. efforts at regime change targeting both countries. It also reassures U.S. allies and partners whose policies and practices on human rights and democracy have alienated past U.S. administrations. If accompanied by greater military, economic, and diplomatic strengthening, the new pragmatism on human rights and democracy is less likely to be seen as appeasement.

The drawbacks are that this policy choice still exacts security and economic costs and may prompt unfair burden-sharing among allies and partners. It also sacrifices the political support at home and abroad that comes from the United States promoting its values and could undermine the vision of the world order that has been long defended by the United States.

*An example mixing strengthening and accommodation: The United States avoids both the perceived excess of primacy and the sacrifice of core American interests.* As explained by Steinberg in this volume, this policy choice favors strengthening, views primacy as unrealistic, and avoids accommodation at the expense of key U.S. interests, including American values. Judging that some accommodation will be essential to the stable management of international relations, the United States should be prepared to take steps, consistent with its core interests, to reduce the danger of unwanted rising tensions with both China and Russia as it shores up U.S. leadership. Examples could include sustaining the long-standing *modus vivendi* with China vis-à-vis Taiwan and implementing restraints on U.S. ballistic missile defenses that might undermine Russian and Chinese nuclear deterrence. In addition, as discussed above, the United States could pursue cooperation with Russia on Syria, arms control, and the Arctic as well as with China on North Korea and development in Central Asia and elsewhere.

The potential benefit of this policy choice is prolonged U.S. strengthening while managing tensions without a major sacrifice of U.S. interests. As the United States becomes stronger, it can use selective accommodation as part of its toolkit to foster less contentious U.S. relations with both Russia and China that are advantageous for broader interests of international leadership.

The risk is that Russia and China may focus on U.S. strengthening and dismiss the United States' nuanced approach toward accommodation. Americans seeking primacy may view deference to Chinese and Russian interests involving Taiwan, missile defense, and other issues as ill-advised concessions weakening U.S. options in the protracted contest with Beijing and Moscow.

## Seeking Advantage with Positive and Negative Incentives toward China and Russia[10]

Several participants in the NBR project, including those from China and Russia, remain convinced that the closeness of Chinese and Russian interests and identities makes U.S. efforts to seek an advantage by exploiting Sino-Russian differences unlikely to succeed under foreseeable circumstances. Others disagree and favor one of the following options.

*Tilt toward China and away from Russia.* This policy choice views Russia as the more troublesome of the two powers, and it seeks to isolate the country further by emphasizing the United States' common ground with China while increasing sanctions on Russia. It could involve maintaining strict sanctions and heightening military pressure against Russia while developing more common ground with China on North Korea, easing trade and investment tensions, and showing U.S. support for China's Belt and Road Initiative in Central Asia and other areas near Russia. U.S. energy production could also compete with Russian energy exports to China, and

---

[10] In addition to the main options in this section, another related option supported by two NBR project participants is keeping Russia and China on the defensive and off balance while exploiting perceived differences. This policy choice involves positive and negative incentives. For example, the United States could (1) join China's Belt and Road Initiative, thereby promoting Chinese expansion in Central Asia and adding friction in China's relations with Russia, (2) propose studying intermediate-range ballistic missile deployments in Asia, despite the restrictions of the Intermediate-Range Nuclear Forces (INF) Treaty, as a means to work with Russia to get China to limit its ballistic missiles, thereby adding friction in China-Russia ties, and (3) encourage Japan, India, and Vietnam to expand ties with Russia, concurrent with U.S. strengthening of ties with all three Asian powers to challenge Chinese regional expansion. Such positive steps by the United States toward China or Russia could divide the two countries, reducing their cooperation on issues at odds with U.S. interests. At the same time, supporting China in Asia could alienate Japan and other U.S. allies and partners; weakening the INF Treaty could alienate U.S. allies in Europe as well as Japan; and tactical U.S. moves regarding Russia and China may be seen as signs of weakness, prompting greater challenges from China and Russia to U.S. interests.

in the process keep energy prices down, weakening Russia's economy and complicating Sino-Russian energy cooperation.

The benefit of this policy choice is that it is in line with existing U.S. policy toward Russia. It also provides the opportunity for the United States to privately warn China that common interests are in jeopardy as China collaborates with Russia. The perceived forecast is that Russia would feel more vulnerable and seek more cooperative relations with the United States.

The risk is that this policy choice may not work as forecast; China and Russia may be too close to be divided without more accommodation from the United States. Meanwhile, Russia may be prompted to lash out and play the spoiler. Russian actions could involve closer collaboration with Iran in support of conflicts in the Middle East that undermine U.S. interests, more direct military pressures and threats in Europe, and intensified overt and covert efforts to disrupt European democracies and support authoritarian regimes.

*Tilt toward Russia and away from China.* This policy choice involves the United States wooing Russia by easing sanctions and military pressures with the goal of managing the perceived larger and longer-term strategic danger posed by a rising China. This option would involve an intensification of U.S. trade and investment pressures, a buildup of U.S. and allied forces around China's rim, and vocal opposition to China's expansion of control in disputed regions, self-serving trade and investment in the Belt and Road Initiative, and perceived subversion of nearby countries and leading developed states through covert influence peddling and overt propaganda. The United States would signal an interest in consulting and possibly coordinating with Russia in strengthening their respective relations with key Asian opponents of Chinese dominance, notably India and Vietnam, and defending the common U.S.-Russian interests in sustaining the independence of Japan and the Korean Peninsula in the face of China's growing power.

The advantage of this policy choice is that it would build common ground with Russia, including in mutual areas of concern over possible Chinese dominance. Russia resents its junior-partner status in relations with China and is clear-eyed on how China requires increasing deference from its neighbors as it rises in power and prominence. Beijing, worried about a U.S. tilt toward Russia amid a hardening U.S. position toward China, has a lot at stake in workable ties with the United States. The expectation is that China would moderate policies toward the United States to preclude closer U.S.-Russian ties at odds with Chinese interests (e.g., closer U.S.-Russian relations with Japan, India, and Vietnam and cooperation on arms control and the Arctic).

The risk of this policy choice is that it may not work as forecast. China and Russia may be too close to be divided without more accommodation from the United States.

*An example favoring a tilt toward Russia.* In chapter one of this volume, Ellings joins NBR project proponents of this policy choice in seeing dire consequences stemming from growing China-Russia coordination and collaboration at the United States' expense, with the potential of a two-front war. Viewing China as the main threat to the United States, proponents of a Russian tilt object to existing U.S. restrictions on interactions with Russia. Moreover, they view Moscow as deeply concerned about Russia's ever-growing subservience to a dominating China and malleable to greater attention involving a mix of U.S. and allied pressures and inducements. Some in this group favor easing U.S. sanctions and other accommodations at the outset of heightened efforts to woo Russia away from China. Ellings and others disagree with such initial compromises. They favor a nuanced coordinated strategy between the United States, other Western countries, and Japan employing existing sanctions and other tough policies along with inducements of mutual benefit that would follow greater U.S. and allied interchange and agreement with Russia. Moscow presumably would be inclined to pursue this path of cooperation with the United States and its allies and partners in order to achieve greater international independence and prominence.

This option would have the benefit of restoring Russia's historically strong linkages with the West and stalling the recent trajectory of Russian dependence on China. A more independent Russia with close ties to the West would serve as a brake on China's ambitions in Eurasia. If done in close coordination with the United States' European and Asian allies, U.S. inducements toward Moscow would avoid the danger of being seen as appeasing Russian aggression.

The risk is that Putin may be unpersuaded by U.S. inducements while continuing strong antipathy toward the West and close relations with China. Russia may view these inducements as signs of weakness, prompting the country to cooperate more closely with China in seeking advances at the expense of the declining Western powers. Russian and Chinese officials could also use the positive U.S. initiatives toward Russia to divide the United States from European powers committed to sanctions against Russian aggression.

## An Uncertain Future

The current outlook for U.S. policy in dealing with the negative consequences of Sino-Russian relations remains bleak. There are no easy fixes for the United States. The drivers of cooperation between China and Russia continue to overshadow the brakes on forward movement at the United States' expense. Limits on their cooperation prompt the two governments to continue to avoid entering a formal alliance or taking substantial risks in support of one another in areas where their interests do not overlap. Longer-term vulnerabilities include Russia's dissatisfaction with its increasing junior status relative to China, China's much stronger interest in preserving the existing world order, and opposition to Russian and Chinese regional expansion from important lesser powers in Europe and Asia seeking U.S. support.

The Trump administration's National Security Strategy and National Defense Strategy focus on strengthening and other countermeasures against the dangers posed by China and Russia. As explained in Steinberg's chapter and in the discussion in this chapter, those and other strategies arguing for peace through strength can be viewed as seeking to preserve U.S. primacy. This approach, however, is deemed as one-sided and unrealistic by Steinberg and many participants in the NBR project. They argue that some accommodation will be essential to the stable management of international relations. Meanwhile, the impact of the strategies is complicated and arguably diluted by Trump's avowed unpredictability and his repeated controversial initiatives seeking better relations with Putin and Xi amid other signs of policy disagreement within the Trump administration on how to deal with Moscow and Beijing.

China and Russia form an authoritarian axis that is intentionally reshaping the strategic landscape in Asia, Europe, and the Middle East. Their coordinated efforts pose a complex set of interrelated challenges. The question that now confronts the United States and its allies and partners is how to respond to these challenges with an integrated and multilateral strategy spanning the security, economic, and diplomatic spheres. The failure to do so will jeopardize the U.S.-led international order that has sustained over 70 years of peace and prosperity since the end of World War II.